# ANCIENT AMERICA

TIME
LIFE
BOOKS
®

———

GREAT AGES OF MAN

*A History of the World's Cultures*

# ANCIENT AMERICA

by

JONATHAN NORTON LEONARD

and

The Editors of TIME-LIFE Books

TIME INCORPORATED, NEW YORK

THE AUTHOR: Jonathan Norton Leonard is a staff writer for TIME-LIFE BOOKS. For 20 years he worked for TIME Magazine as Latin American and Science editor; married to a Peruvian, he speaks Spanish fluently and, from his own travels and studies, is familiar with the regions covered in *Ancient America*. He has written many books; among the most recently published are *Flight into Space*, *Exploring Science* and the volume entitled *Planets* in the LIFE Science Library.

THE CONSULTING EDITOR: Leonard Krieger, now University Professor at the University of Chicago, was formerly Professor of History at Yale; Dr. Krieger is the author of *The German Idea of Freedom* and *The Politics of Discretion* and co-author of *History*, written in collaboration with John Higham and Felix Gilbert.

THE COVER: A Mixtec gold pendant portrays Xipe Totec, the ancient god of spring, wearing a bearded mask and an ornate headdress of filigreed floral shapes.

TIME-LIFE BOOKS

EDITOR
Maitland A. Edey

TEXT DIRECTOR          ART DIRECTOR
Jerry Korn             Sheldon Cotler

CHIEF OF RESEARCH
Beatrice T. Dobie

*Assistant Text Directors:* Harold C. Field,
Ogden Tanner
*Assistant Art Director:* Arnold C. Holeywell
*Assistant Chiefs of Research:*
Monica O. Horne, Martha Turner

PUBLISHER
Rhett Austell

*General Manager:* Joseph C. Hazen Jr.
*Circulation Director:* Joan D. Manley
*Marketing Director:* Carter Smith
*Business Manager:* John D. McSweeney
*Publishing Board:* Nicholas Benton,
Louis Bronzo, James Wendell Forbes

GREAT AGES OF MAN

SERIES EDITOR: Russell Bourne
Editorial Staff for *Ancient America:*
*Assistant Editor:* Carlotta Kerwin
*Text Editors:* Robert Tschirky,
William Longgood
*Picture Editor:* John Paul Porter
*Designer:* Norman Snyder
*Assistant Designer:* Ladislav Svatos
*Staff Writers:* Sam Halper, John Stanton,
Jeffrey Tarter, Bryce Walker
*Chief Researcher:* Peggy Bushong
*Researchers:* Kathleen Brandes,
Jacqueline Boel, Kaye Neil,
Johanna Zacharias, Arlene Zuckerman

EDITORIAL PRODUCTION
*Color Director:* Robert L. Young
*Assistant:* James J. Cox
*Copy Staff:* Marian Gordon Goldman,
Barbara Hults, Dolores A. Littles
*Picture Bureau:* Margaret K. Goldsmith,
Barbara Sullivan
*Traffic:* Douglas Graham
*Art Assistants:* Anne Landry, Mervyn Clay

The following individuals and departments of Time Inc. gave valuable aid in the preparation of this book: the Chief of the LIFE Picture Library, Doris O'Neil; the Chief of the Time Inc. Bureau of Editorial Reference, Peter Draz; the Chief of the TIME-LIFE News Service, Richard M. Clurman; and Correspondents Rafael Delgado Lozano (Mexico City), Tomas A. Loayza (Lima), Maria Vincenza Aloisi (Paris), Barbara Moir (London), Ann Natanson (Rome), Elisabeth Kraemer (Bonn) and Traudl Lessing (Vienna).

# CONTENTS

# INTRODUCTION

"This country," wrote Simón Bolívar, the great South American liberator, "was guided by an instinct that can be called the wisdom of nature itself. There were no known models for its creations, and its doctrines had neither teachers nor examples, so that everything about it was original, and as pure as the inspiration that comes from on high." Bolívar was referring to Peru, the land of the Inca, but his words apply to the entire hemisphere. No one has better described the mysterious isolation in which all of the ancient American civilizations arose, sealed off from the rest of the world by ocean barriers until the great adventure of Christopher Columbus.

The theater in which the pre-Columbian peoples developed their cultures was immense, extending from pole to pole. Man did not arise from the land itself; he came from Asia by way of the Bering Strait, traversing cold and inhospitable zones where life depended on the hunting of animals. Continuing his advance in search of more favorable regions, he reached the beautiful Valley of Mexico and the plains of Yucatán. Then he passed on into South America and climbed to the high Andes where the climate is wonderfully healthful and the sky has infinite depth and luminosity.

In fully tropical lands arose the admirable culture of the Maya: great stone cities characterized by the mingling of nature, technical accomplishments and an original architecture. The ways of the Maya were peaceful, and they ruled their destiny by a calendar that appeared to join time to the infinite.

In the fertile Mexican highlands, archeologists have found evidence of a long cultural evolution culminating in Tenochtitlán, the Aztec capital, sited where Mexico City now stands. With a population exceeding European cities of the time and a splendor that dazzled its Spanish conquerors, Tenochtitlán was a vigorous, warlike city-state. Its culture had developed under the whip of fierce barbarian invaders, but nevertheless it grew to rule over a wide domain that came close to being a true empire.

Genuine empires appeared in the Andean highlands. They reached their fullest and ultimate expression in the Inca Empire, whose efficient central government and generally benevolent policies toward its subject states made it more than a mere confederation. Gradually there arose a kind of welfare state that combined the predominance of an elite with an intense concern for social well-being. Until it fell before the Spaniards, its success was so extraordinary that the Spanish chronicler Fernando de Santillana exclaimed: "Never was there hunger in that land."

Such, briefly, is the cultural picture of America before Columbus. To write his brilliant and delightful text about it, Mr. Leonard has combined the testimony of the early Spanish chroniclers and missionaries, the illustrious travelers, the sociologists and especially the observations of the modern archeologists and anthropologists.

The author of these lines does not feel qualified to tread the rocky path of judgment in the field of ancient American anthropology, which is full of conflicting theories and opposing opinions; that is the domain of the specialists. Yet he does feel confident that a book such as Mr. Leonard's is a splendid contribution to intellectual understanding, and a stimulating invitation to further discussion.

AMBASSADOR VICTOR ANDRES BELAUNDE
*Chairman of the Peruvian Delegation*
*21st Session, United Nations General Assembly*

# 1

# THE EARLIEST AMERICANS

For more than 20 years after Christopher Columbus discovered America, the newly revealed lands proved a disappointment. Columbus had promised much. "Their Highnesses can see," he wrote to King Ferdinand and Queen Isabella of Spain, "that I shall give them as much gold as they want . . . slaves, as many as they shall order, and I shall find a thousand other things of value." But the anticipated wonders had not materialized, and the small Spanish settlements in the Caribbean were held in angry suspense like the audience of a theater whose curtain has failed to rise.

On the thousands of miles of coastline explored, no civilization or substantial wealth had yet been found. The primitive inhabitants, misnamed "Indians" because Columbus thought he was near India, had hardly any possessions, and when they were forced by the Spaniards to work as slaves, they died almost at once. There was plenty of good farmland, but the fierce adventurers who swarmed across the Atlantic had no love for farming. Fresh from fighting the Moors in Spain, they were eager for gold and glory—and neither was in sight.

Only a steady trickle of rumors kept their hopes alive. During Columbus' last voyage, in 1502, he met off the coast of Honduras a canoe "long as a galley" with a thatched cabin amidships, a 25-man crew and a cargo that included copper hatchets and bells. The female passengers were not naked like other Indians. They wore decent cotton dresses and covered their faces modestly like Moorish women. The canoemen pointed toward the west and seemed to be saying in pantomime that a rich land lay in that direction.

Columbus was not much interested. Intent on searching for a strait that would take him to India, he sailed south toward Panama. But later voyagers brought similar reports, and gradually the conviction grew that civilized lands were hidden somewhere in the west. In 1517 an expedition set out from Cuba and found hostile but reasonably civilized people with stone houses and temples living in Yucatán. Hopes soared; swords clattered in dusty parade grounds. Perhaps the curtain of glory would soon rise.

The curtain rose indeed, and not in their gaudiest dreams could the Spaniards have imagined the

A JADE DEATH MASK, *finely wrought from more than 200 pieces of the semi-precious stone, covered the face of a Maya chieftain whose remains were found in the sarcophagus of a 13-century-old tomb in Chiapas, Mexico. The whites of the eyes of the mask are made of shell, the irises and pupils of obsidian.*

truth about the countries they were about to conquer. Only a few hundred miles from Cuba lay Mexico, parts of which had been civilized for more than a thousand years. Its dominant city, Tenochtitlán, the capital of the Aztecs, had reached a dazzling peak of splendor. It was no mere camp of barbarians but one of the biggest cities of the 16th Century world with some 300,000 inhabitants. Built in a lake and linked to the shore by causeways, it had canals for streets like Venice, a system of aqueducts, great temple-pyramids, well-regulated markets, barbershops, parks, even a zoo.

Though generally resembling a big European city, Tenochtitlán was strikingly different in many ways. No beasts of burden or wheeled vehicles could be seen crossing its causeways because there were no large domesticated animals in ancient Mexico, and none of the ancient American peoples understood the principle of the wheel, or at least they made no practical use of it. The farmers of Tenochtitlán grew crops unknown in the Old World and for livestock they raised turkeys and edible fat little dogs, both of them Mexican specialties. The city's nobles wore robes of brilliant feathers fitted together as delicately as fine embroidery and traveled in gorgeous litters borne on the shoulders of retainers. Its soldiers fought in quilted cotton armor and wore helmets shaped like the heads of ferocious beasts. The weird religion that dominated the city's life was the bloodiest ever devised by man.

The Aztec capital was only the beginning. Scattered over southern Mexico and down the mountain spine of Central America were dozens of sizable cities and hundreds of smaller centers, some of them tributary to the Aztecs, others fiercely independent. Standing silently among them were enormous ruins of long-dead civilizations about which all knowledge had faded from memory.

Far to the south, beyond the Isthmus of Panama, stretched a second unknown realm. In some ways

the Inca Empire of Peru was more remarkable than Mexico. Its ruler was a living god, descendant of the sun. His power was absolute for 2,500 miles along the towering range of the Andes from southern Colombia to central Chile. His capital, Cuzco, more than two miles above sea level, glittered with finely worked gold, the largest accumulation of gold in that age.

Peru was probably the world's best-governed country in the turbulent 1500s. Well-built roads threaded its great mountains, crossing precipitous gorges on suspension bridges. A message service of trained relay runners kept Cuzco in touch with all parts of the empire. Irrigation canals and other skilled engineering works such as agricultural terraces ensured plenty of food, and a nationwide social security system took care of the basic wants of individuals. The humblest Peruvian citizen had his duties and rights, paying taxes to the state in the form of his own labor and drawing on the state's reserves in time of need. In spite of some primitive aspects such as lack of a written language, Peru bore an astonishing resemblance to a modern welfare state.

The most remarkable thing about the ancient American civilizations, however, was their inde-

pendent development. Hidden behind their oceans, they had grown from the simplest beginnings with little help from each other and probably none of importance from the Old World. Their people did not suspect that the rest of the world existed, and no hint of their existence had reached Europe or Asia. Their isolation was without parallel. All the European and Asian centers of civilization, from Rome to Japan, developed in direct or indirect contact with each other. Ideas, inventions, knowledge and goods circulated among them for thousands of years, enriching the heritage of all. Only Mexico and Peru remained outside the cultural pool, and this made their confrontation with the invading Spaniards in the first half of the 16th Century an event unique in history. Never before had there been a meeting between men of different civilizations with no previous knowledge of each other. Never again could it happen on this earth.

The result of the meeting was disaster. In a few nightmarish years both Mexico and Peru collapsed into ruin. Millions of their people died of warfare, famine, slavery, European diseases and lack of will to live under foreign rulers. Behind them they left deserted cities, crumbling temples, uncultivated fields. Hundreds of years would have to pass before either country approached the population or prosperity that it had enjoyed at the start of the 16th Century.

To understand how these impressive civilizations grew to their strange magnificence unknown to the world and vanished so suddenly, it is necessary to go back to their dim beginnings. Tracing each step in their rise from savagery to high sophistication and their ultimate downfall is a fascinating exploration through time, but the story is incomplete and full of controversies. Even those advanced stages climaxing their development are not altogether clear, chiefly because native written records are entirely lacking for Peru, and the few that do exist for Middle America—the region reaching from Mexico to Costa Rica—cannot be completely deciphered. Moreover, the eyewitness accounts left by the Spanish conquerors are often conflicting and open to question. But a great deal is known nevertheless, and more is learned every year as archeologists patiently search ancient ruins to reconstruct the history and customs of the extraordinary people who lived there long ago.

The earliest entries in the record are vague and few, but one thing is certain to start with: man is not native to the New World. No primitive kinds of man, such as Java man or Peking man, have ever been found there, and none of the apelike primates from which man evolved. There are, in fact, no apes at all, living or fossil, in the Americas. Anthropologists agree that the remote ancestors of the American Indians were varieties of the species Homo sapiens, or modern man, who evolved in the Old World. They settled the New World during the last stage of the Pleistocene (Ice Age), and they did so only after they acquired cultural equipment—clothing, shelter, tools—adequate to keep them alive in cold climates.

Driven by enemies or in search of food, they came in small bands by way of eastern Siberia, the Bering Strait and Alaska. This route was never easy. Perhaps they used boats or rafts of some sort, or crossed the water gap on the winter ice. Sometimes the strait was dry land because water withdrawn from the oceans by Ice Age glaciers lowered the sea level by more than 200 feet, but immigrants who walked across the Bering land bridge were faced by another obstacle. During periods when the sea level was low, the glaciers were large, and impassable ice sheets in southern Alaska and western Canada blocked the way to the south.

The immigrants may have walked across the land bridge when the strait was dry and then lived for many centuries in ice-free regions of Alaska and western Canada until recession of the glaciers opened a path to more appealing parts of North America. Possibly this intermittent mechanism operated several times, injecting new waves of Siberians into the New World.

Until comparatively late times none of these Asian immigrants could have been Mongoloid in the modern sense because the true Mongoloids typified by the Chinese had not yet evolved, or at least had not reached eastern Siberia. The immigrant waves may, in fact, have been quite diverse physically. The chief backing for this theory is that American Indian groups show a great deal of variation. In general the farther they live from the Bering Strait—and thus the earlier they can be presumed to have left Asia—the less Mongoloid they look, some of them possessing strikingly prominent noses, long heads or wavy hair, in contrast to the flat noses, round heads and straight hair that the typical Mongolians have today. Successive waves of immigrants, each being a little more Mongoloid, would account nicely for this sort of variation. The Eskimos, who crossed the Bering Strait at a relatively recent date, have the most Mongoloid appearance of all.

Some anthropologists believe, however, that the immigrants were fairly uniform and that all the Indian groups into which they divided can be accounted for by "genetic drift" and adaptation to climate. Genetic drift is a random hereditary change that takes place in small, isolated groups of people. If a band of 30-odd primitive hunters is dominated by two or three vigorous males, later generations of the band are likely to show the individual traits of these few men. Perhaps they will be taller than members of bands whose dominant males were not as tall. Or perhaps their skins will be lighter, or their noses longer. In large populations where there is a great deal of intermarriage such personal traits soon average out, but in small groups they tend to be perpetuated and accentuated. If a small group prospers and multiplies, it may grow into a large tribe possessing as stabilized characteristics the personal peculiarities of a few remote ancestors.

In creating the widely different peoples of the Americas, genetic drift must have been helped by the extremes of climate that the spreading immigrants encountered. American Indians who live in hot, humid countries, for example, tend to be smaller and more slender than inhabitants of colder regions; the Indians of the Andes have larger lungs and a greater amount of blood than most people, adaptations that enable them to live more efficiently in the thin air of high altitudes.

The oldest traces of man in the New World that can be definitely dated are well-made flint spear points found mingled with the bones of extinct animals. Carbon 14 tests, which measure the extent of decay of radioactive carbon in organic material, prove the bones—and thus the points associated with them—to be about 12,000 years old. But many anthropologists think that the first pioneers from Asia arrived much earlier and spread widely. Scattered over North and South America are collections of crude stone tools, such as choppers and scrapers, that mark their campsites. Among the

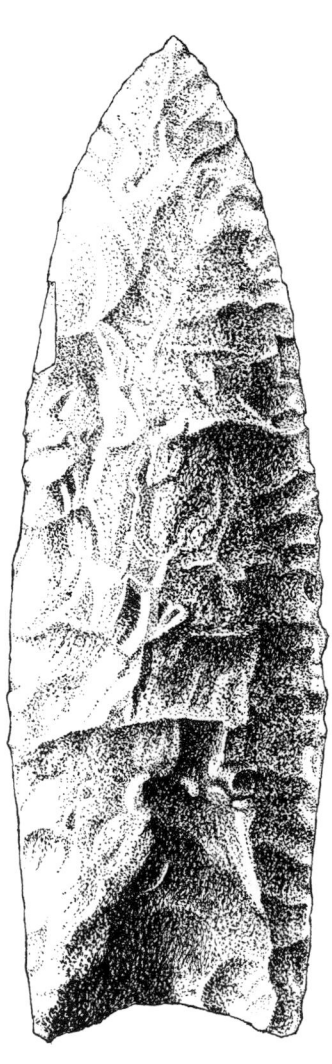

A GROOVED STONE POINT, *which was attached to a spear shaft, marked a revolutionary advance in weaponry: it enabled hunters to kill big game.*

tools are no elegant "points" (arrowheads or spearheads), and this lack suggests that the early immigrants may have left Siberia as much as 20,000 or even 40,000 years ago, before point-making had become established there.

None of the tool collections have been dependably dated, and so there may be other explanations besides extreme age for their crudeness and their lack of projectile points. The people who made them may have known how to fashion points but for some reason did not always do so. Another possibility is that they had become culturally decadent, forgetting the skills of their ancestors in the same way that Europeans of the Dark Ages forgot many Roman techniques.

In spite of these arguments against man's vast antiquity in the New World, it is widely believed that the Americas once had a thin population that lived on an extremely low cultural level. Hardly anything is known about these shadowy people ex-

cept by conjecture. To judge by the crudity of their weapons, they hunted only game that was easy to kill and combed the country for fruits, nuts and roots. The first small bands that ran the gantlet of the glaciers certainly found themselves in a paleolithic paradise, with no human enemies or competitors and plenty of edible animals that had not learned how dangerous man can be. Under these ideal conditions they may have multiplied explosively and expanded swiftly throughout the New World. But they seldom could have been numerous in any particular place; it takes a great deal of country to feed even a few families of primitive hunter-gatherers.

These most ancient Indians must have led rather furtive lives, afraid of large animals and rarely able to obtain their flesh for food. But about 12,000 years ago came a dramatic change. Chief proofs of it are the beautifully made spearheads found sparingly in many parts of the United States and Mexico. They are called "Clovis points" after the place near Clovis, New Mexico, where they were first discovered. A typical point is five inches long and well sharpened by flaking. The base is slightly concave, with a broad groove skillfully chipped from each face of it. This fluting thins the center of the base, making it easier to fasten the point securely in the split end of a wooden shaft. The edges near the base are carefully dulled by grinding to keep them from cutting the tight sinew wrappings that held the spearhead on the shaft.

The Clovis spear was a very effective weapon, and there is no doubt about what it was used for. At the original Clovis site as well as at many other places, typical Clovis points occur among the bones of mammoths, the great hairy elephants that were contemporaries of very ancient hunters on the grasslands of North America. Probably the hunters did not make frontal attacks on these exceedingly dangerous beasts. A more likely tactic would have been to stalk a mammoth, wound it with as many thrown spears as possible, then follow it, harass it, and when it weakened kill it with a spear-stab to a vital organ. Modern African Pygmies hunt elephants in this way. Sometimes a single spear is thrust into the animal's belly; then the Pygmies patiently track their victim until it is close to death from peritonitis.

The Clovis mammoth hunters may also have used other methods. Their favorite hunting grounds seem to have been near ponds or boggy places into which mammoths might be driven and mired and then easily slain. Sometimes Clovis points are found among the bones of several mammoths tangled together. This may be evidence that the hunters stampeded groups of the heavy beasts over a bluff or into a ravine. They killed bison and other big animals too, many of which, such as American camels, are now extinct. But at the same time they did not ignore smaller game, nor did they feel themselves above eating vegetable food when all game was scarce.

While the appearance of Clovis points is firmly dated at around 10,000 B.C., the origin of the deadly spearheads is uncertain. They may have been developed by people who had been living in North America for 10,000 years or more, slowly improving their equipment for coping with the world around them. Or perhaps a wave of immigrants brought improved stoneworking skills from Siberia and perfected the Clovis points soon after they arrived. In any case, the fluted points were an American invention; nothing like them has come to light in Siberia.

So successful was the new technique of big-game hunting that it soon spread to the eastern woodlands of North America where the prime quarry was the tree-browsing mastodon, a close relative of the mammoth, and to Mexico where Clovis points have been found. Isolated spearheads of Clovis type

appear as far south as Panama, and the ability to make effective stone projectile points eventually spread down the length of South America. It may have been carried there by the actual migration of people whose superior weapons enabled them to displace or absorb the original inhabitants. On the other hand, it may have spread by cultural diffusion, which is an anthropological way of saying that news of a good thing travels fast.

The accomplishment of big-game hunting was a revolution that raised the status of American man over much of the two continents. With mammoths and other massive animals on the year-round menu, the food supply became more secure and the human population undoubtedly increased. But eventually there came a change of climate that, combined with the growing and hungry population, spelled extinction for the mammoths and many other edible species.

For thousands of years, while the cold breath of the glaciers still blew down from Canada, the climate of western North America had been moist and cool, and lush vegetation supported great herds of grazing animals. About 7000 B.C., when the glaciers had retreated, the climate began to grow hot and arid, and by 5000 B.C. the face of the land had changed drastically. Rivers dried up; deserts spread; cacti grew in places that had formerly been covered with grass or forest. The herds of game diminished or disappeared altogether.

These changes were not felt strongly in the eastern parts of North America and on the Great Plains, where the Indians continued to live chiefly by big-game hunting, but Indians in the west and in Mexico were forced to develop different ways of making a living. They hunted and trapped small desert animals and learned to make greater use of seeds and other vegetable foods that could be stored for consumption during hungry months. Compared to killing mammoths, one of which would feed a whole band for weeks, this was a laborious and humble way of life. But it was effective; it enabled small populations of pre-agricultural Indians to survive under desert conditions much more severe than those of the present. This desert-living technique, heavily dependent on seed gathering, was the base from which true agriculture gradually developed. And without established agriculture, bringing freedom from constant food foraging, and thus permitting settled communal life with leisure to follow creative pursuits, there could have been no flowering of civilization in the New World.

The first faint beginnings of agriculture did not appear in the American Southwest, where the desert culture was in full swing, and no one knows why not. One possibility is that plants suitable for domestication were not available there. Whatever the reason, the first progress toward agriculture was made in Mexico or farther south, and plentiful finds in once-inhabited caves tell step by step how it was done.

The Mexican state of Tamaulipas on the Gulf of Mexico just south of Texas is largely arid, with many caves so dry that fragile vegetable matter in them lasts undecayed for thousands of years. In 1954 Richard S. MacNeish of the National Museum of Canada excavated two of the caves and found stratified debris of human origin dating (by carbon 14 tests) as far back as 7000 B.C. Patiently he identified plant and animal remains to determine the diet of the cave's inhabitants. From 7000 to 5000 B.C. the Tamaulipans had been almost entirely gatherers of wild plant foods, which they dried and stored in baskets and net bags. They did some hunting, as proved by a few projectile points, but it was not important, and the only plants that were probably domesticated were gourds for use as containers, chili peppers and pumpkins with edible seeds. These contributed almost nothing to their total diet.

In layers of later debris the number of domesticated plants increased to include red and yellow beans, but not until about 2500 B.C. did a tiny primitive variety of cultivated corn (maize) make its first appearance. In other parts of Mexico corn was by then on its way to becoming the most important New World crop, but it had little effect on the diet and way of life of the Tamaulipans for another thousand years. Long after most of Middle America was fully agricultural, Tamaulipas remained essentially in the food-gathering state. MacNeish decided that the Tamaulipans, in spite of their early pioneering with pumpkins and beans, were hopelessly conservative or perhaps too much handicapped by their arid climate. He decided to move farther south in search of a more progressive region where the key crop, corn, may have first been domesticated.

The origin of domesticated corn had been for years a favorite puzzle for botanists. Cultivated corn cannot seed itself; if the ears are left unharvested, the seeds or kernels do not scatter and grow; they remain wrapped in the tight husk and eventually lose vitality. But no wild corn that could seed itself had ever been found. When MacNeish started his work, a well-established theory held that wild corn had never existed and that the first cultivated corn was a hybrid between cornlike grasses that still grow wild in Mexico and neighboring countries. This explanation was shaken when fossil grains of corn pollen were found in test wells bored deep under Mexico City. They came from mud laid down 80,000 years ago, which is long before the earliest human immigrants could have arrived in the New World. So there must have been wild corn once. But how did it turn into cultivated corn that can propagate itself only with the aid of man?

MacNeish and his colleagues found the answer to the corn puzzle in the valley of Tehuacán southeast of Mexico City, where another series of dry caves offered deep, stratified layers of human debris. In the layers that dated from about 5000 B.C. they found tiny cobs of a corn that was almost certainly wild. They were less than an inch long and their individual kernels, smaller than peas, had apparently been surrounded by a thin husk that opened at maturity and allowed the seeds to disperse, fall to the ground and reproduce their kind like the seeds of other grasses.

For more than a thousand years the people who sheltered in the caves of Tehuacán gathered wild corn only, but larger cobs were found in the debris dating after 3400 B.C. Two or three inches long and much thicker than the wild type, they were surely the result of selection and cultivation. In later strata they were still larger and showed signs of hybridization with closely related cornlike grasses. This crossing added vigor (as hybridization of corn still does) and gave the cobs the appearance, if not the size, of modern corn. After 3000 B.C. the cultivated corn of Tehuacán was productive enough to support a considerable population dependent largely on agriculture.

But what happened to wild corn? MacNeish and Harvard botanist Paul C. Mangelsdorf produced a likely answer to this puzzle too. They think the wild plants were never very common and that they grew naturally in just those places, mostly near streams, that the first farmers chose for their cultivated fields. Wild corn that was not displaced in this way was subjected to hybridization by wind-blown pollen from the ever-increasing stands of domesticated corn. Wild plants that fell victim to such botanical rape produced tightly wrapped ears like cultivated corn. Since these could not disperse their seeds, they had no progeny. Only in places remote from cultivation could wild corn continue to reproduce itself. As agriculture spread and these strongholds fell, wild corn became extinct.

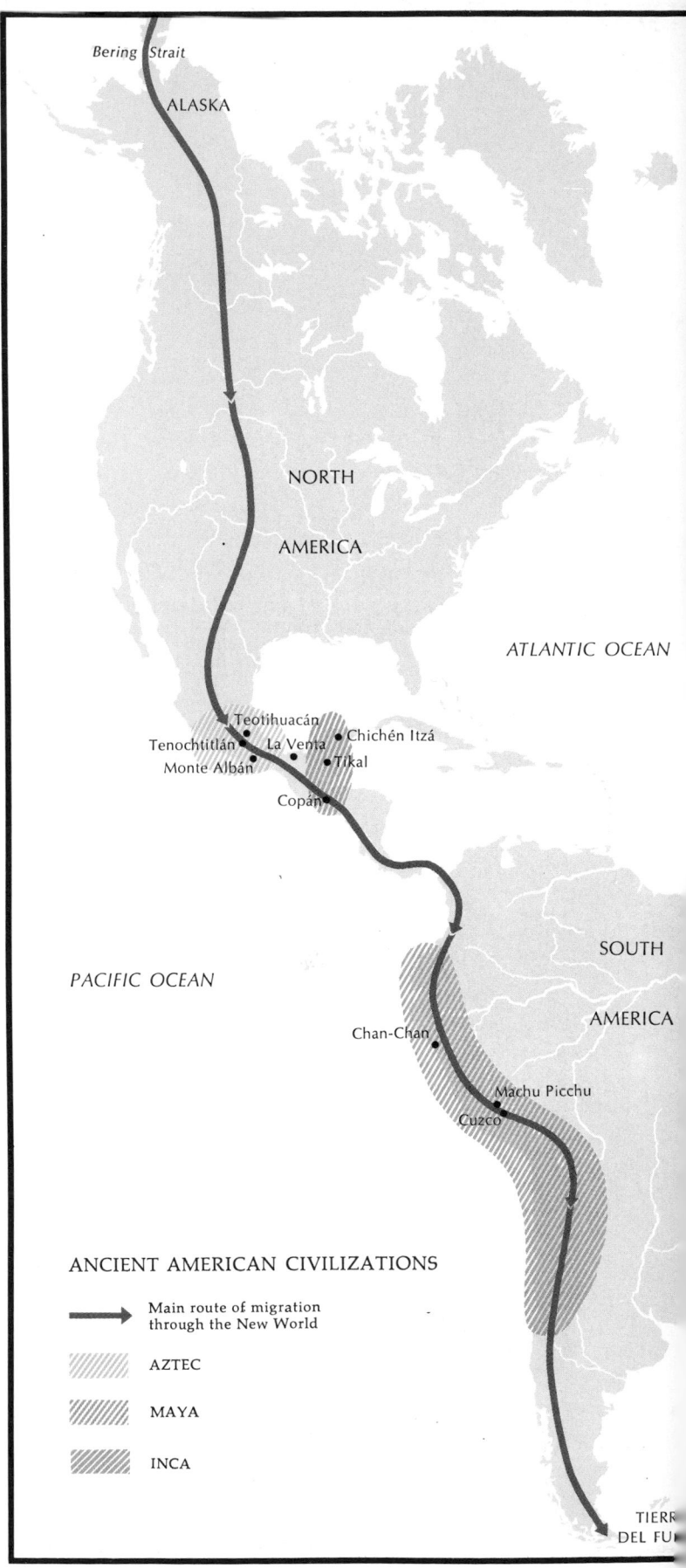

ANCIENT AMERICAN CIVILIZATIONS

→ Main route of migration through the New World

░ AZTEC

░ MAYA

░ INCA

MAJOR CULTURES *developed in three distinct areas along the main route followed by prehistoric man in migrating from Siberia to the New World. Names within each area indicate key cities and ceremonial centers.*

The valley of Tehuacán could not have been the only place where corn passed through its stages of domestication. The inhabitants of many other valleys where wild corn grew must have brought it under cultivation in different forms that interbred intricately as pollen was blown across mountain ridges and as Indian farmers selected superior ears for use as seed. Corn is an extraordinarily flexible plant. Although its first productive varieties were native to cool uplands, it soon threw off types that throve in hot climates at the foot of the mountains. By 2000 B.C. the magical crop was well established in most parts of Middle America and was moving across the Isthmus of Panama and on to South America.

Corn was the major crop in most places, but it was not alone. Shortly after it was domesticated, the climate of Middle America changed for the better. The long, hot, dry spell that had lasted since 5000 B.C. was replaced by cooler, wetter weather. Deserts diminished; intermittent rivers started flowing the year round; isolated groups of farmers who had developed their own kind of agriculture began to communicate, and they exchanged cultivated plants. The backward people of Tamaulipas no doubt contributed their beans and pumpkins to the growing pool and in turn received superior varieties of corn and other crops from the south. Helped by the better climate, agriculture spurted. Every little valley along the mountain spine of Middle America happily found itself in possession of a long list of useful plants capable of supporting a settled life.

The same thing was happening in the Andean lands of South America. The first plants domesticated there were different; root crops such as white and sweet potatoes were much more important than in Middle America. But it was not long before the best domesticated plants of each main region moved into favorable parts of the other region.

When corn reached Peru, it quickly produced, perhaps by crossing with native grasses or local types of wild corn, an extraordinary galaxy of new varieties, some of which have flat kernels almost as big as quarters.

The crop plants domesticated by the ancient Indian plant breeders of Middle and South America play a vital role in feeding the modern world. Corn is a primary food in most countries that are not too cold and sunless for its cultivation. It even competes with the native rice in parts of the Far East. White potatoes developed by the highland Indians of Peru have become such a firmly established staple in lands with coolish climates that it is hard to imagine life there without them. Sweet potatoes of the South American tropical forest are equally important in warm countries. Kidney beans (Mexican) are the poor man's source of protein nearly everywhere except the Far East. Peanuts (Peruvian) are not only an important industrial crop in many places but they are an essential part of the diet in large parts of Africa. In addition, the long list of Indian contributions to the world's food includes lima beans, tomatoes, peppers, most kinds of squash and pumpkins, avocados, cocoa, pineapples and many lesser crops. Nor were the Indians' contributions limited to edible plants. Tobacco was widely cultivated in ancient America when the early explorers arrived, and they quickly introduced Europe to its pleasures.

Agriculture had become a way of life in Middle America by 2000 B.C., and the landscape showed very small villages in favorable locations, each surrounded by patchy fields of corn and other vegetables. In most places the villagers cultivated the land by the "slash-and-burn" system used by nearly all primitive farmers and still common in Latin America. Each year new patches of forest or scrub were cleared and the debris burned. If there were any sizable trees, they were girdled by stone axes and felled by piling brush around their trunks and burning them through. Crops were planted in the ashes. For two or three years they grew well, but soon the soil fertility was exhausted or weeds took over. The land was allowed to return to brush, and a new patch was cleared. After resting for 10 or more years the exhausted land recovered its strength and could be cropped again. This system of farming required a large amount of land used intermittently to grow sufficient food to support one family.

The earliest farmers lived in pit houses with floors below ground level. By 2000 B.C., however, the fashion in housing had turned to wattle-and-daub construction, which is a framework of poles interwoven with cane or brush and plastered with clay. The roofs were of thatch made with grass, palm leaves or anything similar that was handy. This was an excellent house for warm climates; the Middle Americans built it for thousands of years, as proved by innumerable impressions of the construction materials preserved in the baked clay where a house burned down. Houses of just this kind are still built by millions in Indian parts of Latin America.

Pottery—like settled agricultural life, a sign of cultural progress—was made in the more advanced Mexican villages just before 2000 B.C. Shortly thereafter came the odd clay figurines that remained a conspicuous part of Mexican culture for thousands of years and which may indicate an incipient religion. Typically they are four or five inches long and represent a female figure, nude except for a headdress; some of them show girls who would be hailed as charming anywhere. Year after year and century after century these figurines were produced in vast quantities, apparently to be thrown away or buried with the dead. So numerous are they that the ground in many parts of Mexico

is full of their fragments, and the strange little faces peep out of freshly turned soil. Their styles changed many times. Male figures appeared, usually dressed at least in loincloths, and some of the female figurines also acquired clothes. In later years the figurines were made in clay molds, some of which survive and are used to make semigenuine relics to sell to tourists.

Anthropologists have no confident explanation for the long-lived and vigorous cult of the figurines. The early female ones obviously had some connection with sex and reproduction. Perhaps they were symbols of fertility that were sacrificed (that is, broken or thrown away) to petition some god for increased crops or family. Later they may have acquired more general significance, like the custom of burning candles as small offerings at Christian shrines. No one really knows their purpose, but the figurines are extremely useful in dating other remains found with them or in tracing the movements of ancient peoples. An anthropologist well acquainted with the figurines can tell at a glance, and with considerable accuracy, when and where one of them was made.

For a thousand years, between 2000 and 1000 B.C., the agricultural villages made progress slowly. They grew bigger and more numerous, fired better pottery, raised more and better crops and expanded into new territory. By 1000 B.C., a firm agricultural base for civilization reached like a ribbon of life from central Mexico to southern Peru, more than 4,000 miles in all, but nothing that resembled true civilization had yet appeared. Except for the figurines there is little evidence of art or religion, and no traces have survived of political organizations above the village level. Around the year 1000 B.C. ancient America appears to have been waiting for a stimulus, an impulse that would launch the energies of its peoples into the spiritual and material adventure of becoming civilized.

CARVED FROM JADE, *an inscrutable Olmec figurine holds a child thought to represent the offspring of a jaguar god.*

# A GROUP PORTRAIT

In the vast and varied lands of ancient America there dwelt a diversity of peoples, each with its own personality and way of life. Many of these civilizations left a vivid record of themselves in the wealth of sculptured figures that archeologists have unearthed around their settlements. Some of the figures, like the Olmec image above, hint at an overpowering concern with ritual and religion. Others are more worldly: Maya sculpture displays a sophisticated flair for beauty, that of western Mexican villagers an eye for humor; Aztec figures, on the other hand, frequently evoke brutality and death. In a few cases virtually nothing survives of an ancient culture but its small self-portraits in clay, lava rock or jade, yet often these provide remarkable insights into its people's lives.

FROZEN IN RITUAL POSES, *seven-inch-high stone figurines perform a cryptic ceremony beside upright blades of jade. Archeologists discovered the group, arranged*

# THE MYSTERIOUS OLMECS

The first major civilization of the New World was that of the Olmecs, an enigmatic people who inhabited the jungles along Mexico's Gulf Coast as long ago as 1000 B.C. The images they left of themselves and their gods have masklike expressions

s it is here, buried in sand beneath an Olmec ceremonial court.     A GODLIKE HEAD *has the strange feline eyes and mouth characteristic of Olmec sculpture.*

or snarling, jaguarlike features; rigid and anonymous, they suggest a society pervaded by a dark, powerful religion. From such sculpture, and from the ruins of religious centers, scholars have deduced that the Olmecs' priestly rulers once held sway over thousands of peasants through ceremonies that were believed to control rainfall and jungle spirits. By exacting tribute and labor from their subjects, these rulers built impressive temples and spread their influence throughout Middle America.

# VILLAGE ARTISTS

Unlike the austere Olmecs of the eastern forest, the village farmers of western Mexico seem to have enjoyed an earthy and sensuous life. Their pottery figures, made as funeral offerings to the dead, depict not sinister gods but colorful anecdotes from their everyday existence. Most are treasures of the commonplace: women nursing babies, lovers embracing, ball-

THUMPING A DRUM, *a villager accompanies a dance.*

GRINDING CORN, *a woman prepares to make tortillas by mashing presoaked grain with a flat stone.*

LOST IN THOUGHT, *a farmer sits peacefully with one knee drawn up. Though often depicted naked, village men wore cotton clothing and ornaments made out of sea shells.*

players, circles of dancers, musicians with flutes and drums.

Buxom girls were modeled in endlessly varied poses; chieftains and dignitaries in elaborate costumes parade past tiny clay houses raised on stilts. Potbellied little *techichi* dogs are shown curled up asleep, or barking and comically wagging their tails. Pottery in the shape of pumpkins, corn and gourds suggests abundant crops. Isolated from the great centers of American civilization, the Mexican farmers who are portrayed in these lively sculptures never built temple-cities or conceived a dramatic religion. Instead they remained devoted to their land and their rustic village communities, enjoying a comfortable prosperity for over a thousand years.

PLAYING INSTRUMENTS, *one musician (left) scrapes a bone cut with ridges to produce a rhythmic rasping sound, while another blows a flute into a pot used as a resonator.*

AN OLD WOMAN *is depicted with ear ornaments and a scandalized expression.*

A HELMETED WARRIOR, *holding a weapon in one hand, prepares to hurl a stone.*

A VILLAGE BEAUTY, *nicknamed the "Pre-Columbian Mona Lisa" by archeologists, wears a collar and rings in her ears and nose.*

A MAYA ARISTOCRAT, *wearing a long breechclout and huge, doughnut-shaped earrings, flings out one of his arms in an extravagant gesture.*

# A SOCIETY OF TALENT AND EXUBERANCE

The Maya of southern Mexico and Central America were skilled artists and architects who often displayed a passion for the flamboyant. Nearly every exposed surface of their temple-cities was embellished with hieroglyphic symbols and carvings of mythical monsters.

The priests who inhabited the temples dressed in equally exotic garb: golden jaguar skins, blood-red robes, ornaments of green jade, the iridescent feathers of quetzal birds, and towering, flower-topped headdresses *(left)*. Some Maya aristocrats and priests even filed their teeth and inlaid them with semiprecious stones, wrapped their children's heads tightly with cloth and splintlike boards to elongate the skulls, or hung beads from their foreheads to create permanently crossed eyes—a special mark of beauty.

This taste for elaboration affected all of Maya life. A fantastic array of divinities, rank upon rank, peopled the Maya universe and accounted for every phenomenon of nature. Thirteen distinct heavens and nine hells surrounded the earth; each day of the week was regarded as a living god whose behavior had to be predicted through an intricate calendar system. To propitiate all the gods took a perpetual round of sacrificial ceremonies, incense burning, fasting and prayer, which helped give priests a firm hold over Maya farmers and villagers.

# THE GRIM INHABITANTS
# OF HIGHLAND MEXICO

Centuries of conflict over highland Mexico's fertile valleys left a stern mark on the peoples who inhabited the region. The priestly elite of early cities like Teotihuacán and Monte Albán thrived by commanding the labor of peasants in surrounding villages—and may in turn have been overthrown by these same peasants, finally goaded to revolt. More probably,

A STERN EXPRESSION *dominates an ancient Mexican mask of painted clay. Decorated with ear plugs and a feather plume, it was once part of an incense burner unearthed in the ruined metropolis of Teotihuacán.*

A GODDESS OF DEATH *has the truculent stance of a warrior, but wears elegant ornaments. She was a deity in the Zapotecs' ceremonial center of Monte Albán—an enormous sanctuary built for the glory of the gods.*

like many other Mexican cities, they were ravaged by the Chichimecs, fierce nomadic tribes of the northern regions who seized fertile areas from older peoples and built military empires out of them. When the Spanish entered Mexico in 1519 they found the country seething with hatred against the most recent of these empires, that of the Aztecs, whose rapacious armies exacted heavy tribute from the land they conquered.

The harsh life of ancient Mexico stemmed from religions that treated human life cheaply. Gods of war and death held high places in the Mexican pantheon. To propitiate them and demanding gods like Xipe Totec, the highland peoples ultimately went to war to get supplies of victims for their altars.

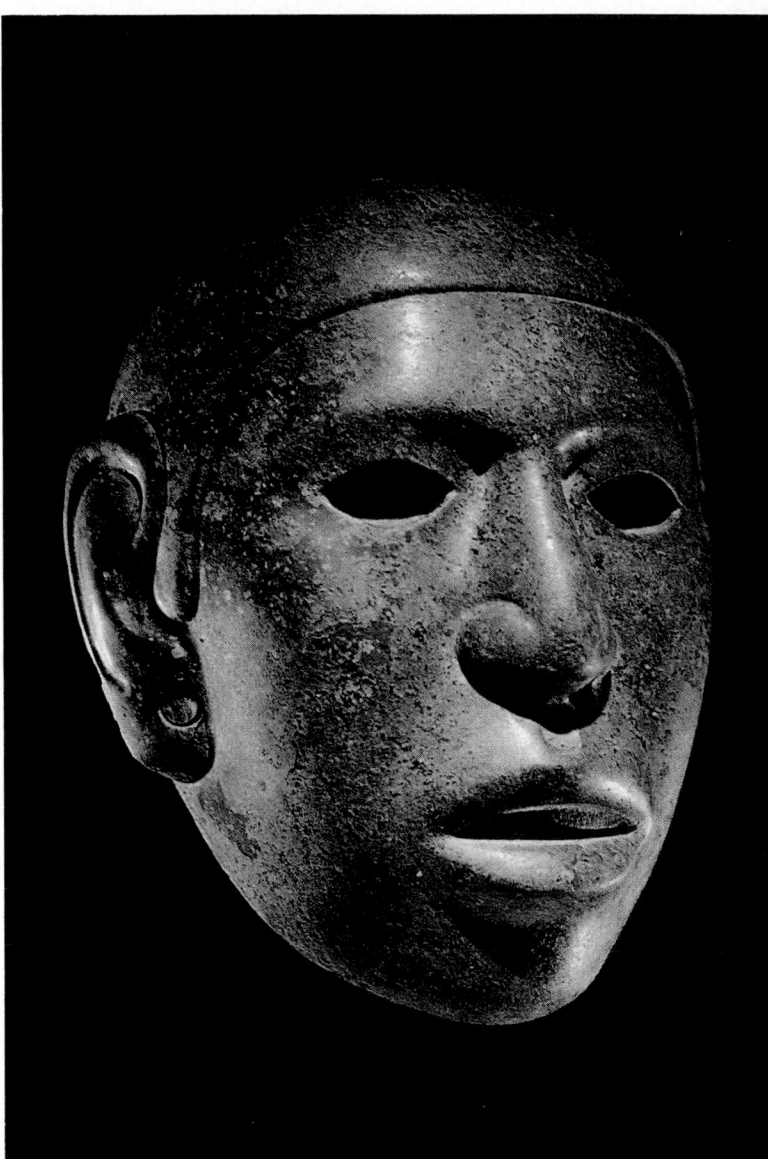

A WARRIOR'S FACE, *this Aztec sculpture has blunt, uncompromising features. The Aztecs, who started as a band of nomads, conquered much of Mexico before being themselves overthrown by the Spanish.*

PAYING HOMAGE TO NATURE, *a priest wears the flayed skin of a young victim to appease Xipe Totec, the god of spring. This grisly ceremony symbolized the earth taking on a new mantle of foliage each year.*

27

A NAZCA POT *uses a bright blaze of color to depict a rotund woman, whose face and wrists carry ceremonial tattoos. Even today Peru's Indians paint such designs.*

# VERSATILE TECHNICIANS OF PERU

The early peoples of Peru developed high levels of technical skills and social organization which the later Inca put to good use. They learned how to channel water into desert valleys through intricate irrigation systems and how to span deep mountain gorges with suspension bridges. Their farmers bred new plants to withstand varied climates; by the time of the Spanish conquest some 30 food crops were under cultivation. They also raised llamas, which yielded them both wool and the New World's only native beast of burden.

The advancement and variety of these early Peruvian societies is strikingly reflected in their arts. In the south, the Nazcas wove swirling, abstract patterns into gauzy cotton cloth and painted flat, brilliantly colored features on their ceramic ware. In northern Peru, Mochica sculptors perfected a strongly contrasting style. Displaying a new and sensitive appreciation of individuals, they executed highly realistic portraits of people of all stations, ranging from beggars to warriors and statesmen.

A SEATED CRIPPLE *(left), sculpted by a Mochica artist, has one stump leg and holds a heavy staff. The hollow figure, equipped with a spout in back, was used to hold beer for ceremonial use.*

A PORTRAIT OF A RULER *(right), this Mochica head displays features of a vigorous intelligence. No other American people took care to commemorate important men with such fine likenesses.*

# 2

# THE GREAT STONE CITIES

By the beginning of the First Millennium B.C. the inhabitants of Middle America had come a long way from the nomadic savagery of their Siberian ancestors. Their small agricultural villages had flourished for centuries from Mexico to Costa Rica, and the villagers had gradually been improving their living techniques. They now possessed good pottery and good cotton cloth. More important, their crops were better, especially their corn. The fat, well-filled ears of the newer varieties yielded so much grain that a man could feed his family for a year with little more than 10 weeks of work in the cornfields. He had other duties, such as tool-making, and to vary his diet he hunted or fished. But at least he was free of the ceaseless search for food that is the lot of so many people without effective agriculture. His leisure time above the demands of subsistence could be put to higher uses: religion, warfare, art or the building of civilization.

Until very recently no one knew when or where the first civilization in Middle America got its start. The whole region is cluttered with enigmatic ruins. Enormous pyramids cluster on barren hilltops or rise suddenly above flat plains. In tangled tropical jungles great stone buildings, encrusted with carvings, stand empty and abandoned, and the heads of great stone snakes gape their dragon jaws. Few of these relics are identified even by legend. Most of them were known to Indians of historic times only as places where gods once came to earth.

At first archeologists knew as little, but their knowledge increased as they carefully excavated the ancient sites and discovered others. Gradually they pushed back into the past the time when the early civilizations appeared in Middle America. For awhile the spectacular Maya ruins in the jungles of lowland Guatemala and adjoining areas were thought to represent the earliest of these cultures. But some archeologists sensed dimly a much older tradition that showed itself in many parts of Mexico in the form of strange and characteristic figures in stone, pottery or jade. Most of them had thick Negroid lips, flat noses and an odd open-mouthed snarl like that of an unpleasant baby about to cry. Some of the "babies" had fangs and more closely resembled jaguars than human beings.

Sculptures in this style were most plentiful in

AN ANCIENT URN *is shaped like a jaguar with bared fangs and a scarf knotted around its throat. The 36-inch-high vessel was found in a refuse bed at the site of Monte Albán in present-day Mexico, and dates from between 200 B.C. and 200 A.D. The jaguar cult was particularly strong in Monte Albán, which was a burial ground and ceremonial center of the Zapotec Indians.*

A CEREMONIAL AX HEAD *depicts an Olmec god who combines the attributes of man and jaguar. This stylized face, with its flamelike eyebrows and drooping mouth, is characteristic of Olmec figures.*

the Mexican states of Tabasco and Veracruz on the Gulf Coast. The region is low, hot and humid, with rainfall reaching 120 inches annually. Sluggish rivers wind through jungly swamps; the air hums with mosquitoes, and troops of howler monkeys swing through the treetops. Few people live there now, but archeologists have found abundant evidence that in this unlikely region the cultural pattern was struck that prevailed in Middle America without fundamental change for more than a thousand years.

The creators of the ancient Gulf Coast culture, generally called Olmecs, are of uncertain origin. Old poems in Náhuatl, the language of the Aztecs, tell of a land on the eastern sea that was settled so long ago that "no one can remember." Its name, Tamoanchán, is not Náhuatl but Maya and means "Land of Rain." So the Olmecs may have been related to the Maya, at least linguistically.

As early as the middle of the 19th Century reports had come from this coastal region of gigantic stone heads with Negroid features. No one paid much attention then; Mexico is full of fascinating relics. But interest in the Gulf Coast gradually increased as other monuments were reported there.

In 1938 Dr. Matthew W. Stirling of the Smithsonian Institution pushed alone into the giant-head country and soon found a long-reported stone head near the village of Tres Zapotes in Veracruz. Six and a half feet tall and weighing 10 tons, it showed the thick drooping lips and flat nose that are the hallmarks of Olmec sculpture.

Dr. Stirling returned to the Gulf Coast in 1939 and later, at the head of well-equipped expeditions which struck an archeological bonanza. The greatest finds were made at La Venta, a small sand and clay island surrounded by coastal swamps in the state of Tabasco. Scattered about the island were innumerable relics of the distant past, including four of the great stone heads, strangely carved al-

tars, and a clay pyramid 110 feet high. Deep under the surface of the ground were found three pavements of flat green stones laid out in a pattern that was probably meant to show the stylized face of a jaguar. These mosaics must have been religious offerings of some sort; almost as soon as they were finished they were covered with layers of colored clay and never again disturbed.

For a few years after their discovery, La Venta and other Olmec sites were believed by archeologists in the United States to date back no further than 300 A.D. But a group of Mexican archeologists led by Dr. Alfonso Caso of Mexico's National Museum and Miguel Covarrubias, the eminent authority on ancient Mexican art, insisted that they were much older. Their view was confirmed by the carbon 14 dating method, developed in the late 1940s. Tests on charcoal found at La Venta pushed back the date of the site to 800 B.C. Since La Venta was a highly developed center, it could not have been the first Olmec effort, and so the inception of their culture is now generally placed at 1000 B.C. —a date when the Golden Age of Classical Greece was still 500 years in the future.

All through Olmec culture runs the theme of the jaguar. In some carvings jaguars are shown fairly realistically; in others the features of jaguars and men are subtly combined, sometimes the beast predominating, sometimes the man. Many carved faces look like those of jaguars while retaining the drooping mouths of the Olmec "babies."

Today the jaguar is not considered a particularly dangerous animal and seldom attacks man; but to a forest-dwelling Indian armed with nothing better than a stone-pointed spear, it must have seemed the dread spirit of the jungle. Very likely the Olmecs or their predecessors began worshiping jaguars as a sort of totem-animal typifying strength and power. Later they developed this simple animism into a sophisticated cult centered around a race of supernatural beings—part man, part beast—who were the offspring of a jaguar and a human. Some scholars believe that the Olmec baby-faces were intended to show "were-jaguars," or men with sacred jaguar blood. Whatever the reasoning behind it, the cult of the jaguar, Middle America's first formal religion, was enormously successful. It stimulated its homeland, the sweltering Gulf Coast, to incredible efforts and later spread its influence over much of Middle America.

The Olmecs may have developed their civilization, jaguar cult and all, without help from any source. No solid evidence exists to indicate otherwise, but it may be more than coincidence that the Chavín culture of northern and central Peru appeared at about the same time and was also preoccupied with jaguar gods or were-jaguars. The many Olmec-like sculptures in the state of Guerrero on Mexico's Pacific Coast led Covarrubias to suggest that Olmec culture may have made its first appearance there. If this is the case, it may have been started by seaborne Peruvian missionaries carrying the jaguar gospel by boat along the coast. Or perhaps it worked the other way around, with the Olmecs spreading the seeds of their culture and the cult of the jaguar to Peru.

No matter where or how Olmec culture began, there is no doubt about the widespread effects produced by its peculiar art style and religion. Typical Olmec sculptures, figurines and rock carvings have been found not only in Guerrero but as far north as Mexico City and as far south as Honduras. Whether the style was carried there by Olmec colonists, war parties, merchants or jaguar-cult missionaries may never be known.

The greatest achievement of the Olmecs was their invention of the system of religious leadership that was the basis of all Middle American civilization. La Venta, their principal center, was not a city in the ordinary sense. The island on which it stood had an area of about two square miles that could feed no more than 30 families by the slash-and-burn method of farming. There is no trace of an ancient residence area. The place was purely a ceremonial center, a holy shrine to which the inhabitants of a large district came at intervals to take part in religious rites and which they supported with food and labor.

The priests of La Venta must have had a powerful hold over their communicants. They kept the place going for at least 400 years, no doubt eating well, dressing in gorgeous finery and pursuing their odd custom of burying mosaics and offerings made of jade and stone that must have cost the disposable time of thousands of men for centuries. There is no stone at all on the island; the nearest source of the hard basalt from which the large monuments are carved is 80 miles away. One stela—a tall, narrow monument carved with figures and inscrip-

Map labels:

CHICHIMEC · HUASTEC · GULF OF MEXICO · MEXICAN PLATEAU · TOTONAC · SIERRA MADRE OCCIDENTAL · SIERRA MADRE ORIENTAL · Santiago River · Pánuco R. · Tajín · Lerma River · TOLTEC · Tula · Lake Chapala · VALLEY OF MEXICO · Teotihuacán · BAY OF CAMPECHE · Tenochtitlán · Tlaxcala · Remojadas · Xicala · TARASCAN · Toluca · AZTEC · Cholula · Tuxtla · La Venta · PACIFIC OCEAN · Cuernavaca · Tehuacán · Tres Zapotes · OLMEC · Palenc · Balsas River · Isthmus of Tehuantepec · Usumac · SIERRA MADRE DEL SUR · Tilantongo · MIXTEC · Monte Albán · Mitla · Tehuantepec · ZAPOTEC · GULF OF TEHUANTEPEC

Inset map labels:

Tamaulipas · Yucatán · Veracruz · CARIBBEAN SEA · Jalisco · Hidalgo · Michoacán · MEXICO · Tabasco · BRITISH HONDURAS · Guerrero · Oaxaca · Chiapas · GUATEMALA · HONDURAS · PACIFIC OCEAN · EL SALVADOR · NICARAGUA · COSTA RICA · ▨ Extent of Middle America

MIDDLE AMERICAN CULTURES

0    Miles    200

tions—weighs 50 tons; some of the great heads weigh 40 tons. The stones must have been cut in the mountains, dragged by painful inches to the nearest river, loaded on rafts and floated to La Venta. Among a people equipped only with stone tools and muscle power, such feats are proof of religious devotion, or fear, of prodigious intensity.

It is possible that the priests of La Venta eventually organized some sort of army to collect goods and labor by force, but this may never have been necessary. The susceptibility of Middle American Indians to religious discipline has always been notable, and remains so to this day. Most likely the peasants freely gave their corn to the shrine and willingly pulled the great stone blocks on their slow way to La Venta. They must have derived some satisfaction from doing so. Revolts were apparently rare, and soon the idea of the ceremonial center as a social control mechanism spread to many parts of Middle America.

One of the first offshoot centers set up by Ol-

mec missionaries or priestly aristocrats was Monte Albán, near the present Mexican city of Oaxaca and about 200 miles southwest of La Venta. This impressive group of stone pyramids and other ceremonial buildings stands on a mountain spur that looms high above three fertile valleys. The structures now visible were built long after Olmec times, but when archeologists tunneled into them they found earlier buildings, some of which contained large flat stones with Olmec-like figures carved in bas-relief. The stones had been used merely as construction material and must have belonged to a still-older structure that was torn down.

The bas-reliefs are called *danzantes*, or "the dancers," and they depict naked men in curious limp poses. The carvings are rather coarse, but their thick lips and flat noses indicate how strongly the people who carved them—probably Zapotec Indians whose descendants still live in the neighborhood—must have been influenced by the Olmec art style. It is not likely that the men were really

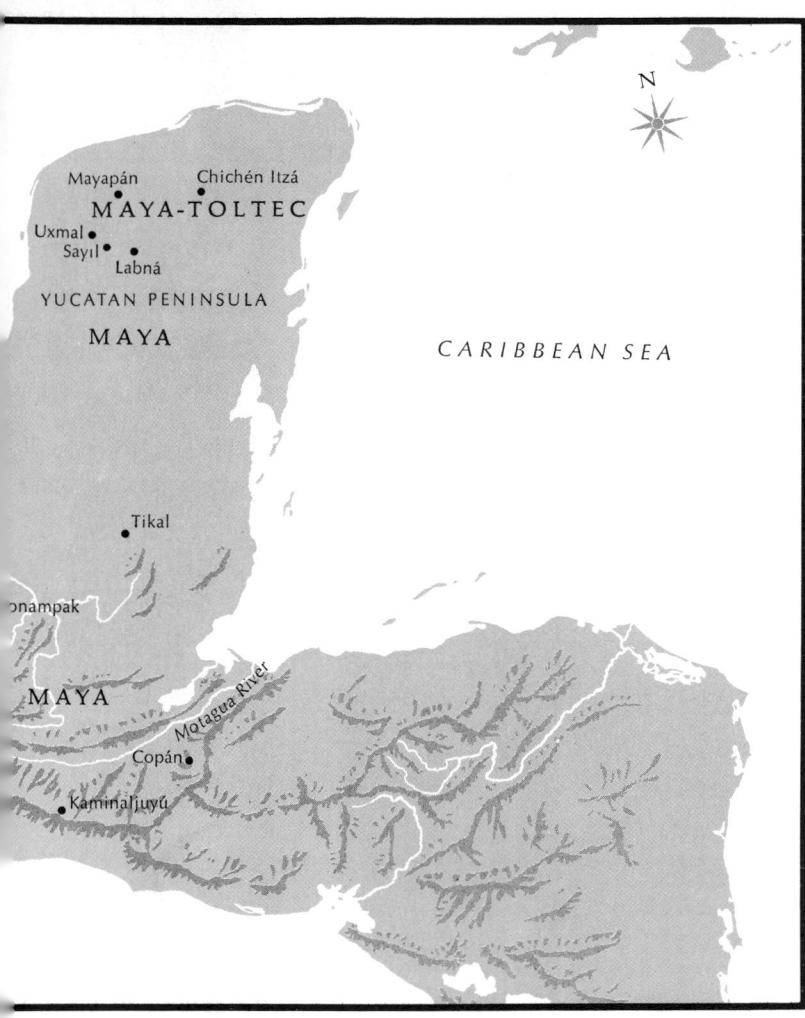

They did this, apparently, for 1,400 years. The first shrine was built on Monte Albán about 500 B.C. and the site kept its appeal as a ceremonial center until 900 A.D., in spite of several changes of religion and probably of population in the valleys below. Even long after the shrine was deserted the mountain remained sacred, and its slopes were used for tombs of the distinguished dead.

Monte Albán was only one of many Olmec-influenced centers. The warriors or missionaries of the jaguar god also spread south into Guatemala and El Salvador. One of their principal sources of influence may have been a kind of writing—the oldest in the Americas—developed by the Olmecs or perhaps by their Zapotec converts. No examples have been found at La Venta itself, but many of the danzantes at Monte Albán have crude (and thus far uninterpreted) glyphs—usually the faces of men, birds or animals—carved near their heads or mouths as if the figures were saying something.

No matter how crude, the glyphs were a potent intellectual tool. They must have set their exclusive possessors, the priests, high above the illiterate masses, enabling them to communicate secretly by written messages and to draw wisdom from sacred records of the past. These early glyphs were so successful that all forms of writing used in Middle America apparently descended from them.

When Olmec influence began to expand through Middle America, the mountain-walled Valley of Mexico, where Mexico City now stands, was remote from the mainstream of cultural development. Its villagers raised their corn, modeled their pottery figurines of fertile pretty girls and kept their leisure time for their own use. But even into this backwater Olmec influence penetrated. From clay pits in the village of Tlatilco near Mexico City have come typical Olmec figurines. They may have been brought in by traders, but more likely they

dancers. Their open mouths, closed eyes and flaccid limbs suggest that they represent corpses. Many have been sexually mutilated, and blood flows from the wounds in curling streams. They were no doubt human sacrifices, the vanguard of the army of sacrificial victims that marches through ancient Mexican history.

Other Olmec traces at Monte Albán are pottery incense-burners with man-jaguar faces, showing that the jaguar cult had established itself in the region around Oaxaca. It certainly carried with it the powerful social invention of the ceremonial center. Monte Albán itself is waterless and barren and could never have supported an appreciable number of farmers, but its commanding position above the rich valleys made it an impressive place for priests to ply their trade. Processions of worshipers must have climbed its slopes bearing gifts for the priests and victims to be sacrificed. After watching the stirring ceremonies, they returned to their farms with the renewed goodwill of the gods.

indicate the presence of Olmec missionaries, or converts of their converts, who reached the valley before 500 B.C. and established themselves as spiritual leaders of its resident population. The first known fruit of their collectivizing influence is a pyramid of sorts found at Cuicuilco on the outskirts of Mexico City. Cuicuilco's pyramid is not impressive. It is an oval earthen mound about 390 feet long, faced with rough stones and rising by four stages to a height of 75 feet.

In spite of its crudity, the Cuicuilco pyramid was a real ceremonial center on the Olmec model. Begun about 300 B.C., it was enlarged twice and probably remained in use for many centuries as the chief focus of religious activities in the Valley of Mexico. About 300 A.D. the nearby volcano Xitli gushed out a flood of glowing lava that buried the pyramid 20 feet deep. Cuicuilco was probably abandoned before Xitli erupted. Perhaps new people came into the valley or a more potent religion drew its supporters away. But even as it declined in importance a new kind of center was being built at Ostoyahualco across the lakes that then filled much of the valley. From developments begun at Ostoyahualco around the beginning of the Christian era grew the great Teotihuacán civilization, one of the most splendid of ancient America.

The new center had raised platforms for ritual use, but they did not stand alone in the age-old Olmec pattern, drawing worshipers from scattered villages. Around them was a zone of residences. What sort of people lived in them is not known; they could not all have been priests. They may also have been artisans and merchants. They huddled close to the sacred structures, and their presence gave Ostoyahualco, or Teotihuacán I as archeologists call it, some of the character of an Old World metropolis and made it the first true city in Middle America.

Teotihuacán I is known today only to archeolo-

gists who have traced its almost obliterated platforms and walls. But its people must have been vigorous and their social-religious organization exceptionally powerful, for next to it and over it rose a similar but much bigger city that between 300 and 700 A.D. spread over nearly seven square miles. This was Teotihuacán, whose enormous pyramid complex, 30 miles northeast of Mexico City, is today the most spectacular sight in Mexico and one of the most impressive in the world.

Teotihuacán could not have grown haphazardly; it must have been planned by master architects with a taste for austere lines and magnificent distances. Through the city runs the broad Avenue of the Dead, nearly two miles long and lined with low, stone-faced structures. Beside this central concourse stands the flat-topped Pyramid of the Sun, 700 feet square at the base and as high as a modern 20-story building—a colossal edifice built of earth and sun-dried bricks and sheathed with stone. The

smaller Pyramid of the Moon rises at the northern end of the avenue, and near its south end is a great square enclosure walled with massive build-ings and called the Citadel.

Inside the enclosure is the Temple of Quetzal-cóatl, the famous Feathered Serpent and the most attractive god of the Mexican pantheon, a culture hero revered as a bringer of knowledge and civili-zation. Enormous stone heads of the Serpent pro-trude from one side of this temple-pyramid and alternate with odd staring faces that probably rep-resent the rain god Tlaloc. When these buildings were in use they were covered with smooth lime plaster and brightly painted. Traces of the paint, generally red, can be seen where a plastered sur-face has been protected by fallen debris.

Religious ceremonies in this majestic setting must have been awe-inspiring. On such occasions crowds of city dwellers and pilgrims from distant places watched the solemn priests, all plumes and glitter, as they paraded across the courts to the mutter of deep-voiced drums and climbed in pro-cession up the steep stairs of the pyramids. It is easy even now to stand at one end of the Avenue of the Dead and see in imagination the ancient peo-ple gathered among their pyramids to worship with such fervor their fantastic gods.

The names of the Pyramids of the Sun and Moon and of the Temple of Quetzalcóatl are traditional, but they come from later Aztec legends, and al-though the Aztecs were greatly impressed with Teotihuacán and made pilgrimages to its ruins, they knew hardly anything about its builders. The name Teotihuacán means "Place of the Gods" in Náhuatl and a myth tells that the gods gathered there after the sun had died. One by one they threw themselves into a fire so the sun would rise again and give light to the world.

The pyramid complex is only the center of Teo-tihuacán. Surrounding it are hundreds of brush-

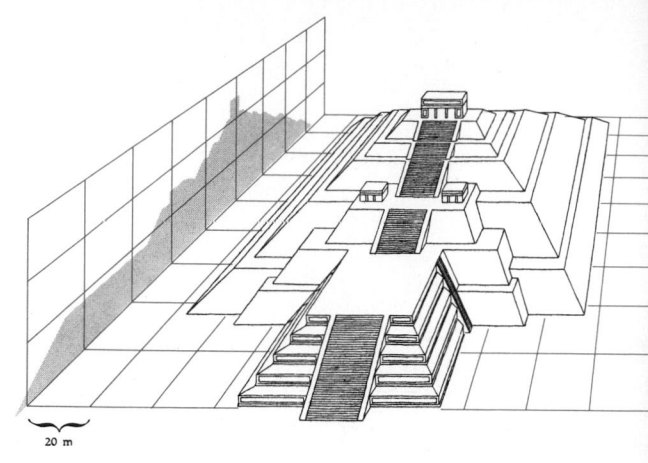

A: PYRAMID OF THE MOON

covered mounds and hummocks extending in all directions. The larger mounds contain small pyramids or structures that presumably were subsidiary shrines, like the lesser churches that cluster about St. Peter's in Rome. Many of the hummocks are the remains of palaces where priests or other important persons lived.

Some of the palaces have been excavated and they hint at the elegant life of the elite of Teotihuacán. The buildings had clay roofs supported on posts and wooden beams. These supports have disappeared, but the floors and often large parts of the walls are intact. The many rooms are always arranged around a courtyard paved with plaster and equipped with drains to carry rain water away.

The frescoed walls show the luxury of these ancient apartments. Across them march processions of priests, gods or allegorical animals painted in reds, greens, blues and yellows that are still bright today. A favorite subject is the rain god Tlaloc or his priests who scatter large drops of water and dispense from little bags the crops, flowers and butterflies that are the gifts of the rain.

One famous palace painting, *The Paradise of Tlaloc*, shows the innocent after-lives of men who died by drowning, lightning or other causes connected with rain or water. Tlaloc took care of their souls, and in the painting they are seen as small, bright, happy figures dancing, playing children's games (some of which are still played in Mexico) and chasing butterflies. From their mouths come curling shapes that represent speech or song.

The palaces of Teotihuacán with their predominantly religious wall paintings might still be considered parts of a ceremonial center, but among them and for miles beyond are remains of humbler buildings and courtyards closely packed together and intricately threaded by alleys. These provided living space for at least 50,000 people. This number of city dwellers was unprecedented for Mexico,

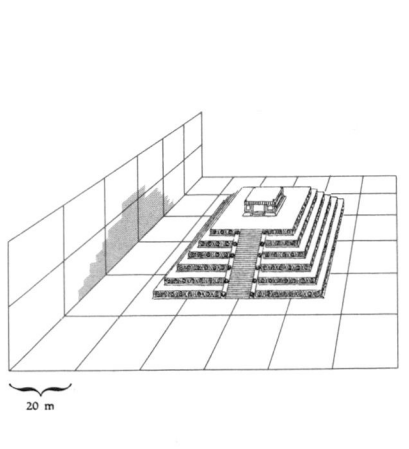

C: TEMPLE OF QUETZALCOATL

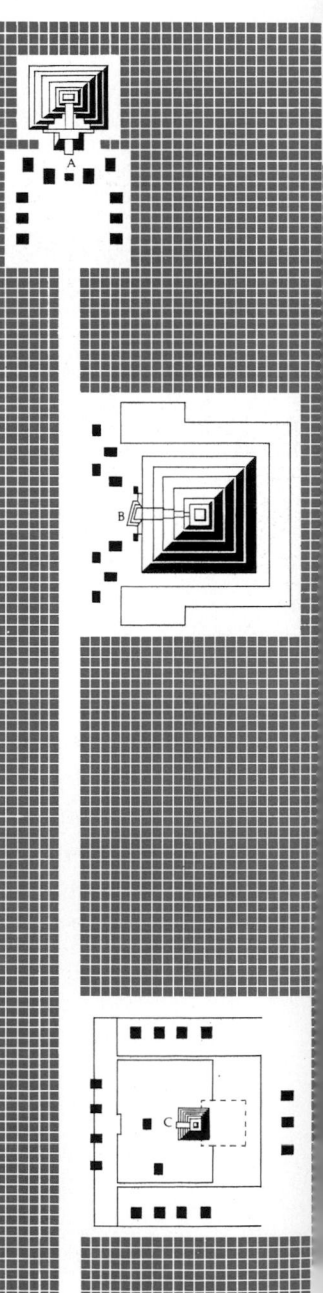

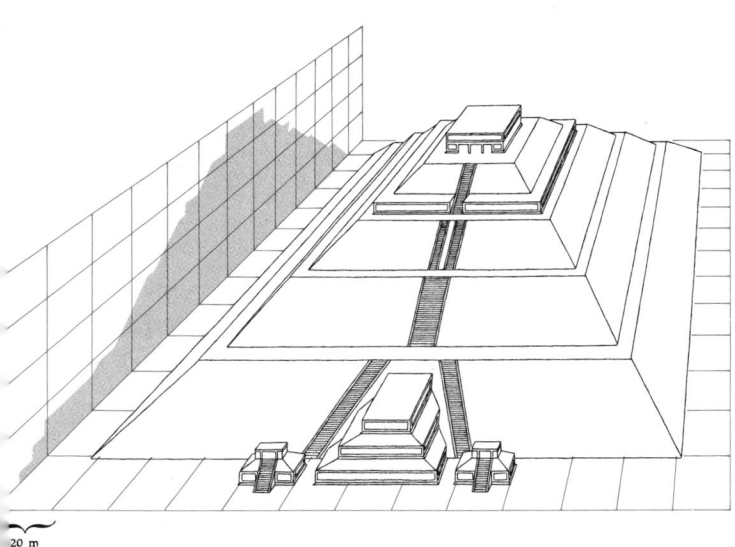

B: PYRAMID OF THE SUN

THREE MASSIVE PYRAMIDS, *now partly in ruins, adjoin Teotihuacán's main thoroughfare, the two-mile-long Avenue of the Dead. Their locations, in broad plazas dotted with smaller ceremonial structures, are shown in the diagram at the left on a metric grid similar to those used by archeologists; each square in the grid is 20 meters, or some 65 feet, on a side. An artist's re-creation of each pyramid, drawn against an enlarged grid of the same dimensions, shows its relative size and details of its construction. The largest, the Pyramid of the Sun, has a base some 700 feet square, almost as wide as Egypt's colossal Pyramid of Cheops.*

and it meant that there must have been some great improvement in agriculture; the slash-and-burn method of farming could not have raised enough food to support such a multitude. One possibility is that people of Teotihuacán may have developed the system later used by the Aztecs of building artificial islands, called *chinampas*, in the shallow lakes of the valley. Composed chiefly of reeds and silt from the lake bottom, chinampas are enormously productive, and they may well have been the secret that fed the city.

Teotihuacán seems to have been a rather peaceful place. Soldiers and weapons are not prominent in its art, and the favorite gods were the beneficent Tlaloc and Quetzalcóatl. The bloodthirsty gods that rose to power in later times are notably absent, but this does not mean that human sacrifice was unknown. One of the gods of Teotihuacán was the very ancient Xipe Totec, who was worshiped in a most unappealing way. The sacrificial victim, often a young woman, was skinned with an obsidian knife and the skin was removed in one piece. Then a priest put it on like a garment and danced solemnly around an altar. This ritual celebrated the coming of spring, when nature puts on a new coat of fresh young vegetation.

During its heyday Teotihuacán spread its influence to all civilized parts of Middle America. Its building styles and methods were copied, many of its gods were worshiped; and its pottery and other manufactures were traded to distant places. Specially prized were bowls and tall lidded jars of a thin, bright orange ware whose fragments are still commonly found all over Middle America, looking like bits of orange peel in the dark soil.

The main influence of Teotihuacán may have been cultural and religious, but there is evidence that the city's political control reached far beyond the Valley of Mexico, carried by armed settlers led by priest-aristocrats. Architectural features in the city of Kaminaljuyú in distant Guatemala are strikingly similar to those of Teotihuacán.

Around 700 A.D. the great city fell. It was looted and burned, its people were massacred or dispersed, and its influence ceased suddenly. The plaster flaked from its pyramids, and weeds and bushes took root in the mud mortar between the exposed stones. The city appears to have succumbed to an invasion of fierce barbarians from northern Mexico. They may have pressed on Teotihuacán for years, but were held back by the armies of the civilized valley. Then came a moment of weakness, perhaps a dynastic or doctrinal struggle among the priestly rulers of Teotihuacán. The barbarians—Chichimecs, or "Sons of the Dog"—saw their opportunity and destroyed the city.

Other civilized places held out for a while but a dark age fell gradually over most of Middle America. Monte Albán, which continued to flourish as a ceremonial center under Teotihuacán influence, became a graveyard, and other Classic centers were abandoned. The Valley of Mexico itself would not recover its cultural leadership for 300 years; when it did it worshiped new and fiercer gods.

While the Valley of Mexico was still reaching for its first period of dominance around the dawn of the Christian era the brilliant and isolated civilization of the Maya was taking shape far to the south. The Maya were a special breed with a distinctive language and the peculiar profile—sloping forehead, prominent curving nose and full lips—that is endlessly depicted on their ancient monuments and is still common among their descendants in modern Yucatán. The Maya have been called the Greeks of the New World, but the appellation is not accurate. The Maya were the Maya; they were like no other people, and their civilization was like no other.

It was once believed that the Maya had their roots in the cool Guatemalan highlands where several old and comparatively crude centers had been found, but the discovery of the more ancient Olmecs shifted attention to them as the original source of the Maya culture. Olmec writing seems ancestral to the more elaborate Maya glyphs, and the great Olmec social invention, the ceremonial center, was carried to its extreme by the Maya. It now appears likely that Olmec influence spread slowly southeast to northern Guatemala, where the climate is not unlike that of the sweltering Olmec heartland on the Gulf Coast of Mexico.

The land where the civilization of the Maya first crystallized is a low, hot rain forest embracing the modern Guatemalan province of Petén, the lowlands of the Mexican state of Chiapas and nearby parts of Honduras and British Honduras. Most of the region is now smothered in jungle 150 feet tall, but in Classic Maya times, roughly 300 to 900 A.D., the area was a hive of activity. Hundreds of great temple-crowned pyramids and thousands of lesser buildings were raised with enormous effort to honor or placate the gods.

A Maya city still untouched—and there are plenty of them—is a strange and somewhat frightening sight. From a high-flying airplane the jungle looks like an endless expanse of massed broccoli, the rounded treetops standing close together and giving no glimpse of the ground. If the airplane circles lower, a few crumbling walls of light-gray limestone appear above the green, like rocky islets poking out of a sea. Sometimes the eye catches a glimpse of a steep-sided pyramid rising from below.

Approached on foot the scene is strikingly different. The jungle floor is deeply shaded, with only occasional flecks of sunlight filtering through from the sky. There is little undergrowth; the ground is soft with rotting humus, and great trees stand solemnly with thick vines dripping down from their tops. Their buttressed trunks march up the sides of the pyramids, and exposed roots writhe like boa constrictors, prying the stones apart. Trees often sprout from the very apex of a pyramid and they cover lesser structures completely.

Many of the Maya sites have been partially cleared and to a degree restored. They are crowded with structures of many kinds, most of which were rebuilt over and over again. The steep-sided pyramids, the buildings most typical of Classic Maya, have smaller and older pyramids inside them. The custom of renewing old pyramids by covering them with new ones was widespread in Middle America, but no one carried it further than the Maya. They covered other structures too; some of their great courtyards are paved with as many as 15 stucco floors, each overlying important remains of an earlier era.

A traveler passing through the land of the Maya in 700 A.D. would have found footpaths leading past groups of one-room thatch-roofed houses surrounded by cornfields cultivated by the slash-and-burn system. The high jungle had been eliminated centuries before, the great trees killed by girdling with stone axes and felled by repeated burning. In most places the population would be sparse.

Every few miles the well-trodden footpaths would lead to a minor ceremonial center with a small pyramid supporting a temple, a paved court and a few low stone buildings. The place would probably be deserted, but if the traveler happened to arrive on the right day, he would discover it thronged with most of the people of the district. Some of them would be bartering local produce or handicrafts at a market near the temple-pyramid. The rest would have come, bearing appropriate offerings, to witness religious ceremonies that they firmly believed controlled the round of the seasons and the growth of their crops. Hundreds, if not thousands, of such regional centers dotted the land of the Maya. Their priests were comparatively simple men, perhaps part-time farmers.

At longer intervals the paths would converge and widen. More houses would stand along them, and the traveler would encounter files of men with burdens of corn, quicklime or dressed stones. He would feel the excitement of approaching a great city, and at last around a turn of the path he would see tall pyramids crowned with intricately carved temples painted in brilliant colors.

A really great ceremonial city was never empty. Young men came there to study for the priesthood. Skilled artisans were forever at work on the buildings. Craftsmen were constantly busy carving stone, baking pottery and making gorgeous costumes for the high priests.

On days of major ceremonies the city throbbed with excitement. Traders from distant places displayed their exotic wares, and peasants and priests from minor centers crowded its great paved courts. These ceremonies were solemn occasions, for the priests of a major temple were closest to the gods, and everyone knew that the lives of all men, down to their smallest details, depended on the gods' favor. The crucial ritual must follow exactly the glyphs in the mysterious books kept within the temple. If all went well and the gods were pleased, life would continue happily. But angry or neglected gods were sure to send disaster.

Skillful and versatile Maya artists have left a vivid picture of the priests who directed this intense activity. In stone carvings, wall paintings and vase decorations they sit or stand in rigid poses, their fingers making subtle gestures like those of Balinese dancers. Haughtily they receive offerings or tribute, give orders to subordinates, pass inflexible judgment on captives or offenders. They look like frosty aristocrats, and that is what they were, but they presumably did not rule by force.

The Maya city-centers did not form an empire. There is no evidence of a dominant capital. They were a loose federation bound together by similarity of culture and the parallel interests of the high priests, whose power depended on their education and intellectual superiority over their peasant subjects. They had books on bark paper and other writings, most of which cannot now be read. They could count and figure; they had invented the arithmetic concept of zero long before Europeans adopted it from the Orient. By long-continued astronomical observations they had learned to predict accurately the movements of the sun, the moon and the planet Venus. They knew the length of the year, including the final fractional day, with extraordinary precision. The calendar derived from this knowledge permitted them to carve accurate dates in stone on their major buildings.

Such soaring knowledge gives power, especially when no rivals are on hand to contest it. Maya society had no strong secular leadership. There must have been soldiers, but they seem to have had no power in government, and if there was a merchant class it was a humble one. The priest-aristocrats were hereditary rulers with an almost total monopoly of knowledge, wealth and power, which they used to channel the energies of the people into their insatiable building programs and their own support.

On the whole they governed well. The land of the Maya suffered little from war, and most of the foreign influences that affected it, such as the introduction of gods from Teotihuacán, were absorbed without much strife. Some stelae have been found deliberately defaced or broken and thrown on dumps. Possibly these indicate brief periods when the Maya peasants revolted against the rulers. A few carved scenes show bound prisoners. But in general the Classic Maya period seems to have been peaceful and its people remarkably conservative. Their religious and social customs changed very little over the centuries and they accomplished their feats of building with primitive tools and techniques that show few improvements during the long life of their civilization.

But about 550 A.D. there came a 50-year interval when ceremonial building stopped. Shortly thereafter, all Teotihuacán influence vanished completely, and so the break in the busy life of the devout and artistic Maya may have been related in some way to difficulties at Teotihuacán, perhaps the beginning of the wars with the Chichimec barbarians.

The Maya revived and prospered for 300 years more both in the lowlands of Guatemala and in Yucatán, where they built such splendid cities as Uxmal and Sayil. Then, about 800 A.D., their civilization in the southern lowlands began to decline; by 900 A.D. they had collapsed. All construction stopped; the great and small cremonial centers were abandoned. Some Maya, presumably members of the peasant class, without aristocratic leadership, lived among the ruins for awhile; then the jungle swept over them. Maya civilization continued for centuries in northern Yucatán, but the Maya heartland in Guatemala and neighboring lowlands remained almost uninhabited, as it is today.

Many explanations have been advanced for the sudden collapse of the Classic Maya civilization. Disease, soil exhaustion and change of climate have all been blamed, but none of these reasons satisfies scholars. More convincing is the case for some political or social change that drastically weakened the obedience of the Maya peasants to the priest-aristocrats. Perhaps the continued turmoil in central Mexico had something to do with it. New sects built around violent new gods may have started the deadly religious struggles that are the usual fate of theocracies.

With the lowland Maya died the last of the Classic cultures of Middle America. The new civilization about to arise would be even more vigorous, but harsher and in some ways less civilized.

**THE TEMPLE OF THE WARRIORS**, *one of the last great Maya ruins, is seen from the top of Chichén Itzá's Castillo.*

# A RACE OF MASTER BUILDERS

Building monuments was a religion for the ancient Maya. Spurred on by their priests, this mysterious people raised majestic stone cities to their gods. At least 80 major Maya sites, some with temples more than 200 feet high, still dot the landscape of Middle America. The earliest of these cities began to flourish in the Third Century in the tangled rain forest of Guatemala; the last great ones were built in the 10th and 11th Centuries in the plains of northern Yucatán. Much about the culture they represent still puzzles archeologists, but they stand today as one of the most varied and sophisticated architectural records in history.

THE PYRAMID OF THE SUN, *the most imposing monument in all of ancient America, rises 213 feet above the arid plains at Teotihuacán. Priests once climbed its steps to a temple at the peak.*

Although the Maya civilization flowered mainly in Guatemala and Yucatán, it was strongly influenced by the culture of Teotihuacán in central Mexico. Once the largest city in the Americas, Teotihuacán had about 50,000 inhabitants who lived in adobe houses and worshiped at massive stone pyramids, which still dominate the landscape 30 miles north of Mexico City. From the Fourth to the Eighth Centuries, its influence spread through Middle America, and Maya architects and craftsmen borrowed its building designs and decorative motifs. Even after Teotihuacán fell to barbarians in 700 A.D. its prestige lingered: centuries later the Aztecs revered the deserted city as "the place of the gods," and their rulers made pilgrimages to its ruins.

A PRECIPITOUS STAIRCASE, *flanked by stone snake heads, ascends the Temple of Quetzalcóatl, the ancient Mexicans' serpent god. Large carved panels (right) form the sloping side of its pyramid.*

Tikal—the first great Maya city, an oasis of civilization amid the jungles of Guatemala

A RUINED TEMPLE *looms in profile against a twilight sky. Framed in the entrance, an archeologist photographs the floodlit interior of the shrine.*

No location in Middle America would seem less hospitable to man than the sweltering rain forest of Guatemala. A tangle of cedar and mahogany trees chokes the landscape, and torrential rains leach most of the richness from the soil. Nevertheless, in these unlikely surroundings the Mayas built their first great temple cities.

Tikal, the earliest major Maya site, is also one of the most spectacular. Two steep-sided pyramids, facing each other across a broad plaza, rise like prehistoric skyscrapers from the jungle floor. At their summits are temples crowned with tiaralike superstructures that were once embellished with mysterious religious symbols fashioned in painted stucco or carved stone. Surrounding them, some 350 lesser temples and palaces crowd an area of six and a half square miles.

Tikal's two facing towers date from the Eighth Century. But archeologists delving under a huge acropolis nearby have uncovered structures built a thousand years earlier. Beneath the topmost temples they have found level upon level of older buildings, encasing one another like layers of an onion; every few decades, the old shrines seem to have been replaced.

The frenzy of building and rebuilding at Tikal apparently lasted through the Ninth Century. Then, mysteriously, the site was abandoned. The stones began to crumble and the jungle moved in to claim the palaces and the temples of the priests.

A SOARING PYRAMID, *being restored by University of Pennsylvania scholars, forms a 100-foot-high platform for Tikal's Temple of the Giant Jaguar.*

Copán—in the highlands of Honduras,
a serene, well-ordered center of intellectual life,
dedicated to art, science and sacred games

A CEREMONIAL BALL COURT *with sloping stone sides was the arena in Copán for a popular Maya game. Played with a hard rubber ball, it resembled a rugged version of volleyball.*

A RITUAL STAIRCASE, *which once led to a temple on an elevated terrace, bears the longest known inscription in Maya hieroglyphs, written in 2,500 carved symbols across its steps.*

Even in the intellectually oriented Maya civilization, the city of Copán stood out as a cultural center. Inscriptions on its stones indicate that conferences were held there on mathematics and the Maya calendar. The site abounds in magnificently carved statues inscribed with complex astronomical notations. The surrounding structures also carry inscriptions—notably the intricate and as yet only partly deciphered carvings that adorn the "hieroglyphic staircase" *(left)*, which archeologists believe may chronicle the city's history.

Copán's inhabitants were not only astronomers and sculptors. On a paved court *(above)* they played a ball game which was popular throughout Middle America. But at Copán many of the games were religious, and priests may have divined the future from their results.

# Labná—in the low-lying hills of Yucatán, a monument to a Maya renaissance

In the Ninth Century, as the ceremonial centers declined in the Guatemalan forests, Maya culture reached a second flowering in the sun-drenched hills and plains of Yucatán. In this setting Maya architecture took on subtle differences in style. No longer did temples soar 200 feet or more; the roof combs at their tops grew less imposing, and entwined ornamental figures in stucco gave way to abstract designs in stone.

Labná, once a major city in the peninsula's low, scrub-covered hills, exemplifies the new style. Its most imposing feature is a large gateway structure pierced by a 20-foot-high pointed arch *(right)*. This kind of arch, known as a corbeled type, was used by the Maya to roof temples, but only in Yucatán was it built to stand on its own. Probably used for ceremonial processions, it is decorated by stone replicas of farmers' cottages.

Near the gateway rises Labná's only remaining temple. Though it is crowned by a traditional ornamented roof comb, seen here in profile, the mound it rests on is far lower and gentler than the steep-sided pyramids of the rain forest—as though its builders no longer felt the need to boost their shrines above the jungle trees.

Uxmal—a city of plazas and palaces with a grim portent of the future

AN ARROW-SHAPED ARCH, *recessed near one end of the Palace's façade, was built in ascending, corbel fashion, then partly walled up to create a room inside. The columns in front once carried a portico.*

A SKULL AND CROSSBONES *decorate an altar at Uxmal. Such macabre designs, unusual in Maya architecture, reflect the influence of a later, harsher culture brought in by the Toltecs from central Mexico.*

The architects of Uxmal, one of the largest and finest of the Yucatán cities, evolved a style as expansive as the countryside itself. Their majestic palaces extend hundreds of feet and abut plazas broad as football fields. The 19th Century traveler John L. Stephens, whose writings first excited the interest of the modern world in Maya culture, compared Uxmal with the great Egyptian ruins at Thebes.

Civil pomp and the arts, more than religion, seem to have inspired Uxmal's builders. Temple-pyramids are outnumbered by huge horizontal buildings, like the Palace of the Governor *(left)*, whose long frieze of geometric patterns is considered one of the most beautiful in ancient American art. The peaceful lives of the Maya are reflected in its motifs, such as masks of the rain god, ascending in diagonal rows, and stone latticework recalling the weave of textiles. But symbols on other monuments, like the skull carving above, show the influence of warlike Toltecs, who swept Yucatán in the 10th Century and abruptly altered the path of the Maya renaissance.

RANKS OF COLUMNS *(right), a Toltec innovation, march by the Temple of the Warriors. A vaulted stone roof once covered them.*

A RECLINING FIGURE, *which may have received sacrificial offerings on its belly, faces the Castillo, Chichén Itzá's main temple.*

When the Toltecs invaded Yucatán, they established their regional capital in the conquered Maya city of Chichén Itzá. There they replaced the benign Maya deities with their own bloodthirsty gods and forced Maya craftsmen to rebuild the city along Toltec lines. Temples were erected to Tezcatlipoca, the Toltec war god, and decorated with carvings of grim-faced foot soldiers; weird, recumbent figures called *chac-mools* were placed outside.

Over the next century the Maya and Toltec cultures gradually merged. But the fierce new strains persisted. At last, under the pressure of constant civil warfare among Chichén Itzá and other neighboring cities, the great monuments slowly deteriorated and the Maya's proud civilization collapsed.

# 3

# AN AGE OF
# WARRIOR-KINGS

A MASSIVE STONE SOLDIER *in full battle dress stands at the base of a pyramid-temple erected to the supreme Toltec deity, Quetzalcóatl, near the Valley of Mexico. Along with identical statues shown dismantled beside him, the 15-foot-high figure served as a column to support the temple's roof.*

After the fall of Mexico's great city of Teotihuacán in about 700 A.D. came centuries of darkness and confusion that affected all Middle America. The character of its civilization changed. Old-style unfortified cities dominated by scholarly priests of a rather mild religion gave place to warrior city-states whose rulers made fighting and conquest a way of life. Their cities were often fortified, and the religion they followed was anything but mild.

The great change was brought about by the Chichimecs—fierce barbarians from the north who stormed into civilized Mexico in successive, destructive waves over a period of 500 years. But the Chichimecs, while they caused the total collapse of some high cultures and drastically altered the structure of others, also carried with them the seeds of future greatness. Ancient Mexico's most celebrated and most dynamic people, the warlike Aztecs, who were at the height of their power when the Spaniards arrived, sprang from Chichimec ancestors. So did the vigorous Toltecs who preceded them—and who laid the foundations on which the Aztecs built the civilization whose savagery and splendor astonished its Old World conquerors.

Although the name Chichimec means Sons of the Dog in the Aztec language, it was not intended to be derogatory; it simply signified that the invaders were nomads. Even in this sense, however, the name was inaccurate. The Chichimecs were not mere hunter-gatherers; if they had been they would have been too few to be dangerous. Like the crude Germanic tribesmen who overwhelmed the Roman Empire in the Fifth Century, they had enough agriculture to support considerable populations. Remains of their farming settlements have been traced deep into the wild mountains and deserts of northern Mexico.

When Teotihuacán fell, either through internal weakness or external assault, the first bands of Chichimecs swarmed over the Valley of Mexico and beyond, bringing terror wherever they appeared. Feathered and painted like the Sioux or Comanches of later times but in greater numbers, they attacked peaceful cities with blood-chilling battle cries, slaughtering here, enslaving there, raping and plundering. But sometimes they must have

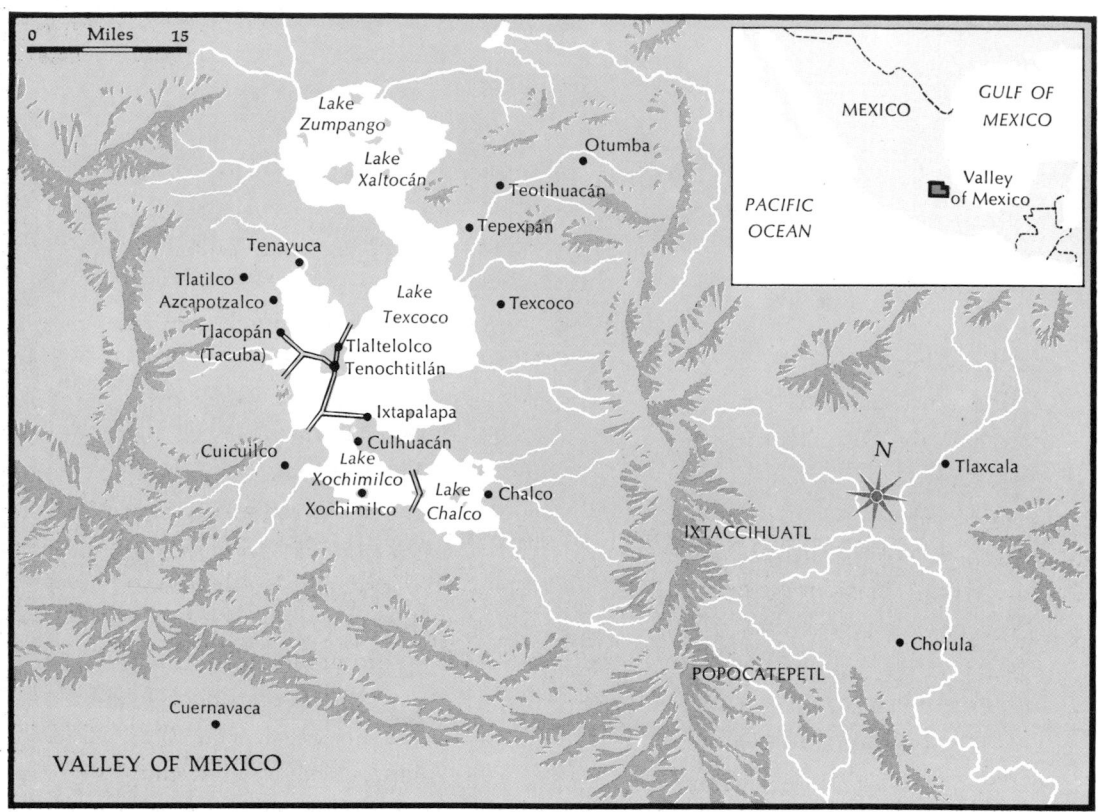

THE VALLEY OF MEXICO *was the seat of the mighty Aztec Empire. In this fertile basin of central Mexico (inset), the Aztecs built their capital, Tenochtitlán, an island fortress in Lake Texcoco. Most of the valley was once covered by five lakes, but only Texcoco remains, much reduced in size.*

stopped to stare with awe at the magnificent temples and pyramids whose builders could no longer protect them.

Like most barbarian invasions, the Chichimec conquest did not occur everywhere at once, nor was it ever complete. Some cities in the Valley of Mexico accepted Chichimec rulers and were protected by them; some resisted for considerable lengths of time. Several cities outside the valley preserved enough of their old and well-developed cultures to exert a strong influence on later peoples. They can be compared to Byzantium, which resisted the barbarous invaders of the Roman Empire and sheltered important features of Greco-Roman civilization until the Renaissance in Western Europe.

Gradually order returned to Mexico and its central valley. Some of the Chichimecs were assimi-

lated by the valley's ancient civilization and helped its survivors repel fresh invaders from the north. Others built crude cities of their own and gradually improved them as their cultural level rose. By about 970 A.D. one of these cities of ex-barbarians, Tula of the Toltecs, whose ruins lie 50 miles north of Mexico City in the present state of Hidalgo, had concentrated enough population and power to dominate not only the key Valley of Mexico but many distant parts of Middle America.

At this point the recorded history of Mexico begins. Scraps of information about the Toltecs of Tula are preserved in the Aztec poems and legends that were memorized for many generations like the Homeric poems of the Greek Heroic Age. After the Spanish conquest some of this memorized literature was written down by educated Indians or recounted to Spanish chroniclers. The legends are more colorful than factual, but many contain real facts which scholars have separated from their mythical trimmings and confirmed by archeological findings.

The story of the Toltecs begins with a legend describing them as a Chichimec tribe that prowled down from the north early in the 10th Century, led by a king named Mixcóatl, settling at Culhuacán, a few miles south of modern Mexico City. Mixcóatl may have been a legendary ruler, but his son, Topiltzin, actually lived. Although many myths accumulated about him, he is the first flesh-and-blood personality in Mexican history.

As a youth, Topiltzin studied for the priesthood and eventually became a high priest of Quetzalcóatl, or the Feathered Serpent, the very ancient god of Teotihuacán and the patron of learning and civilized skills. When Topiltzin ascended the Toltec throne, he changed his own name to Quetzalcóatl. This was not an act of self-deification; high priests of the time were often called by the names of the gods they worshiped. But the change of name caused endless confusion. Both ancient Indian legend-makers and modern historians have often mistaken Topiltzin-Quetzalcóatl, the man, for Quetzalcóatl, the god.

Around 950 A.D. Topiltzin moved the Toltec capital to Tula, beyond the northern end of the Valley of Mexico. He populated the new city, so the legend tells, partly with Nonoalca (Deaf and Dumb People)—which is just a way of saying that he brought to Tula people unable to speak the Toltecs' language. They were undoubtedly survivors of the Chichimec onslaught from the Valley of Mexico or elsewhere who had preserved elements of Teotihuacán civilization. Their artistry was beyond that of the Toltecs of the time, who were still only a few generations removed from Chichimec barbarism, and Topiltzin put them to work

carving statues, making fine pottery and building temples.

Topiltzin-Quetzalcóatl made Tula into a great city and taught its people all the civilized arts. His piety and celibacy were much admired, but he made the fatal mistake of trying to establish the gentle, beneficent Quetzalcóatl as the principal god of Tula. This did not appeal to the dominant Toltecs of the city, who already had gods more to their warlike taste. Chief among them was Tezcatlipoca, a warrior god who demanded to be fed frequently on the warm blood and still-beating hearts of human sacrificial victims.

The legend goes into great and often conflicting detail about the way the Tezcatlipoca faction defeated Topiltzin and his gentle god, Quetzalcóatl. One curious version is that one evening Tezcatlipoca disguised himself as an old man, used his divine persuasive powers to get Topiltzin drunk and then left the king's own sister, the charming Quetzalpetlatl (Feathered Mat), in the room with him. In the morning Topiltzin realized that he had lost his chastity and was hopelessly disgraced. So he abdicated the Toltec throne and with a group of devoted retainers went into exile.

Scholars, concluding that this story was based on fact, have interpreted it to mean that Tula was torn by religious conflict between devotees of the old civilized gods of Teotihuacán and those of the fierce war gods brought by the Toltecs from the savage north. The followers of the war gods won, as symbolized by Topiltzin's departure.

In the rest of the legend the man and the god are blended together. After leaving Tula, the exiled Topiltzin-Quetzalcóatl spent 20 years at Cholula, a famous cultural and religious center. Then he set out for the seacoast; one of the many versions of the story says that he sailed out into the ocean on a raft made of interlaced snakes, another that he rose to the sky and turned into the Morning Star. But before he left he promised to return from the direction of the rising sun, and he specified the date—a date corresponding to 1519 in the European calendar. This legend, known all over Middle America, was to have disastrous consequences for the Aztec civilization; by one of history's most remarkable coincidences, on the date of Quetzalcóatl's predicted reappearance the first conquistadors were to arrive in Mexico.

The ancient Tula, which has been partially but carefully restored, does not look much like Teotihuacán or any of its offshoots. The delicate artistry of that classic age is largely lacking; instead the place is characterized by a fierceness and strength. The principal feature so far restored is a low, five-stepped pyramid topped by a wide platform once occupied by a large temple. Standing in a row on the platform are four stone columns in the shape of armed warriors 15 feet tall. These columns and four square pillars carved with warriors in bas-relief supported the temple's timber roof. In front of the pyramid is a vestibulelike area with many more square pillars, and sections of others lie scattered around the site. Such pillars and the grim warriors that they often depict are characteristically Toltec. Wherever they occur in Middle America they indicate Toltec influence.

Although the Toltecs had refused to replace all of their blood-hungry gods with less sanguinary ones, they were nevertheless considerably influenced by the traditional religion of Teotihuacán. Some of its old gods appear in stone friezes ornamenting Tula's pyramid. Among them is Quetzalcóatl, represented by many-feathered rattlesnakes with upraised tails and rattles. One complicated monster is believed to be the very ancient rain god Tlaloc in combination with various snake and bird elements.

Tezcatlipoca, the war god and master of life and death, is not among the gods portrayed on the pyramid; perhaps the structure was completed before the victory of his sect and the exile of Topiltzin. But there are many signs that the cult of human sacrifice was in full swing at Tula. Repeated over and over on the pyramid are carvings of an eagle, symbol of the sun, eating a human heart. Other carvings show an eagle vessel meant to contain the hearts of victims, and an altar where their heads were displayed is decorated with skulls and crossbones. Since skulls and crossbones are common on ancient ruins along parts of Mexico's Gulf Coast, they may well have been the inspiration for the black flag of the pirates who prowled the Caribbean in the 17th and 18th Centuries.

In some ways Tula was a new kind of city. Instead of rising defenseless from a flat plain like Teotihuacán, its temples and large residential sections crowned an easily defensible hilltop. The city was built, after all, on the Chichimec frontier and must have been under continual threat of barbarian attack. Far from being dominated by priests, the Toltec capital was a city of soldiers, obeying military leaders and supported by wealth exacted from conquered populations. As the hub of ancient America's first clearly defined tribute state, it set the governmental, economic and religious pattern that was to prevail throughout most of Middle America until the Spanish conquest.

Within a generation after Tula's founding around the middle of the 10th Century, Toltec armies, probably an amalgam of many different races and tribes, had spread over most of Mexico. They dominated both coasts and reached south to Guatemala and far into the country of their Chichimec ancestors in the north. About 1000 A.D. they achieved their most spectacular advance, sweeping into northern Yucatán and overwhelming centers where the late Maya civilization was still flourishing. They probably invaded by sea; some accounts, obviously influenced by later legends, say the invasion was led by Quetzalcóatl himself. The Toltecs may have destroyed some Maya centers, but in return they built, with the help of Maya artisans, a large part of the strikingly beautiful city of Chichén Itzá that stands gleaming in the sun on a dry, scrub-covered plain.

The architecture of Chichén Itzá is Maya, but there are many signs that Toltecs dominated the place, bringing with them their religion of death and human sacrifice, and their altars decorated with carved skulls. Maya sculptors were not entirely unacquainted with the subject of sacrifice, but now more than ever before they used their artistry to depict this ghastly but dramatic act.

Chichén Itzá had a special kind of sacrifice unknown in Tula of the Toltecs. To the north of the city's most imposing structure, the temple-crowned pyramid called the Castillo, is the famous Sacred Well, a deep *cenote*, or sinkhole, in the limestone bedrock. When the rains failed or the priests saw other signs of divine displeasure, they consecrated young girls specially selected for their beauty and hurled them into the well along with jewels and other objects of great value. According to Spanish chronicles, written centuries after the well had claimed its last victim, the girls were thrown into its depths at sunrise. If they survived until midday, they were taken out and asked to repeat any messages or special instructions that the gods may have given them.

For many years the tale of Chichén Itzá's Sacred Well was dismissed as a fanciful legend. But dredging has since retrieved from its murky waters an extraordinary collection of treasures. Mingled with the bones of victims who did not receive the favor of the gods have come hundreds of offerings that include exquisite gold and jade jewelry, sacrificial knives of obsidian with jeweled handles, and masks and plaques of copper or gold. Many of the golden ornaments are believed to have been made in distant Panama.

The Toltec influence emanating from Tula in Mexico not only profoundly affected the Maya of Yucatán but also penetrated to some degree into what is now the United States, particularly the Mississippi Valley. Some earthen mounds in that region, used simply as burial places, may date from as early as 1000 B.C., but after about the 10th Century A.D., when the Toltecs began their rise to power, large temple-supporting mounds reminiscent of Tula's pyramid were built there. The people who worshiped their gods on these mounds were probably not Toltec immigrants; the religious ideas that inspired them may have been passed from tribe to tribe, or possibly they were brought in by venturesome traders from Toltec-dominated lands.

Tula was destroyed about 1160 A.D., probably by another wave of the Chichimec barbarians who throughout Toltec times never ceased to be a menace from the north. Its site was deserted, but the name Toltec lived on. Warlike groups of people claiming Toltec ancestry dispersed over Mexico and as far south as Nicaragua, settling where they could or installing themselves as the ruling class of the cities they conquered.

The destruction of Tula and the breakup of the Toltec empire did not cause so severe a collapse of Mexican civilization as had the fall of Teotihuacán nearly 500 years before. Fresh bands of Chichimecs roamed the country, as fierce and merciless as ever; but many city-states held out against them. The Mixtecs, for example, who for years had maintained a magnificent center at Mitla in mountainous country southeast of the Valley of Mexico, continued their civilization undisturbed. They even expanded into the region around Oaxaca, occupying the ancient and long-abandoned Zapotec ceremonial site of Monte Albán and using some of the Zapotec

## A LYRICAL LANGUAGE

*Náhuatl (pronounced Nah'-wahtl), the language used by the Aztecs and still spoken by some central Mexicans, has a rich, harmonious vocabulary. Some Náhuatl names used in this book, with their pronunciation and meanings, are listed below.*

CULHUACAN *(Cool-wah-cahn'): "Crooked Hill." The first city of the Toltecs, founded by King Mixcóatl in the Ninth Century.*

HUITZILOPOCHTLI *(Wee-tsee-loh-pohtch'-tlee): "Left-handed Hummingbird." War and sun god, the Aztecs' principal deity.*

MICTLANTECUHTLI *(Meek-tlan-tay-coot'-li): "Lord of the Underworld." God of the dead, who wore a mask of a human skull.*

MIXTEC *(Mish-tec'): "Cloud People." A highly cultured civilization of the Oaxaca valley, noted for its use of picture-writing.*

NEZAHUALCOYOTL *(Nets-ah-wahl-coy'-ohtl): "Hungry Coyote." A Texcocan king who was also a noted poet-philosopher.*

OAXACA *(Wah-hah'-cah): "Place of the Mimosa." A valley inhabited by the Zapotec and Mixtec peoples, now a Mexican state.*

QUETZALCOATL *(Ket-sahl-coh'-atl): "Feathered Serpent." The god of creation, inventor of agriculture, and patron of learning.*

TENOCHTITLAN *(Ten-och-tee-tlahn'): "Near the Cactus." The Aztec capital, founded in 1325 on an island in Lake Texcoco.*

TEOTIHUACAN *(Tey-o-tee-wah-cahn'): "Place of the Gods." An early ceremonial site located near present-day Mexico City.*

TEZCATLIPOCA *(Tehs-cah-tle-poh'-cah): "Smoking Mirror." A warrior god who observed the deeds of men through a mirror.*

TLALOC *(Tlah'-lohc): "He who makes things grow." God of rain and lightning, who lived on the tops of high mountains.*

TLAXCALA *(Tlahs-cah'-lah): "Place of Bread." A region in central Mexico whose inhabitants fought the Aztecs with Cortés.*

XOCHIMILCO *(Show-chee-meel'-coh): "Field of Flowers." A village south of Mexico City noted for its "floating gardens."*

tombs there for their own priests or rulers. From one of these Mixtec burials, the celebrated "Tomb No. 7," came the richest find ever unearthed in Middle America—more than 500 beautifully worked objects of gold, silver, jade, turquoise and other precious materials.

The Valley of Mexico itself seems to have assimilated the new waves of Chichimecs without any serious setback. Its population soon recovered, supported by bounteous farming on artificial islands, or *chinampas*, built along the margins of the lakes. Warfare was continual for more than 200 years among the city-states, large and small, but none of them gained control of the whole rich valley, the key to mastery of all Middle America.

That achievement was reserved for the Aztecs, who made their first appearance around 1200 A.D.

Descendants of the last Chichimec tribesmen to push into central Mexico, the Aztecs were destined to grow in a few centuries from a handful of savage outlaws into lords of the Valley of Mexico, with a large and gorgeous capital city and armies that exacted tribute from dozens of terrorized city-states. The Aztecs were the culmination of ancient Mexican civilization, and the climactic battle between them and the conquering Spaniards would mark that civilization's end.

Several surviving chronicles of the Aztecs describe their origin and rise, but some of these reflect a deliberate attempt to rewrite history. After the Aztecs had become powerful, they decided to conceal their humble origin by replacing it with a more honorable and impressive past. They transformed themselves into descendants of the Culhuas, citizens of the city of Culhuacán and the most ancient and aristocratic Toltec remnant in the Valley.

Earlier chronicles, beneath their mythological embroidery, are more factual. They show the Aztecs as a small, harried tribe of impoverished nomads whose ancestors emerged from a cave at an unidentified place in northwestern Mexico called Aztlán, from which the name Aztec is derived. For many years the tribe had only one cherished possession, the wooden image of a terrible god wrapped in a bundle. It was carefully guarded by four priest-chiefs and carried on all of the tribe's wanderings, just as the early Hebrews carried their Ark of the Covenant through the wilderness of Sinai.

Like many gods of other religions, the god in the Aztecs' bundle was of partly human descent. His mother, according to one legend, was a devout and elderly widow with one daughter and "four hundred" (that is, innumerable) sons. One day as she was piously sweeping a sacred precinct she picked up a small ball of feathers endowed with supernatural powers. She tucked it between her breasts and eventually found herself pregnant. Her children did not accept her condition as a divine honor; they considered it shameful and decided to punish her with death, but as they advanced to kill her, she heard a voice inside her saying "Do not be afraid." Her child leaped from her womb a full-grown man and armed with a "serpent of fire," or lightning. With this favorite and formidable weapon of gods he promptly slew his mother's hostile children. Thus was born Huitzilopochtli, the fearsome war god of the Aztecs.

When Huitzilopochtli's name is translated literally, it has the singularly harmless meaning of "left-handed hummingbird," but certainly few who knew him thought of him as harmless. Of all the gods of ancient Mexico, Left-handed Hummingbird was the most greedy for human blood. In the time of the Aztecs' glory thousands of victims paraded each year to his altars to have their spurting hearts torn from their bodies.

That time of glory was far in the future. During the Aztec wanderings in the 13th Century, Huitzilopochtli could not have enjoyed much human blood,

but nevertheless he made himself useful. According to the priests who guarded his image, he gave divinely wise advice whenever they asked him for it, and the advice was always followed.

Huitzilopochtli's advice was better than most, but for a good many generations some of his followers must have had their doubts. When the Aztecs first entered the Valley of Mexico, they were shunted from place to place like gypsies. All the good land in the valley was owned, and none of its cities wanted these hungry and dangerous barbarians to settle near them. At last, after many vicissitudes, the Aztecs persuaded Coxcox, ruler of the ancient Toltec city of Culhuacán, to give them a piece of sterile, snake-infested land. Here they built a temple for their god, killed and ate the snakes and seemed on their way to settling down and becoming just another group of assimilated invaders.

But the bloody ways of the Aztecs soon alienated their benefactors. The priests of Huitzilopochtli asked Coxcox for his attractive and dearly beloved daughter, saying that they wished to honor her with a very special ceremony. The king of Culhuacán complied, and when the girl arrived the priests took her into the temple, flayed her and dressed one of their number in her skin. Then they invited her father to witness the ceremony. When Coxcox first entered the temple he could not see in the darkness, but he lit a fire of incense—and as its flames leaped high he saw the priest dancing before the altar of Huitzilopochtli clad in his daughter's skin.

The result of this outrage was immediate war between the Aztecs and Culhuacán. The Aztecs were quickly driven into the marshes of Lake Texcoco where they hid among the reeds. Huitzilopochtli came with them, and he gave them wise advice. He told the Aztecs crouching among the reeds that they should search for an eagle perched on a cactus and holding a snake in its beak, and there they should build their city. The search did not take

MEXICO'S NATIONAL EMBLEM, *adopted when that nation achieved independence from Spain in 1821, derives from an Aztec legend. In choosing a site for their city of Tenochtitlán, the story goes, the people, following the instructions of the god Huitzilopochtli, sought and found a spot where an eagle was perched on a cactus devouring a snake. There they settled and built their capital. The site is now buried under Mexico City.*

long. On a small uninhabited island, hardly more than a few rocks poking above the marshes, they found the cactus, the eagle and the snake, which today are displayed on Mexico's coat of arms. There they began to build their city, Tenochtitlán, meaning "near the cactus."

This oft-told tale may be more than mere legend; perhaps it is a figurative way of saying that the subtle priests of Huitzilopochtli, claiming the guidance of their god, selected the island for its strategic advantages even before their cruel treatment of Coxcox's daughter. When they saw that their followers were in danger of settling down, becoming humble serfs of Culhuacán and abandoning hopes of greatness, they engineered the girl's sacrifice, knowing perfectly well it would provoke a war. Then they led their planned retreat to the chosen island in Lake Texcoco.

If the priests of Left-handed Hummingbird really planned it that way, they could hardly have done better. The island was in the center of three powerful mainland cities but was not strongly claimed by any, and so the Aztecs had no trouble keeping it for their own. It could be approached for attack only by water, which gave its defenders an important advantage. Relatively secure in their water-walled stronghold, the Aztecs, whose favorite occupation was war, could ally themselves with the city that offered the most for their help, but they could not be easily reached and punished if a war went against them.

The water that protected the Aztecs' stronghold also made possible its expansion. Its inhabitants soon learned to increase the area of their island by filling the marshes with dirt and rocks and by building chinampas, islets made by anchoring wickerwork enclosures to the bottom of the lake and piling them with silt mixed with reeds and refuse. The ease of water transportation was another factor in the growth of the island city. A Mexican city surrounded by land could attain only a certain size, which depended on the productivity of the land near it. Then it was forced to stop growing because its food and other necessities would have to come from distant places; and since the ancient Mexicans lacked wheeled vehicles and beasts of burden, these supplies were limited to what could be borne on the backs of human porters. A city encircled by water had no such limitation; a canoe paddled by a single man could carry the load of many porters.

Tenochtitlán was first settled about 1325, and for awhile the Aztecs supported themselves by trading fish, ducks, frogs and other lake products for corn and beans, and for stone to build a temple for Huitzilopochtli. Whenever they could they fought, furiously and well, and their numbers steadily increased as adventurers, malcontents and refugees joined them on their island. Before many years had passed they were in high demand as allies or mercenaries. Part of the tribe split off and founded the city of Tlaltelolco on a small island in the marshes nearby, but this defection did not stop the mushrooming growth of Tenochtitlán.

The Aztec capital was not alone in its development. Although its leaders in later years claimed much of the credit for the final flowering of Mexican civilization, other peoples also played significant roles. Ever since Teotihuacán times the life-giving lakes that filled the center of the Valley of Mexico—and which were much bigger than they are today—had been ringed with populous cities. Their citizens and ruling classes were of several different origins, but most of them spoke Náhuatl, the same language as the Aztecs. These cities enjoyed a common though not entirely uniform culture that preserved many elements of Mexico's earlier civilizations.

Texcoco, on the eastern shore of Lake Texcoco, for example, was a highly civilized city and the valley's intellectual center. Its king, Nezahualcoyotl, was a patron of the arts and sciences and ancient Mexico's most famous philosopher and poet. His speeches are still quoted by scholarly Mexicans, and some of his poetry is inscribed on the walls of Mexico City's Museum of Anthropology. Like Egypt's Pharaoh Akhenaton of the 15th Century B.C., he toyed with monotheism and even dedicated a temple to "the unknown god, creator of all things." Nezahualcoyotl was also a notable engineer. When Tenochtitlán, at the time his ally, was threatened with flooding by the rising water of the lake, he built a dike 10 miles long to protect it.

Tenochtitlán, a latecomer to this long-established community, won its dominant position in Mexico by playing these and older cities elsewhere against one another. The wars and intrigues by which it succeeded are as complex as the rivalries of the city-states of Renaissance Italy. At first the Aztec nation was a very subordinate ally of the Tepanecs, powerful outsiders from Toluca who almost got control of the valley. At exactly the right moment, presumably selected by Huitzilopochtli, the Aztecs shifted sides and helped Texcoco destroy the Tepanec empire. This adroit maneuver won the Aztecs a foothold on the mainland and rights of tribute from many parts of the former Tepanec domains.

From here on the rise of the Aztecs was rapid, for they exploited the advantages of the tribute state with unparalleled vigor and ruthlessness. Looked at religiously, which is the way the Aztecs viewed it, the system worked as follows: Huitzilopochtli was the prime mover. He hungered for the fresh, bleeding hearts of human sacrificial victims. When the Aztecs gave them to him, he rewarded them with victories. Each victory gathered more captives, more hearts for Huitzilopochtli, more victories for the Aztecs. The thing grew like a rolling snowball. Decade after decade more and more captives taken in battle were led to the temple of the insatiable god. Each time Huitzilopochtli was gratified and duly scheduled for the Aztecs another success in war.

Looked at nonreligiously, the system had a solid base in economics. Besides taking captives from a defeated nation, the Aztecs exacted tribute in food, clothing, weapons and other things that their growing city needed. With these assets in hand, they could equip and maintain more soldiers, fight more wars and increase the flow of both captives and tribute from conquered cities. Other states in other ages, notably Rome, were built on the same principle, but seldom if ever did it work better than it did for Tenochtitlán. The city in the lake spread out over the marshes, its population swelled by soldier immigrants from neighboring warlike tribes.

Tenochtitlán's parade of victories was interrupted by one serious defeat. About 1470 the Aztecs and their allies under the Emperor Axayacatl attacked the Tarascan kingdom in the present state of Michoacán and were disastrously beaten. Axayacatl also failed to overrun the hardy mountaineers of Tlaxcala east of the Valley of Mexico.

But he made up for these failures by smashing the growing presumptuousness of Tlaltelolco, the city originally built on a marshy island but now joined to Tenochtitlán's by man-made land. The people of Tlaltelolco, Aztecs themselves, and old allies of Tenochtitlán, had insisted on keeping a measure of independence. When they arrogantly dared to build a temple-pyramid higher than any in Tenochtitlán, Axayacatl headed an army that fought its way into their main square. As a last resort the women of Tlaltelolco stripped themselves naked and threw filth at the invaders, but even this odd tactic, which must have had some justification in the customs of the time, did not turn the tide of battle. Tlaltelolco was conquered, its rulers slaughtered and its offending pyramid pulled down. The twin city remained the merchants' quarter of expanding Tenochtitlán. Some of its pyramids and other religious buildings have been restored and can be seen in a suburb of Mexico City.

Although they never did conquer the Tarascans and Tlaxcalans, most of the Aztecs' campaigns succeeded. With or without allies, their armies marched to the Pacific and Gulf Coasts, and southward past the Isthmus of Tehuantepec, almost reaching the present boundary of Guatemala. Some of the Zapotecs and Mixtecs around Oaxaca held out precariously, but whether they would have continued to do so is doubtful; when the Spaniards invaded Mexico, the Aztec Empire was in the flush of its power and still expanding. Long files of captives marched toward Tenochtitlán, headed for their moments on the sacrificial stone, and armies of porters carried burdens of tribute to feed and embellish the city in the lake.

By 1519, the year of the Spanish invasion, Tenochtitlán had become a city of great size and magnificence, about five times as big as the London of that time. Most of the oval island on which it stood had been created by filling swampland with silt dredged from the lake bottom and earth brought from the mainland in canoes. And the island was still growing. To feed Tenochtitlán's estimated 300,000 inhabitants, its industrious farmers were encircling the island with an ever-widening fringe of chinampas planted with flourishing crops of fruits and vegetables. A remnant of this very efficient kind of farming can still be seen in the "floating gardens" (which do not really float) at Xochimilco, a short distance south of Mexico City.

In the middle of the belt of chinampas rose the city, connected to the mainland by three long causeways. Cutting it into blocks was a gridwork of canals bordered by narrow pedestrian lanes and crossed by plank footbridges. The meaner houses were of adobe, the better ones of stone and stucco, but all were cleanly whitewashed. Most of them had courtyards, some of which resembled small parks, and everywhere bloomed flowers, which the fierce Aztecs loved inordinately.

Each of the four main sections into which the city was divided had its local market, and two very large ones, in Tenochtitlán itself and in its satellite Tlaltelolco, offered all the products of the Empire. Some areas of these great markets specialized

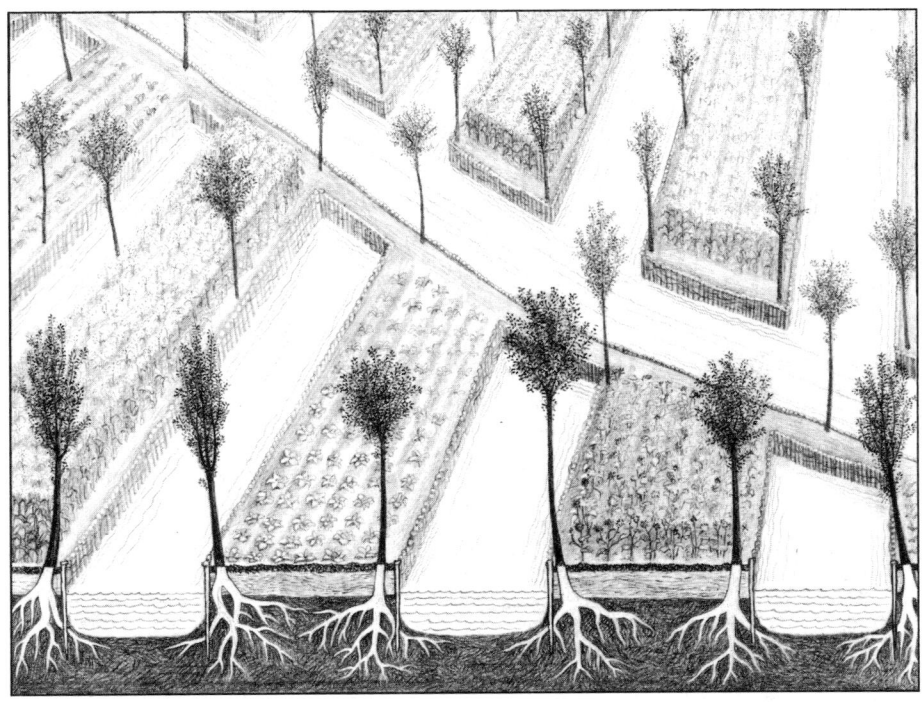

MAN-MADE ISLETS *called "chinampas" supported several crop plantings per year for the Aztecs. Canals were cut through marshland, and the reeds and rotting vegetation were piled between retaining walls; this served as a foundation for beds of topsoil, which were periodically renewed with fertile mud from the canal bottoms. Willows planted at edges and corners retarded erosion.*

in corn, beans and squash or in turkeys, venison and edible dogs. Others displayed cotton cloth, robes of brilliant featherwork and sandals of plaited fiber. From the armorers, soldiers off to the wars obtained new shields, spears or wooden swords edged with obsidian. Noblemen and their elegant ladies patronized the jewelers, who unwrapped before them delicate carvings of jade and other precious stones.

Near the center of the city on wide canals were the palaces of the emperor, the great nobles and the high priests, and in the center itself stood the temple-pyramids and other ceremonial buildings which, in the eyes of the Aztecs, gave Tenochtitlán its reason for being. Enclosed by a stone wall decorated with carved snakes was a wide paved court, dominated by a 100-foot-high pyramid surmounted by twin temples, one sacred to Huitzilopochtli and the other to the ancient rain god Tlaloc. Flanking this immense edifice were the smaller pyramid

of the war god Tezcatlipoca, inherited from the Toltecs, and minor pyramids and altars. One lesser pyramid belonged to Xipe Totec, Teotihuacán's god of springtime, whose priests danced in his honor dressed in freshly flayed human skins.

This sacred precinct was no quiet sanctuary. It was an active industrial center whose principal product was human hearts for the gods. Black-robed priests strode across its pavements or climbed the steep steps of the pyramids carrying censers shaped like clay frying pans and filled with smoking incense for the gods' pleasure. Often they led victims to the stones of sacrifice, which were seldom idle. The victim was thrown on his back over the upward-curving stone, and four priests with long hair matted with blood held him down by his arms and legs. A fifth priest plunged a knife of razor-sharp obsidian into the man's taut chest, reached inside and pulled out the still-beating heart.

Nearly every enterprise of Aztec life, from crop

planting to the launching of a trading expedition, called for the donation of at least one heart to win some god's favor, and during major ceremonies the great enclosure was densely crowded with priests, victims and worshipers. When the Emperor Ahuitzotl consecrated the temple of Huitzilopochtli shortly before 1490, at least 20,000 (some accounts say 80,000) prisoners of war were sacrificed. The Emperor and his near relatives, who were also high priests, took turns plunging the knife for as long as their strength lasted; then they turned the duty over to lesser hierarchs. For four days the files of victims inched toward the curved stone, now surrounded by ponds of blood. Their bodies piled up in tumbled heaps, and their skulls overflowed the skull rack rising in front of the pyramids. For weeks thereafter the center of the city stank of rotting bodies and blood.

To do the Aztecs justice, these scenes of sacrifice did not seem entirely horrible to them or even to the victims. Death itself was not much feared, and ritual death at the hands of the priests was considered an honor. In the case of soldiers captured on the battlefield, it assured them of a glorious after-life, and tales have been handed down of famous captives who had been offered their lives but preferred to die.

Though wholesale human sacrifice was the mainspring of Aztec religion and was regarded as essential for the state's well-being, it did not entirely dominate Aztec life. Along with the grisly ceremonies inside the Wall of Snakes went joyous festivals with feasting, music and dancing, and the upper classes followed a fastidious etiquette that was the antithesis of their religious practices; young noble people for instance, were taught the proper way to hold and smell bouquets of flowers. The court of the emperor was as punctilious as any in Europe. The ruler ate his meals behind a gilded screen, shielded from spectators; when he

traveled he was carried in a litter on the shoulders of noblemen. Whenever he walked, the ground was covered with cloths so his feet would not touch it.

The emperor in 1519 was Moctezuma II, who had ascended the throne in 1502. In his youth, he had served ably as a soldier and later led successful campaigns, but he was the first of the Aztec emperors who was not primarily a military man. Basically, he was a religious intellectual dominated by doubts and worries that did not fit the creed of the Aztec conquest state. He had deeply absorbed Toltec civilization, especially those aspects that had come down to the Aztecs from the even more ancient and more peaceful era of Teotihuacán, and he knew that the gods had once been worshiped without great floods of human blood.

In particular he brooded about the exiled Quetzalcóatl, the giver of knowledge and all good things, who had sailed into the eastern sea and promised to return. That had been more than 500 years before, and the year when the god had said he would return was almost at hand. What would happen then? thought Moctezuma. Perhaps the beneficent god would vanquish the god of death and war. Such thoughts were sacrilegious for an Aztec emperor, but there had been rumors of strange men riding in white-winged ships on the eastern sea.

The rumors were correct; those were the ships of the Spaniards. In their leader, Hernán Cortés, the Emperor imagined he saw Quetzalcóatl, fulfilling his promise to return. Dreading to offend a living god, Moctezuma hesitated to send his warriors to drive the invaders from Mexico. Instead he allowed them to approach the Aztec capital of Tenochtitlán—and in so doing he opened the way to disaster and conquest.

In a very real sense Quetzalcóatl had returned to fight on the side of the conquerors and to wreak his long-delayed revenge on the worshipers of the war gods.

A CHIEF WITH HIS SYMBOLS, *Eight-Deer points to a buck's head and eight circles that represent his name in Mixtec picture writing.*

# THE LEGEND OF EIGHT-DEER

Nearly a thousand years ago a fierce chieftain named Eight-Deer Ocelot-Claw ruled a large area in what is now southern Mexico. Born in 1011 A.D. in Tilantongo, a small town that still stands in the state of Oaxaca, Eight-Deer became chief of his people at the age of 19, upon the death of his father. He was a Mixtec, a member of a proud race also known as the "Cloud People," whose ancestors, according to one legend, came from the skies. Through conquest, strategic marriage and the sacrifice to the gods of potential rivals, Eight-Deer expanded his realm. He married many wives, sired large numbers of children and died at the age of 52, sacrificed in his turn after losing a battle. The exploits of Eight-Deer are preserved in seven books of picture writing called codices. The stories these codices tell are full of mysterious symbolism not completely clear to scholars. But they are beginning to reveal more and more about a colorful—and often bloodthirsty—people who lived 500 years before Columbus came to their shores.

# A PICTURE PAGE FROM EIGHT-DEER'S LIFE

It was the custom to name children after the day on which they were born in the Mixtec calendar, which assigned to each day a name and number. Thus, Eight-Deer was named for Eight-Deer day; later, when he became an important prince, the name of Ocelot-Claw was added. A codex from the British Museum records on one of its colorful deerskin pages, reproduced here, four of Eight-Deer's early military victories; it also shows him paying respect to a dead relative, serving as a priest and making sacrifices to the gods.

**16** *In his royal role as a priest, Eight-Deer (left) holds a deer over a sacrificial block, while his half-brother Twelve-Earthquake Bleeding-Tiger wields a stone knife to extract the animal's heart in a sacrifice to the gods. One god, Thirteen-Reed, calls down to them from the sky; on the ground is the body of a dog already sacrificed. This ritual took place in a town with a ceremonial court, represented by the H figure at lower left.*

**9** *Eight-Deer, in the black body paint of a priest and wearing an eagle headdress, is seen at Three-Lizard's funeral. The dead man, according to the genealogy charts on the back of each page of the codex, was Eight-Deer's great great-grandmother's brother's son, thus three generations removed from the warrior himself. But as an elder statesman, Three-Lizard was a man to be respected and mourned by all.*

**15** *The date for the rites shown above is given as Five-Reed Year (1043 A.D.), Two-Water Day.*

**10** *The date of Three-Lizard's funeral is repeated. It may also refer to the event shown below.*

**14** *Another reed in the ground, above a figure surrounded by walls, indicates that Eight-Deer has conquered a place where people live underground or in caves.*

**11** *Eight-Deer, wearing what appears to be a small black mask, holds an incense burner; he is making an offering to the sun, which is seen as an ornamental orb suspended in a divided tree with dark and light trunks. This is believed to symbolize a divine place dedicated either to the sun or to night and day. The place symbol at the bottom of the picture identifies it as "Alligator Hill." This event is pictured in other Mixtec codices and may refer to an offering to the gods by Eight-Deer on behalf of his departed relative, Three-Lizard.*

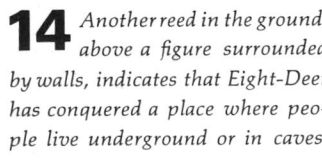

**13** *Eight-Deer's fourth victory is over a place identified with a bird, possibly an eagle. The wall design below is the common symbol for a town or locality.*

**12** *According to this symbol, the next major event in Eight-Deer's life occurs on One-Reed Year (1039 A.D.), Six-Water Day.*

The book this page comes from is 7½ by 10 inches in size and unfolds like an accordion, as shown below, with the first page at the right. That page is reproduced in its entirety at the far right, and is broken into its component parts below. The record begins with the picture shown at the upper right (Number 1), then moves down one column and up the next. The individual scenes, or pictographs, were intended to be read not as a running story but as reminders of important events, which a narrator could point to as he told the tale.

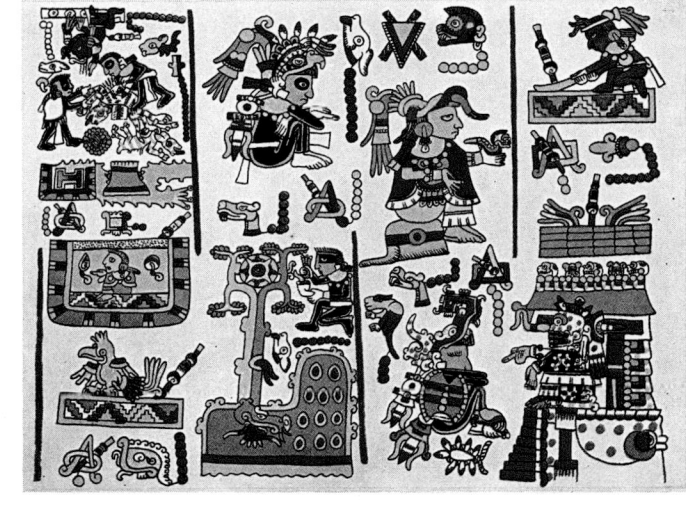

**8** *Directly above Six-Monkey are the symbols for her full name. The triangular device stands for a blouse and the crossed bands signify warfare. Beside these symbols is the monkey head with six dots.*

**7** *Seated on a skin-covered stool while she plays the role of chief mourner for the dead man is a woman named Six-Monkey War-Shirt, an adviser to the rulers of the Cloud People. She holds a pipe-like object with a head in the shape of a skull, thought to be an offering to the Goddess Nine-Grass.*

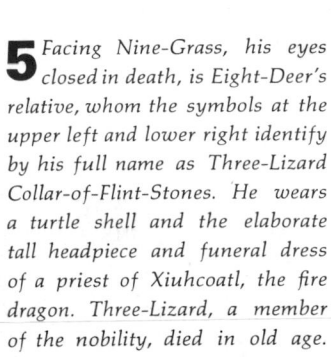
**6** *The date of Three-Lizard's funeral is given here as Six-Reed Year (1031 A.D.), Six-Serpent Day.*

**5** *Facing Nine-Grass, his eyes closed in death, is Eight-Deer's relative, whom the symbols at the upper left and lower right identify by his full name as Three-Lizard Collar-of-Flint-Stones. He wears a turtle shell and the elaborate tall headpiece and funeral dress of a priest of Xiuhcoatl, the fire dragon. Three-Lizard, a member of the nobility, died in old age.*

**1** *The opening picture commemorates one of Eight-Deer's first conquests. The decorated reed or shaft sunk in the ground symbolizes a victory; the wall pattern below signifies a city or place, and the working figure identifies it as a "place where the soil is tilled."*

**2** *This pictograph gives the date of the next event as Two-Reed Year (1028 A.D.), 10-Flower Day.*

**3** *On the above date, a reed records Eight-Deer's conquest of a place "where the grass bends." At the time he was only about 16.*

**4** *Some years later the codex tells of the death of one of Eight-Deer's royal relatives, Three-Lizard. The Goddess Nine-Grass, sitting in a temple, presides over the funeral rites. She is adorned with the symbols of death: a skull mask covers her face, her robes are decorated with skulls and bones, and the temple roof is lined with skulls and hearts. She gestures toward the dead man (seen in the following pictograph at the left).* 71

A CEREMONIAL NOSE-PIERCING *is performed on Eight-Deer by a priest, permitting him to wear a nose-plug, the sign of a high official. Eight-Deer will wear a small jade rod stuck horizontally through his nose; other officials sometimes wore gold ornaments dangling from their nostrils like earrings.*

A HIGH-LEVEL CONFERENCE *brings together a well-armed Eight-Deer and a man named Four-Tiger (left), probably a high lord of the Toltecs, a neighboring people. Between them is a bundle of ceremonial objects. Apparently they made a pact; in his next war, Eight-Deer was joined by Four-Tiger.*

# THE WARS AND HONORS OF A KING

For many years Eight-Deer won all of his battles. He killed the males of the royal families he overthrew, and he or his sons married the widows and princesses. Thus he extended his realm from the Mixtec highlands south to the Pacific coast, and perhaps as far north as Cholula. Eight-Deer underwent painful rituals to make himself strong so he could win victories. He knew that if defeated in battle, he would have to be sacrificed, just as he had sacrificed his own vanquished foes.

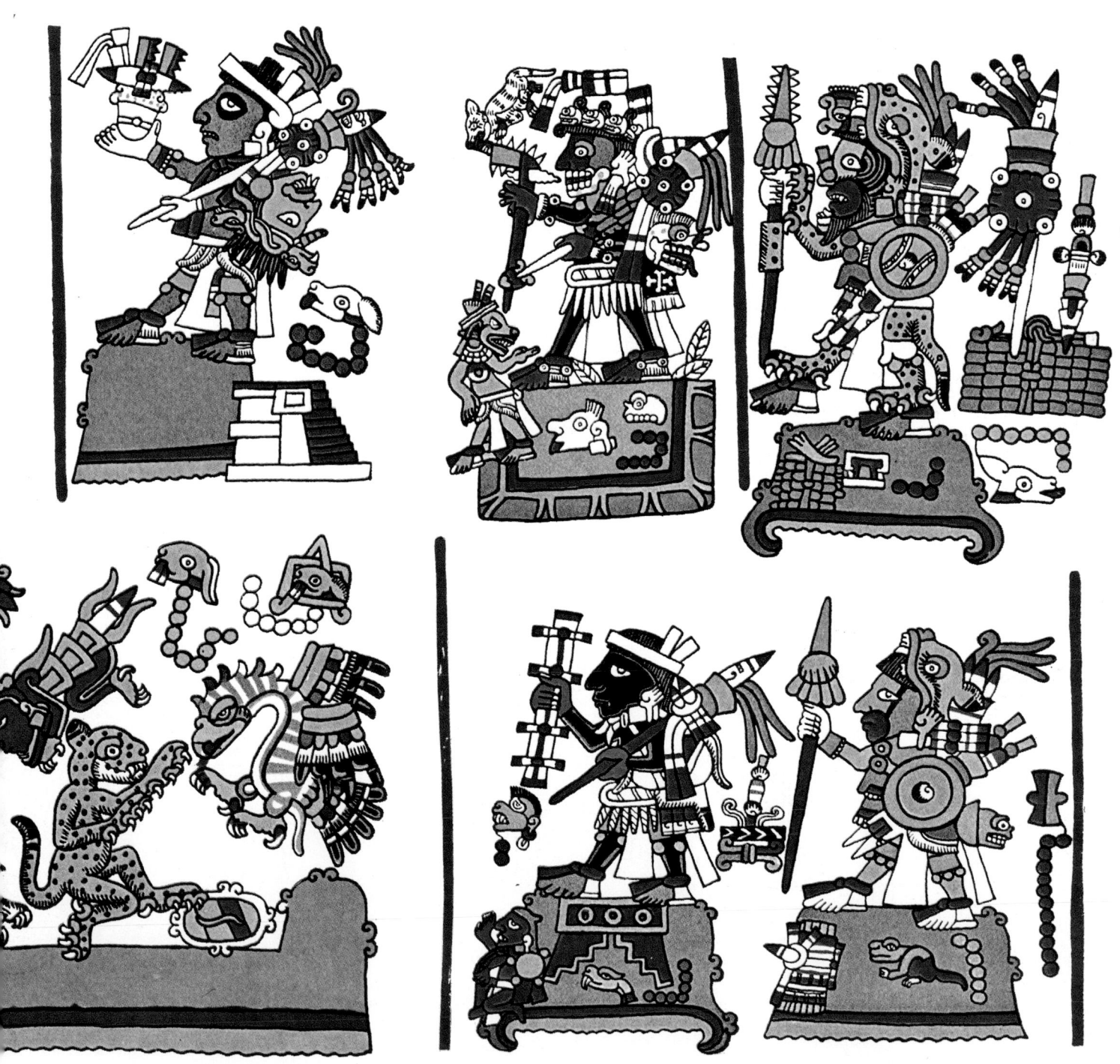

A PROCESSION OF WARRIORS is shown above; each stands on a place symbol, perhaps his home. At the upper right is Eight-Deer; below is his half-brother, Twelve-Earthquake. The other three are probably allied lords. The scene at the lower left is believed to refer to the sacrifice of Eight-Deer's half-brother, Nine-Flower. In codices a fighting eagle and ocelot allude to rivalries or rebellions, suggesting a dynastic conflict.

A STRATEGY OF WAR is discussed in a meeting between Eight-Deer and his Toltec ally, Four-Tiger (lower picture). In the pictograph above, they cross a sea in canoes to attack the town of Xipe-Bundle.

# THE DYNASTIC WAR FOR XIPE-BUNDLE

CAPTURING A YOUNG RIVAL, *Eight-Deer grabs Four-Wind by the hair. Four-Wind, an heir to the ruler of Xipe-Bundle, was only nine years old at the time and probably for this reason was spared.*

THE SACRIFICE OF A PRINCE *comes when Four-Wind's older half-brother, Ten-Dog, is attacked by Eight-Deer and another warrior, clad as tigers. The weeping Ten-Dog, tied to a stone, is killed.*

Intrigue—and the sacrifice of members of his own family—played important roles in Eight-Deer's expansion of his empire. One of his major campaigns concerned an assault on a town with the odd name of Xipe-Bundle (named after its recurrent place symbol, which resembles a bundle of religious articles that pertain to Xipe, the god of spring). The war, described in many Mixtec codices, was fought over who would rule the city.

The plot was set in motion in 1047 when a Mixtec chief named Eleven-Wind, the ruler of Xipe-Bundle, died. Eleven-Wind had three children by one of his wives, who was Eight-Deer's half sister and the full sister of Eight-Deer's half-brother, Twelve-Earthquake. The boys were named Six-House and Ten-Dog, and the girl Thirteen-Serpent. By a second wife Eleven-Wind had another son, Four-Wind.

To prevent either his half-nephews or his half-brother, Twelve-Earthquake, from succeeding to the city's throne, Eight-Deer allied himself with his Toltec friend, Four-Tiger, at a meeting in a ceremonial court *(far left, bottom)*. Then, with other allies, they set out by water *(far left, top)* and later marched across land in pursuit of their goal.

On the way Eight-Deer captured his luckless half-brother, Twelve-Earthquake, and promptly sacrificed him to the gods. Thus he eliminated one claimant to the throne of Xipe-Bundle and could continue his campaign for its dynastic control.

In the following year, 1049, Eight-Deer finally took Xipe-Bundle and captured another of the heirs, Four-Wind. He spared the young boy, who afterward played an important role in Mixtec history. Before long Eight-Deer captured the other heirs, Six-House and Ten-Dog. He eliminated Six-House by ritual sacrifice, and Ten-Dog in gladiatorial combat *(left)*. The path thus cleared, Eight-Deer then married his victims' sister, Thirteen-Serpent; she bore him three daughters and two sons, one of whom also became a great Mixtec king.

# THE RITUALS OF A ROYAL DEATH

Religious ceremonies were at the core of the Mixtec civilization, and of Eight-Deer's life. To win favor with the gods the Mixtecs sacrificed dogs, birds and human beings by opening their chests with a stone knife and ripping out the still-throbbing hearts. They also drank sacred intoxicants, ate hallucination-producing mushrooms and sometimes made the supreme sacrifice by committing suicide. Some of the more athletic Mix-

tecs even dressed in the beaks and feathers of birds and, attached by long thongs to the tops of tall poles, "flew" through the air around the poles in ever-widening circles as the thongs unwound, until at last they reached the ground. (This feat is still practiced at fairs and carnivals in some parts of Mexico.)

No rituals were more important to the Mixtecs than those concerned with death. Their gods had to be placated with the proper observances in order for a dead or dying man to gain immortality. Although Eight-Deer had his half-brother Twelve-Earthquake sacrificed for dynastic reasons, he made sure that in death Twelve-Earthquake received all of the honors due his princely station (below). This was Eight-Deer's guarantee that when his turn came to die—as it did 14 years later— he too would be properly ushered into death and after-life.

FUNERAL RITES *for Twelve-Earthquake are shown in the pictures on these pages. After the sacrifice (lower right), his body is cremated to reduce it to a skeleton (above) at a place identified as Seven-Flower Hill, while five noblemen (left) bring offerings to the pyre. On the opposite page, Eight-Deer sits on a jaguar throne in the elaborate costume* of a king. Below him is Twelve-Earthquake's robed and masked skeleton, toward which priests bring a funeral garment and bowls of paint to decorate the face. Finally, at top left, a jaguar place-symbol and a strange, human-shaped earth form presumably indicate Twelve-Earthquake's burial, after which the dead man's weapons are burned (below).*

# 4

# HIGH CULTURE IN THE ANDES

A BRILLIANT EMBROIDERY, *this detail from a Paracas burial cloth reflects the high skill of textile craftsmen in southern Peru. The figure represents a mythical monster with faces on its long tongue and tail, carrying a trophy head under one arm. The Paracas weavers used up to 190 different colors.*

Far to the south of Mexico, beyond the Isthmus of Panama, lay the Inca Empire of Peru, the second great civilization of ancient America that unknowingly faced the doom of Spanish conquest. In some ways it was more advanced than Aztec Mexico, in others less so. In nearly all ways it was different. An Aztec set down in the Peru of the Incas would have found himself in surroundings almost as foreign as if he had been transported to Spain.

In physical features no other country of the world remotely resembles Peru. Its coast is a desert where rain hardly ever falls and the only inhabitable places are scattered oases watered by small rivers that trickle down from the Andes. The barren hills behind the shore climb steeply rank on rank and culminate in white-capped peaks more than 20,000 feet high. Between the great mountain ranges are fertile valleys with plenty of rain. Those at moderate altitude have the climate of perpetual spring, and both temperate and tropical fruits grow there in lavish abundance. Others are high, thin-aired and cold, and on clear nights the grass glitters bright with frost.

East of the Andes the land slants steeply toward the great hot floor of the Amazon basin. Rain falls here frequently and in torrents. White streams foam down the mountainsides in chains of rapids and waterfalls, and wide rivers wind sluggishly through the jungle flatlands on their way to the Atlantic, 2,000 miles away.

When Francisco Pizarro and his handful of Spanish conquistadors assaulted Peru in 1532 they found the elaborately organized Inca state extending some 2,500 miles from the southern boundary of modern Colombia to the Maule River in central Chile. They also noticed many abandoned ruins. Hills were crested with battlements built by unknown hands, and huddled in dry ravines were clusters of roofless stone or adobe houses unoccupied for 1,000 years. In the highlands of what is now Bolivia, called Upper Peru by the Spaniards, stood the ruins of great stone temples and fortifications whose builders were enigmas even to the educated Inca. All they could say was that these structures had been created by an ancient people or perhaps by giants or gods.

These relics told that Peru had a long and complicated history, but most of the information about it had been lost. The Inca, in spite of their talent for government, had no written language with which to record events, and since they had risen to importance less than a century before the Spaniards overthrew them, their traditions revealed nothing about Peru's distant past. The legends of older peoples, which might have told more, were almost forgotten. So the piecing together of ancient Peruvian history has depended even more than that of Mexico on archeological detective work.

The first people to reach the Andes were primitive hunter-gatherers who pushed across the Isthmus of Panama at least 11,000 years ago, probably a good deal earlier. Their scant traces show that they had only the crudest technology, and they did not bring agriculture with them across the Isthmus; they came long before agriculture began its evolution in Middle America.

Scarcely anything would be known about Peru's very early inhabitants if it were not for the eternal dryness of the soil of the coastal desert, where their remains are most plentiful. Fragile organic materials buried there last indefinitely. Near modern roads through the desert, pieces of ancient cloth can be pulled out of the dust. The fabric may be a thousand years old but it is still soft and strong. Sometimes it takes an experienced eye to distinguish it from cloth recently tossed away by a motorist cleaning a dirty windshield.

Scattered along this rainless coast are low, circular mounds, and carbon 14 tests prove that they date as far back as 3750 B.C. The furtive grave robbers who probe for treasure elsewhere in Peru waste no effort on these humble places—they contain nothing salable—but they are rich with informative relics. The people whose refuse and crumbled house walls built up the mounds lived in permanent dwellings of stone or adobe with roofs of poles and cane. They had no pottery or cotton, but they made cloth of coarse wild fibers, wore leather caps ornamented with pieces of shell, and played on wooden flutes. Not only their possessions are found well preserved in the arid soil; the bodies of their dead and even the lice that infested their clothing have also endured intact.

The villagers ate mostly fish, shellfish, sea lions and sea birds, all of which abound along the coast, and they also gathered wild vegetable foods. By about 2800 B.C., however, they had succeeded in cultivating lima beans and other native plants that now formed an important part of their diet. Whether the villagers' agricultural achievements were original with themselves is uncertain. Their knowledge and skill may have come from the highlands where agricultural villages older than any on the coast or in Middle America may yet be discovered. Or the people themselves may have been highland farmers who migrated down to the sea at certain seasons to catch and dry fish.

Well before 1500 B.C. sedentary village life based on fishing, agriculture, or both, was solidly established in Peru. When cultivated corn was introduced from Middle America or perhaps domesticated independently in the Peruvian highlands, it greatly increased the food supply; pottery arrived, probably from a northern source; and in the mountains the wild guanaco, a relative of the camel, was developed into the domesticated llama and alpaca.

From many impressive remains that had been discovered by the early 1900s, archeologists of that time knew that a great variety of forgotten cultures far more advanced than the early villages had flourished in Peru's temperate highlands and on the coast. These cultures formed a basis for the later Inca civilization, but both their absolute and relative ages were uncertain. Some authorities insisted they were all recent enough to have stemmed from Middle America, which was then believed to

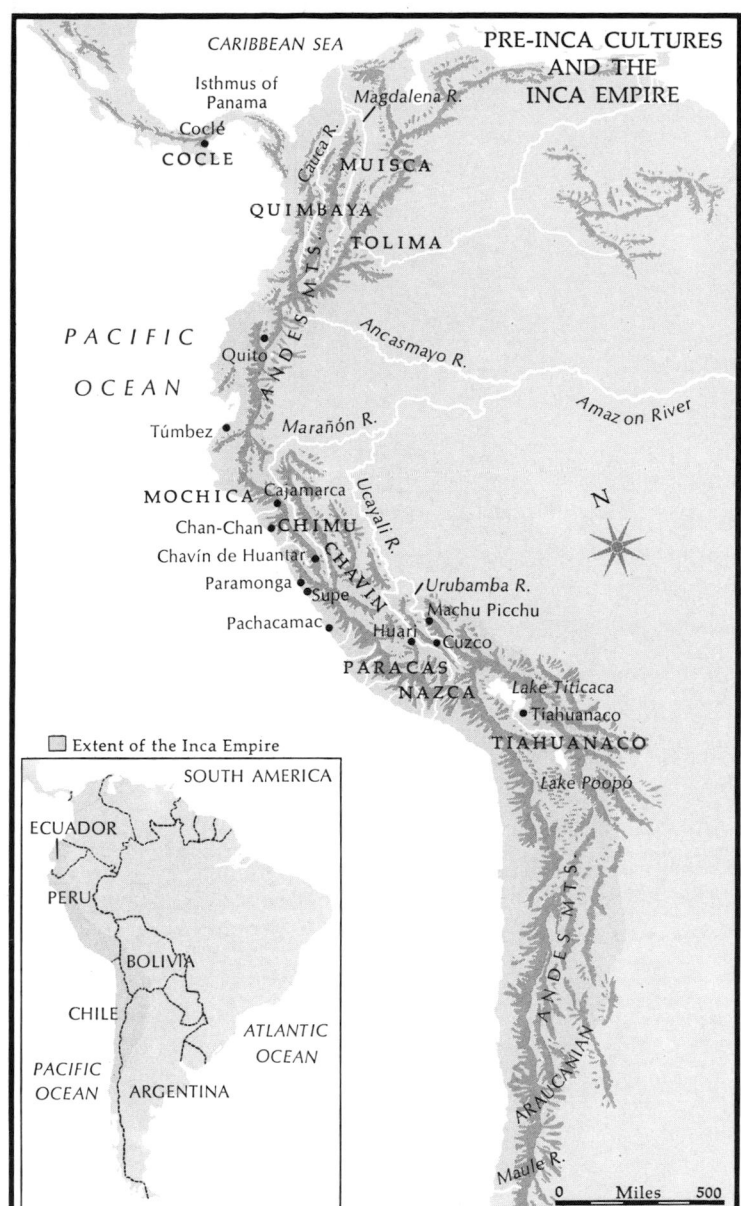

PRE-INCA CULTURES
AND THE
INCA EMPIRE

CARIBBEAN SEA

Isthmus of
Panama
Coclé
COCLE

Magdalena R.

MUISCA

QUIMBAYA

TOLIMA

PACIFIC
OCEAN

Quito

Túmbez

Marañón R.

Ancasmayo R.

Amazon River

N

MOCHICA Cajamarca
Chan-Chan CHIMU
Chavín de Huantar
Paramonga
Supe
Pachacamac

Huari

Urubamba R.
Machu Picchu

Cuzco

PARACAS
NAZCA

Lake Titicaca
Tiahuanaco
TIAHUANACO

Lake Poopó

☐ Extent of the Inca Empire

SOUTH AMERICA

ECUADOR

PERU

BOLIVIA

CHILE

PACIFIC
OCEAN

ARGENTINA

ATLANTIC
OCEAN

ANDES MTS.

ARAUCANIAN

Maule R.

0    Miles    500

THE INCA EMPIRE *encompassed most of the earlier coastal and highland Indian cultures of western South America. It extended about 2,500 miles from Ecuador through Peru and Bolivia to Argentina and Chile (see inset).*

level, stands an enormous stone building called the Castillo, nearly 250 feet square. Inside is a maze of small rooms and narrow corridors, three stories of them, connected by stairways and ramps. Probably no one ever lived in the Castillo. It was a house for gods, not mortals, the mysterious sanctum of a strange religion. In one of its dim galleries a god still stands: a tall stone idol with the fanged grin of a man-jaguar.

A man-jaguar? This strange concept of a god that is part human, part feline was not peculiar to Peru. It was also the central theme of the Olmec culture, Middle America's first successful civilization, which began to flourish in southern Mexico as early as 1000 B.C. But the Olmecs were still unknown when Dr. Tello and his colleagues started their work of tracing man-jaguar faces through Peru. They found them carved on stone, painted on pottery and woven into textiles, and the conclusion was inescapable that Peru's first true civilization was associated with the appearance of a jaguar god.

Many theories have since attempted to explain this association and the part it played in the rise and expansion of the Chavín culture. The most likely one is that some of the villages that had long existed in Peru had become good-sized towns by around 1000 B.C., but they had few if any interests outside themselves. Then came the jaguar god, a symbol of supernatural strength and power whose cult spread from town to town, creating conflict and excitement as a successful, growing religion usually does. It also created unity. Ambitious local medicine men won additional power by becoming priests of the new faith. Certain towns where they performed especially impressive ceremonies before the images of the jaguar god became regional centers of pilgrimage whose fame traveled from valley to valley among the towering mountains and down to the sea and the jungle.

have reached a civilized state shortly after the start of the Christian era. This thinking was radically changed about 1940 by archeologists Julio C. Tello and Rafael Larco Hoyle of Peru and Professor Wendell C. Bennett of Yale University. Their delving into the past led to the realization that at least one thousand years earlier a vigorous culture had spread over a wide area of northern and central Peru. This first Peruvian civilization is known as the Chavín culture, after its most impressive center, at Chavín de Huantar on the high eastern slope of the Andes.

There, in a narrow valley 10,200 feet above sea

The people who worshiped the divine jaguar probably had no central government, political or religious, and there seems to have been no important movement of population. They merely got in the habit of visiting distant shrines in search of divine advice or assistance, and they rewarded the priests handsomely for such services. When this custom was well established, elaborate ceremonial centers like Chavín de Huantar were built. At these shrines artists, craftsmen and traders from various parts of Peru met one another and exchanged ideas, techniques and products, and before long Chavín civilization and the religion that inspired it had spread widely.

Where this unifying religion came from originally is still a great unanswered question. Its general resemblance to that of the Mexican Olmecs is obvious. Both religions appeared at roughly the same time, about 1000 B.C., both centered about the worship of jaguar gods, and both gave rise to ceremonial centers. Each sect also carried with it an artistic style by which its area of influence can be identified. But here the similarities end. Except for their emphasis on man-feline deities, the art styles themselves are different, and there is nothing in Peru like the Olmecs' "baby-faced" sculptures or like the written language apparently invented by the Olmecs or by their converts. Moreover, the Olmecs built little in stone, certainly nothing that approaches the Castillo and other imposing Chavín structures. If the Olmec and Chavín civilizations are connected, they must have separated at a very early stage and thereafter developed independently.

If indeed they are connected, which of the two came first? Which was the magic seed that started all the civilizations of the Americas? Many archeologists favor the Olmecs and believe that some elements of their jaguar cult passed to Peru by sea, skipping the intervening regions. But Peru, too, has its supporters, who claim that the strange but po-tent religion originated on the edge of the Amazon jungle, where jaguars are also plentiful, and then climbed the Andes, descended to the Pacific Coast and advanced by sea to Mexico. There is also a possibility (although there is little evidence to support it) that the original seed of civilization may have come from still farther away, perhaps carried to the South American coast by Asian boats driven across the Pacific by winds and currents.

In any event, Peru's period of cultural unity dominated by the Chavín religion ended rather abruptly about 500 B.C., possibly because the jaguar god had suffered some theological setback that diminished the popularity of his centers of pilgrimage. But Peruvian civilization did not die with the jaguar cult. It merely broke up into many fragments, each isolated from the others and developing in its own special way.

Dozens of these separate cultures have been found, and probably as many more still remain hidden. Some of them rate high in achievements. On the utterly arid Paracas Peninsula in southern Peru, for example, are the 2,000-year-old burial grounds of a people whose textiles are considered superb even today. At one site called Paracas Necropolis, 429 seated mummies were unearthed, presumably of important chieftains or priests, each wrapped in many layers of beautifully woven cloth. The innermost wrapping was a shroud of plain white cotton, in one case 13 feet wide and 84 feet long. Then came layers of smaller colored cloths and garments of alpaca or vicuña wool. Tucked at intervals into the growing bundle were food for the dead man, clothing, weapons, gold ornaments and pottery vessels.

Especially gorgeous are the mummies' large embroidered mantles, which connoisseurs rank among the triumphs of the textile arts. They are worked with tiny figures of fishes, birds, animals, gods or mythological creatures, sometimes mingled with

# TRANS-PACIFIC RIDDLES

Just how isolated was ancient America? Recently archeologists have noted certain resemblances between East Asian and American artifacts and art styles. One theory, which sparks heated controversy among scholars, is that Asian peoples, in voyages eastward, may have made contributions to New World cultures.

EASTERN ASIA                        ANCIENT AMERICA

FELINE DIVINITIES *were worshiped by China's Shang Dynasty (left) and by both the Olmecs of Mexico and the Chavín civilization of Peru (right). Shang and Olmec priests also built similar earthen ceremonial platforms, and used much the same kind of small reflecting mirrors in religious rituals.*

LION-HEADED THRONES *are shown in representations of deities in India (left) and of Maya dignitaries (right). The Maya shared other ritual expressions with Hindu-Buddhist culture, including stepped temple pyramids, doorways with serpent columns and balustrades, and sacred tree forms.*

LOTUS FRIEZES *adorn both Maya and Indian temples. Remarkable similarities occur between these two designs, which portray men reclining between winding lotus stems which they grasp in both hands. Water monsters or fish often occur in the same compositions.*

WHEELED ANIMALS *made in India may have inspired similar figures found in Mexican tombs; the wheel was not otherwise used in ancient America, possibly because of the lack of strong draft animals. Certain types of looms and pottery-making techniques were also shared by Americans and Asians.*

geometrical designs and arranged in complicated patterns. The stitches of the embroidery are minute, each enveloping a single thread of the cloth, and by some miracle of prescientific chemistry the dyes are almost as vivid as when the cloth was made.

Over the centuries the Paracas culture gradually merged into the Nazca culture, which centered in the Ica and Nazca Valleys 100 miles down the coast. The Nazca people continued the Paracas textile tradition, adding many intricate weaving techniques but never quite equaling the finely stitched embroidery of Paracas. The chief glory of the Nazcas is their polished pottery, a single vessel of which may be painted in as many as 11 colors. Designs show great freedom and variety. Some are naturalistic, with fishes, birds, insects and other familiar creatures easily recognizable. Others are highly stylized, showing strange, half-human faces of demons or gods. A common design is a cat-face, sometimes depicted with dramatic flaring whiskers. Memory of Chavín's jaguar god was still strong.

Little is known about the personal appearance or customs of the Nazcas, whose charming pottery and textiles seldom show realistic human forms. But 500 miles up the coast in northern Peru was a contemporaneous culture with a seemingly obsessive desire to preserve for posterity every detail of its life. The Mochicas (a name derived from the Moche River near the modern city of Trujillo) were a vigorous, warlike people who spread their control to several neighboring valleys. From the pottery that they buried with their dead comes an almost photographic knowledge of Mochica life.

Two kinds of pottery predominate, modeled and painted. The modeled vessels are skillful sculptures in clay, and they show practically everything that the Mochicas could have seen or imagined: deer, frogs, monkeys, fishes, owls and many other birds, fruit, vegetables, boats, houses and gods, some of whom have jaguar fangs. Most of all they show people—clothed or naked, healthy or sick, jocular or grotesque, of all ages and both sexes, engaged in every conceivable activity.

Most remarkable of all Mochica pottery masterpieces are the portrait vases, which represent individual persons with lively and startling realism. Many are so subtly made that they seem about to speak. Seldom has the art of portraiture in clay been more completely mastered.

The painted vessels, although they portray people in a more highly stylized and less naturalistic way, tell even more about Mochica life than do the modeled ones. Across their smooth surfaces march delicately drawn figures of all classes and occupations. Chiefs in elaborate litters or seated on raised platforms welcome visitors, receive gifts or give orders to servants. Warriors resembling medieval knights—they are armed with maces and spears and wear crested, conical helmets and tunics emblazoned with heraldic devices—plunge into battle and carry as trophies the severed heads of the vanquished. Hunting scenes show beaters driving game into enclosures where men wait to club or spear the animals to death. Other scenes, less dramatic, depict musicians playing Panpipes or flutes or beating drums or illustrate merchants and craftsmen displaying their wares in the marketplace. Mochica women are not neglected on the painted vessels; they appear in long, shirtlike dresses seated at their looms, carrying burdens on their backs, tending their children.

When it came to building sanctuaries for their gods the Mochicas did not stop at half measures. Near the Moche River stand two enormous ceremonial pyramids called the Temple of the Sun and the Temple of the Moon, built of adobe bricks that last almost forever on this rainless coast. The 60-foot-high base of the Temple of the Sun covers eight acres and is surmounted by a stepped structure towering another 75 feet. The Temple of the Moon rises out of an ancient burial ground and around it the red-brown, dusty desert is littered with sea shells brought as offerings to the shrine, along with bits of pottery and fragments of human bones exhumed by grave robbers. Ritual rooms on top of the Temple have traces of wall paintings, one of which shows axes and other tools with little arms and legs; they are chasing and apparently rebelling against their human makers.

The Nazca and Mochica civilizations, as well as many other regional cultures both coastal and highland, continued with full vigor until about 600 A.D. but trouble was building for them on a cold plateau in the high Andes. At Tiahuanaco, 12 miles south of Lake Titicaca on the boundary between Peru and Bolivia, one of those characteristic institutions of ancient America, a ceremonial center, was taking shape. The site, though it had been long occupied, is uninviting—almost 14,000 feet above sea level and set in a bleak and rocky landscape. But a new god established there was exerting tremendous drawing power. People from the cold plateau, then from farther and farther away, were coming to his holy place, bringing gifts for his priests, building temples for him, enlisting in the armies of his cult. A thrill of religious excitement unfelt since Chavín times was running like an electric tingle along the spine of the Andes.

The name of the new god will probably never be known, but his image is clear, carved on a monolithic temple gateway at Tiahuanaco. The carving is stiff and unrealistic and shows a squat, standing man wearing an elaborate headdress featuring puma heads in profile. His large face is squarish and from his staring eyes fall round tears. There must have been great power in the name and image of the weeping god, for with remarkable suddenness his cult expanded through the Andes and down to the civilized coast. The new god's sym-

bols—puma heads and tears—and the stiff Tiahuanacan art style are found almost as far north as Ecuador and deep into Bolivia and Chile.

Tiahuanaco itself is an enormous ruin, long abandoned, long plundered for building stones, but still tremendously impressive. One of its main units was apparently a fortress or place of refuge; other units were temples, and there are remains of houses, presumably for priests. The masonry is among the most skillful in the Andes; stones, some of them weighing more than 100 tons, are accurately cut and ground to a smooth finish. Often they are held together by copper clamps hammered or cast into "I"-shaped channels.

Who were the Tiahuanacans? They may never be identified, and most likely they were not a single people. Possibly the nucleus of the cult was a group of the Aymara Indians who still inhabit the Lake Titicaca area. Because the center they founded at Tiahuanaco stands in a region too cold for most crops, it never supported a large-scale population. It remained a remote and mysterious holy place ruled by priests who may also have been warriors.

But at Huari near modern Ayacucho in Peru there was a more populous center from which the priests extended their domination northward. Certainly the priests were politicians, for the empire they established deeply affected many cultures and obliterated others, including that of the Nazcas. The vigorous Mochicas of the north tolerated the weeping god for a time, but then resumed their normal flamboyant life. Archeologists call their new emergence the Chimu Kingdom, but the Chimus were only the talented Mochicas in a different phase: richer, more numerous and not so creative.

How long the Tiahuanaco empire lasted is uncertain. Some scholars think it was held together by little more than a proselytizing religion with military aspects, and that it was gone in a century. Others believe that it was fairly stable for several hundred years, with a tight government, armies, garrisons and an elaborate system of roads. A reasonable date for its end is 1000 A.D., though the cult and the government associated with it may have retained power in some places until considerably later.

The empire of the Tiahuanacans was the first to include nearly all of Peru. This was important: it set a precedent; it could be done again. And the remarkable dynasty that would re-establish Peruvian unity was soon to emerge, according to tradition, from a remote valley in the southern highlands. The Inca would prove that the weeping god of the cold plateau had not done his pioneer work in vain.

When the Inca began their spectacular sweep along the Andes, Peruvian civilization had long been prospering. All its material technologies were far advanced. There were, to be sure, many things lacking in Peruvian culture that had long been commonplace in the Old World. As in Middle America, there was no knowledge of the wheel—or if there was, it was not put to practical use. There was no written language, only a system of keeping accounts with knotted strings called *quipus*—a very poor substitute. There was also no money or other convenient medium of exchange. One of the most striking things about Peruvian culture is that it developed so brilliantly without these elements, usually thought indispensable to the growth of civilization.

The Inca did not correct such deficiencies. Their contribution was their extraordinary organizing power. When they came on the scene sometime after 1200 A.D. political organization was already proceeding on the coast. In the north the Chimus had pushed their control over 600 miles of coastline. Farther south along the coast were other groups of valley cultures in the process of grouping into fair-sized nations. The time was ripe for

an even larger nation, one that would extend its domination over both coast and highlands.

The legend of the Inca origin has several versions. According to the best known, four brothers and four sisters, all children of the Sun God, came out of a cave about 18 miles southeast of the present city of Cuzco, and from two nearby caves came a handful of followers. These were the Inca, a word that originally identified a certain group of clans and that later referred to the emperor, "The Inca." Today the term is commonly used to signify all the people of the Inca Empire as well.

According to the legend, Manco Capac, leader of the band, felt himself threatened by one of his brothers, Ayar Cachi, who was so strong that the stones he threw with his sling blasted ravines in the hills. Manco Capac sent Ayar Cachi back into the cave to fetch a sacred llama. Another man went along and walled Ayar Cachi up inside, and there he remains today. The two other brothers eliminated themselves by obligingly turning into sacred stones. That left Manco Capac alone as the first Inca ruler. He had already married one of his sisters, Mama Occlo, who bore Sinchi Roca, second of the Inca line.

Like the Aztecs when they first entered civilized Mexico, the little band under Manco Capac started out as landless wanderers, but they quickly overcame this handicap. Moving toward the fertile Valley of Cuzco, they probed the ground with a golden staff to test the depth of the soil, and when they found a spot they considered good farmland they decided to settle down. During the battle to drive out the established inhabitants Mama Huaco, another one of Manco Capac's sisters, played the key role. She killed an opponent with a stone, tore out his lungs and inflated them. Terrified by this horrible spectacle, the others fled.

Other legends tell of colorful battles in which

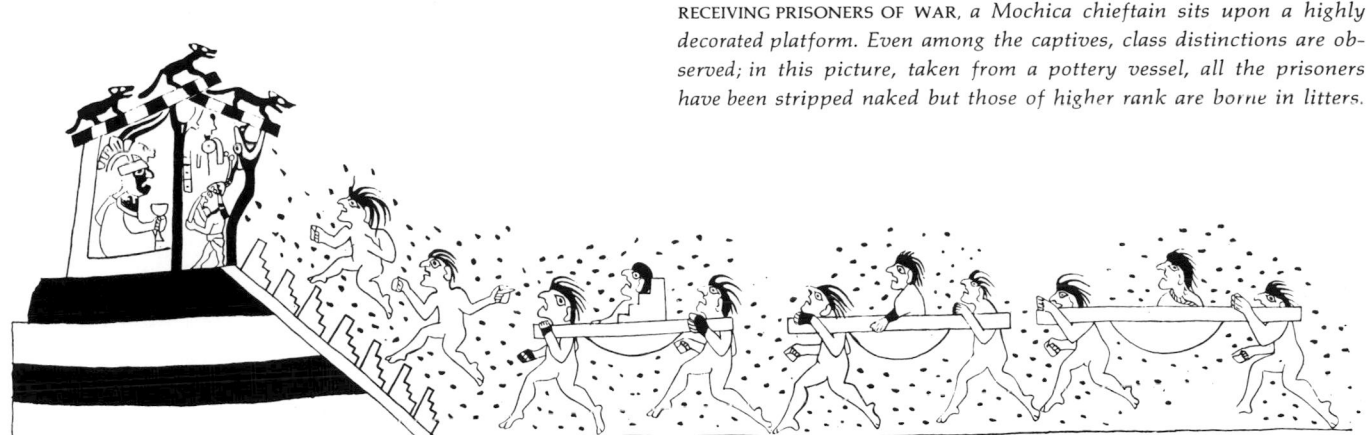

RECEIVING PRISONERS OF WAR, *a Mochica chieftain sits upon a highly decorated platform. Even among the captives, class distinctions are observed; in this picture, taken from a pottery vessel, all the prisoners have been stripped naked but those of higher rank are borne in litters.*

the early Inca were always victorious, but the fighting did not advance more than 25 miles from Cuzco. Often these tales described a tribe as being utterly vanquished and having to be vanquished again a few years later. This means that during the first 200 years after the Children of the Sun and their followers emerged from the cave the Inca remained a small group of people who fought inconclusive skirmishes with their neighbors. In fact, they might never have been noticed except for their ninth ruler, the Inca Pachacuti.

Although his father and some other predecessors may have been at least partly legendary, Pachacuti was a real person, the actual founder of the Inca Empire and perhaps the greatest man produced in ancient America. He was not the first or the favorite son of his father, Viracocha Inca. He was, however, a skillful military leader. Toward the end of Viracocha's reign, Cuzco was attacked by the Chancas, a powerful people to the west of its fertile valley. The battle at first went against the Inca, and Viracocha with his eldest son and heir, Urcon, fled to a mountain stronghold. Pachacuti rallied his forces, defeated the Chancas and took the succession away from his father's favorite, assuming the throne in about 1438. From this point onward Inca history, which was memorized by a corps of official historians, is reasonably precise.

Under Pachacuti the expansion of the Empire was

almost an explosion; wherever the Inca armies marched they met with victory. Their first task was to clean up pockets of independence in the Cuzco region. Then the highland soldiers swept down the fertile Urubamba Valley, which leads to the Amazon forests. Next, with their supply trains of laden llamas and human porters, they followed the white-capped Andes to Cajamarca in the northern highlands, subduing tribe after tribe. Then they doubled south to attack the Aymara on the plateau around Lake Titicaca.

These campaigns were not mere forays in search of booty. They were part of a deliberate plan to unite the diverse lands and peoples of Peru, and Pachacuti's devices for achieving this end were masterstrokes of statecraft with few equals in history. When the Inca Empire began its sudden growth, Peru was an intricate patchwork of tribes and nations speaking dozens of languages and worshiping different gods. Some Peruvians lived in large, civilized cities with centuries of prosperous history behind them; Chan-Chan, capital of the Chimus, for example, had become a splendid city with walled temple precincts, parks and artificial lagoons. Other people clung to life on grim deserts or defied the rest of the world from narrow mountain valleys. In the eastern forests were naked savages, and on the highest ranges were herdsmen who lived with their llamas close to the glittering snow. To establish a united and stable empire in this cut-up land might seem almost impossible, but Pachacuti and his advisors were supremely confident that it could be done by long-range planning.

Though Pachacuti's armies fought ferocious battles when necessary, they often accomplished their objectives by bloodless diplomacy. Before attacking a state the Inca sent ambassadors to explain the considerable advantages of joining his Empire. Behind its lines were peace and plenty, which would be enjoyed by aristocrats and commoners alike. The local rulers would not be displaced; they would continue to rule under Inca guidance. The local religion would be respected as long as it made no trouble. On the other hand the ambassadors made it plain that resistance would lead to unpleasantness. Local leaders would be slaughtered along with their families or dragged off to Cuzco where they might be imprisoned in dungeons filled with fierce animals or poisonous snakes. Confronted by these alternatives and eyeing the veteran Inca soldiers camped on their boundaries—well trained, well supplied, well armed and glowing with the prestige of famous victories—many states surrendered with no resistance at all.

One of the most effective unifying devices employed by Pachacuti and later Inca rulers was the extension of Quechua, the language of the Cuzco region, as a lingua franca. Just as English spread around the world with the expanding British Empire, Quechua marched with the Inca armies. It was made the formal medium of communication between the conquerors and the polyglot population and was taught to local chieftains and young people.

Another statesmanlike but strong-armed policy was the *mitima*, or the practice of exchanging populations. Groups of recently subjugated peoples still considered hostile were moved to places where they would be less dangerous and were replaced by loyal subjects. But the Inca took pains to avoid inflicting unnecessary hardship. For example, they never moved sea-level people to the high mountains where they would have suffered from the cold and altitude. Also, their skilled engineers often provided irrigation systems and other public works that bettered the material condition of the displaced groups.

As the Empire expanded, its roads expanded with it. There had long been roads of varying quality in Peru, but the Inca improved them, linked them together and engineered them according to the terrain. On flat coastal deserts these routes might be no more than twin lines of guideposts while in settled districts they were often walled and bordered with shade trees. Swamps were crossed by earthen viaducts pierced with culverts for drainage, and in the rugged Andes the roads were carried across ravines on suspension bridges and either around high spurs or through them by means of tunnels. On steep slopes they zigzagged to reduce the grade, just as modern Peruvian highways climb in dizzy sequences of tight hairpin turns. In some of the steepest sections they became long stairways cut in the rocky mountainsides. Since they carried no wheeled traffic, only pack llamas and people on foot, the Inca roads were often no more than three feet wide, but they were frequently paved with stone and supported when necessary by solidly built retaining walls.

At intervals along the roads were *tambos*, or way stations. These might be mere huts, but often they were elaborate establishments with roomy storehouses for the use of the army's quartermaster corps and comfortable accommodations for official travelers. On the principal roads, stationed a mile or two apart, waited pairs of trained messengers called *chasquis*. When a running chasqui approached, his waiting counterpart would fall into stride beside him, memorize a verbal message and grab any object to be relayed, then dash for the next relay station. This postal network covered the Empire and in its day was probably the world's fastest communication system. Speeding messages at 140 miles per day over mountain passes three miles high, it gave a tremendous military advantage. The far-ranging Inca armies, guided by swift instructions from headquarters, could concentrate forces for surprise attacks and stamp out revolts before they became dangerous.

As the Emperor Pachacuti grew old, he left active campaigning to his able son, Topa Inca, and devoted himself to administration and to rebuilding and embellishing Cuzco. The plan of the city was largely his creation, and according to the Spanish chronicler Pedro de Cieza de León, who saw Cuzco before it was drastically altered following the conquest of Peru, it was a magnificent capital indeed. "Cuzco was grand and stately . . ." he wrote. "It had fine streets, except that they were narrow, and the houses were built of solid stones, beautifully joined. . . . This city was the richest of which we have any knowledge in all the Indies."

A great plaza occupied the city's center and about it stood imposing temples and other ceremonial buildings. Here, too, were the palaces of the Inca, the houses of the nobles, the offices of administrators and trained interpreters of the knotted-string quipus. The more important of the temples and royal edifices were plated with sheets of gold that gleamed in the bright Andean sunlight, and the first Spaniards who entered the city must have gasped in disbelief. Most of Cuzco's common people lived apart in small villages separated by green, cultivated fields, rather like the satellite centers favored by modern city planners.

Measured by territory conquered, Topa Inca was the greatest of the emperors, and by his time the Inca system had genuine benefits to offer not only its own peoples but the vanquished as well. Its efficient agriculture provided a good food supply, and its roomy warehouses brimming with surpluses were insurance against future crop failures. Promising young men of subjugated peoples might enter the Inca educational system and learn to be admin-

istrators or civil servants; adventurous youths could join the Inca armies and share their glory. Orphans, the old and the sick were fed when necessary out of public stocks. As far as the common people were concerned, the Inca followed the Marxist adage: "From each according to his abilities, to each according to his needs."

Topa Inca began his expansion of empire by advancing northward from Cuzco and along the highlands, conquering state after state and finally subjugating the strongest of all, the Kingdom of Quito, in what is now Ecuador. This left only one important opponent, the ancient and highly civilized Chimus of the north coast. The Chimus had fortified their southern borders with a series of elaborate strongholds. But their emphasis on defense, which suggests the Maginot Line psychology of France in World War II, did them little good. When Topa Inca attacked them from the north, the unexpected direction, they surrendered with little fighting. The Inca did not disturb the Chimus much, however; they merely installed a garrison and took the sons of the rulers to Cuzco as hostages and to be educated in the Inca system of government. Very likely, the advanced and luxurious Chimus had as much effect on the Inca as the Inca had on them.

Using both diplomacy and force, Topa Inca and his armies next moved southward, sweeping through Bolivia and into Chile. As the tropical sun was left behind, the mountains became more barren and the snowline lower. Meeting little opposition, the Inca came at last to the beautiful Valley of Chile, where they defeated northern groups of the fierce Araucanian Indians. South of the valley the country was cold, tangled with thick vegetation and swarming with savage foes. Topa Inca decided to stop at the Maule River near the present town of Constitución. He was 1,700 miles from Cuzco, and nothing ahead seemed of interest. He set up the boundary markers of his Empire and started the long march home.

Topa Inca, like Alexander the Great, was fast running out of worlds to conquer. His next campaign pushed deep into the lowlands east of Cuzco where the forest Indians were sometimes troublesome. Though his mountain-bred soldiers must have suffered from the tropical heat and the insects, he defeated these lowland tribes easily and embarked in a great fleet of canoes down the broad Madre de Díos River, which empties into the Amazon. No doubt the jungle of the Amazon basin looked as repellent to him as it does to most modern travelers. He returned to Cuzco assured that nothing worth conquering lay to the east.

While in Ecuador the great Inca, hoping to find new lands to win, had cruised out into the Pacific in a fleet of sea-going balsawood rafts. Some Spanish chroniclers report that he reached the Galápagos Islands, 650 miles offshore. If he did, he found them as barren and unpromising as they are today. The cruise proved that the west was no better for empire than the east, the north or the south.

Topa Inca died in Cuzco in 1493 after a few peaceful years spent consolidating the Empire. He had no way of knowing that during the year before his death the three ships of Christopher Columbus, freighted with disease, had made their first landfall in the New World.

Topa Inca's son Huayna Capac did little conquering; little remained to be done. He suppressed a revolt in Ecuador and pushed his northern frontier to the Ancasmayo River, the boundary between modern Ecuador and Colombia. During his reign the office of Inca reached its peak of magnificence, perhaps inspired by the exuberant glories of the captured Chimu kingdom. Moving a few miles a day in a plumed and gold-bedecked litter and surrounded by a swarm of courtiers, bureaucrats, concubines, entertainers, soothsayers, soldiers and servants, the Inca made majestic journeys around his enormous dominions. In a very real sense the government

moved with him. The Empire had grown so fast that there had been no time to construct governmental machinery that could function effectively without his leadership.

In 1523 the Inca Empire got its first fleeting look at a European. He was a Spanish adventurer named Alejo García, whose ship was wrecked on the coast of Brazil and who wandered inland and joined a band of savage Paraguayan Indians in a raid on Inca outposts. The raid was easily beaten off; García got back to Paraguay but was killed before he could transmit many details about the fantastic empire in the Andes.

Two years later Huayna Capac was residing in Quito when he heard rumors that white-sailed ships from the north were exploring the coast of Peru, but another event may have impressed him more. According to an Inca legend, a stranger presented himself before the Emperor carrying a black box which he said contained something so important that the Inca himself must open it. Huayna Capac condescended to do this. He lifted the lid of the box and out flew a cloud of moths and butterflies. These were considered evil omens; in this case they proved to presage a plague that was soon raging through the Inca realm.

The plague may have been smallpox, measles or some other European disease deadly to Indians without natural resistance. It may have spread from the Spaniards in Panama or perhaps it traveled overland from forts built by Spanish explorers probing South America's Atlantic Coast. Whatever it was, it killed Huayna Capac so quickly that he did not make an effective choice of his successor, and the ensuing civil war between two of his sons, Atahuallpa and Huascar, tore the Empire apart. Well before Pizarro and his audacious conquistadors attacked Peru, their grim ally, pestilence—by bringing sudden death to Huayna Capac and thus confusing the Inca succession—had struck a crippling blow.

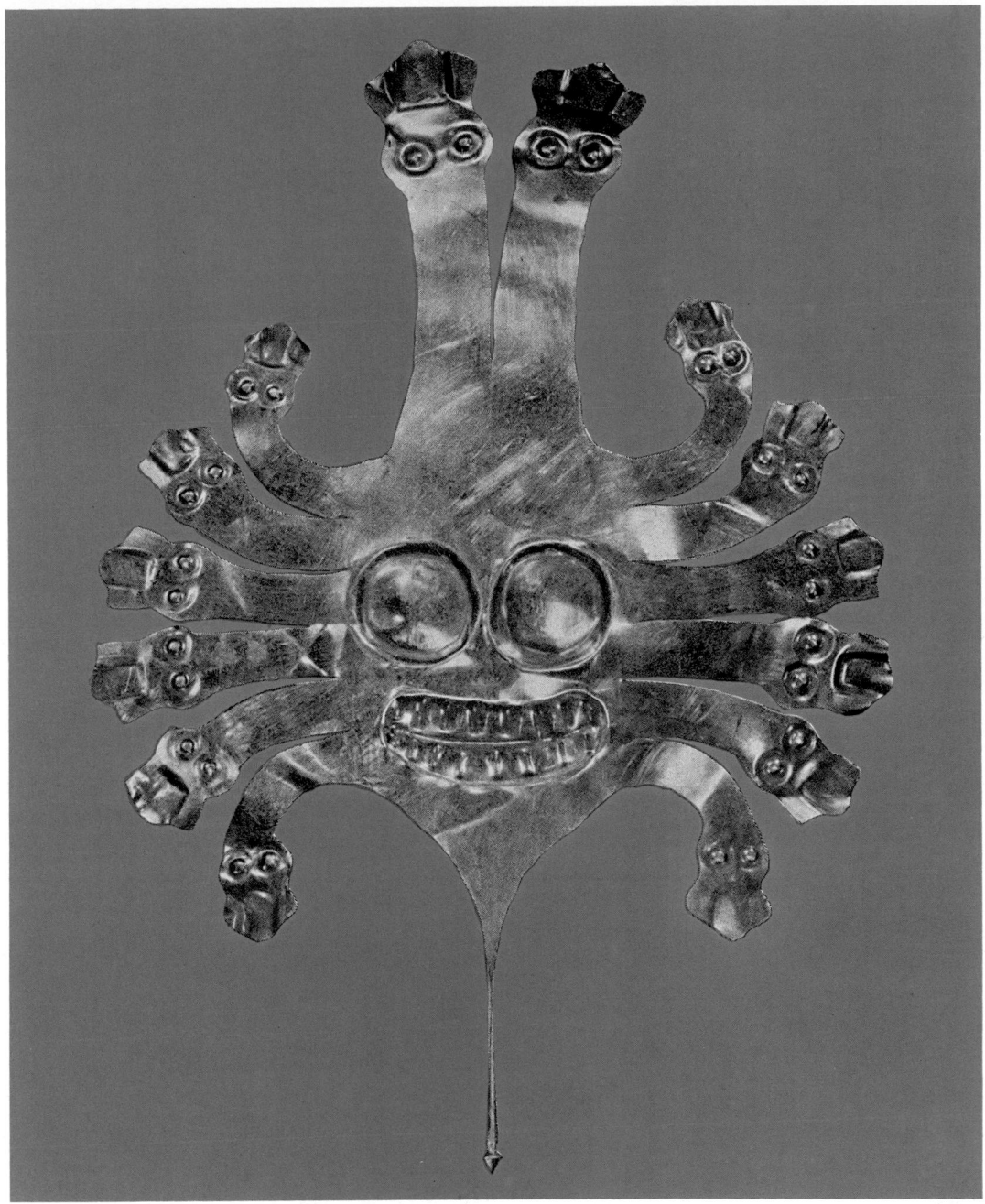

A MEDUSA-LIKE HEADDRESS *of writhing snakes was worn in religious ceremonies by the Nazcas of early Peru.*

# "SWEAT OF THE SUN"

To the conquistadors, gold must have appeared almost as common in America as dirt. It rolled down the mountain streams in nuggets; it appeared in cliff faces; it could be sifted from sand. The metal was used to make everything from ceremonial objects to fishhooks, but the higher Indian cultures associated it with the gods. "Sweat of the sun," the Inca called it, and they displayed it in such quantities that the Spanish were dumbfounded. The workmanship of Indian goldsmiths, one invader wrote, seemed "like a dream . . . not as if made by man's hands."

A SNARLING JAGUAR, *four and a half inches long, was probably designed to be sewn into the vestment of a Chavín priest. Its open mouth, with its clenched teeth and overlapping fangs, symbolized supernatural power; the same device turned up repeatedly in later Peruvian art.*

A LOFTY HEADDRESS, *this ornament of beaten gold stands more than a foot high. Its workmanship and its jaguar-mouth are Chavín inspired, but the piece was made by Mochicas who lived more than a thousand years later. One eye still has its shell inlay, a feature of Mochica work.*

# ANCIENT CRAFTSMEN OF THE ANDES

America's first goldsmiths were members of a Stone Age civilization who lived in Peru some 2,000 years ago. Much of their work might have been unknown today had it not been for a group of children who stumbled upon an ancient grave in 1928 while playing near the Indian village of Chongoyape. The grave contained—in addition to some centuries-old remains—a magnificent trove of gold objects.

The civilization that produced this goldwork was located near a ceremonial center called Chavín de Huantar, dedicated to the worship of a fierce and awesome jaguar. As early as 800 B.C. Chavín goldsmiths were beating gold into thin sheets with stone hammers, cutting it with stone knives and embossing it with slivers of bone. In time they passed on their techniques, and their jaguar-god, to other Peruvian peoples who added innovations of their own. The Mochicas inlaid their goldwork with stones and shells, and a later people, the Chimus, forerunners of the Inca, raised gold into three-dimensional forms by hammering it on wooden molds.

AN ELEGANT BEAKER *in the form of a head was raised from a flat sheet of gold by a Chimu goldsmith near the city of Chan-Chan. The reproduction is somewhat larger than the actual size.*  93

# A HOARD FOR THE HEREAFTER

In the 16th Century, Spain's gold-hungry adventurers melted down and carried off all the Peruvian gold they could lay hands on—some 17,500 pounds of it. But they heard of other objects they could never find: a golden fish bigger than a man's arm; a gold-hung chain so heavy that 200 men were needed to carry it. Fortunately for posterity they also missed many of the tombs filled with gold furnishings; the objects on these pages were among those the conquistadors inadvertently passed up.

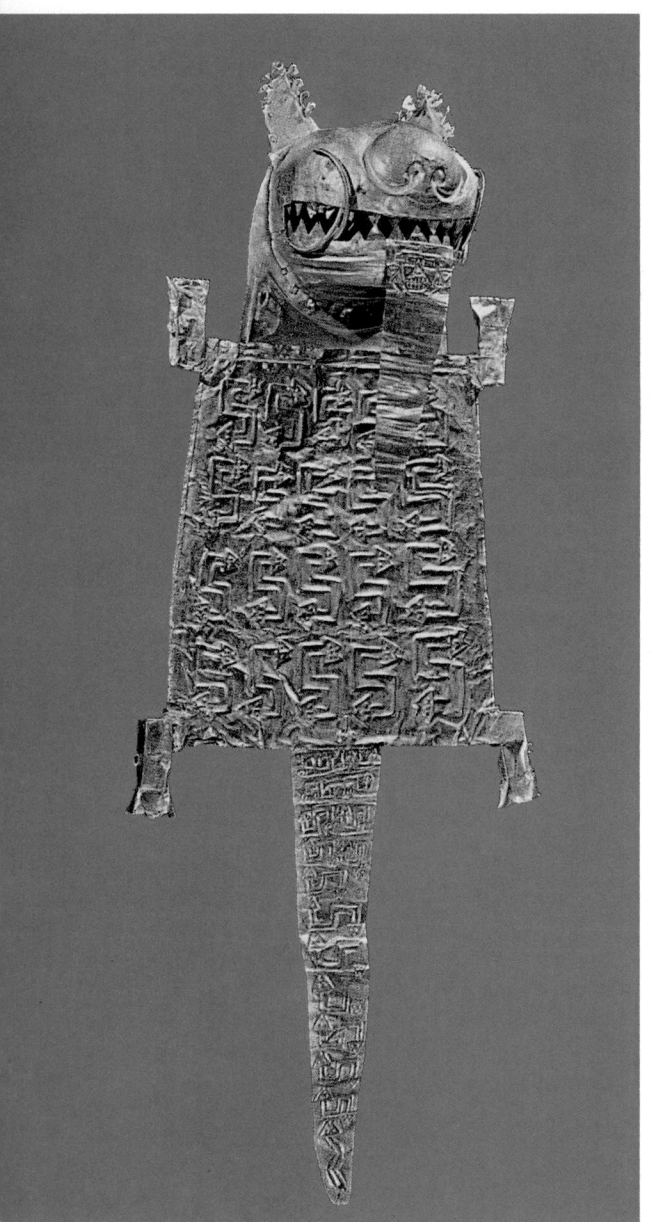

A PUMA-SKIN POUCH, *formed of two sheets of gold soldered together, contained a religious offering of coca leaves, used by Peruvians for their narcotic effect.*

RITUAL CUPS *from the Inca period held libations of fermented corn beer in religious ceremonies*

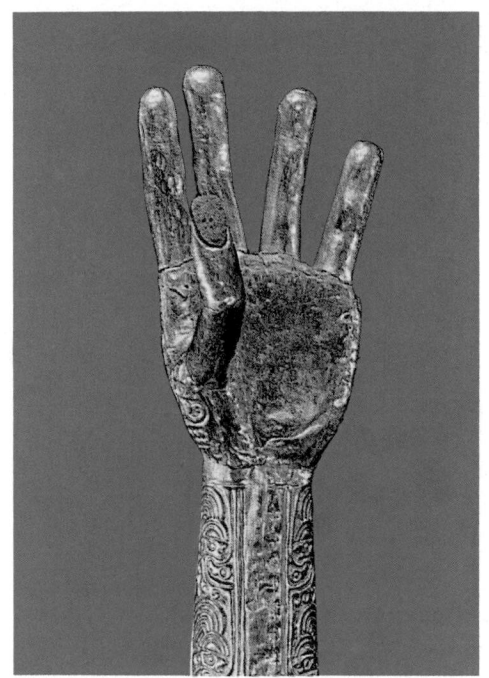

A HOLLOW HAND *from a Chimu tomb may have held burning incense in its palm. The tattoo on the forearm reflects a common Chimu practice.*

A DOLL-LIKE FIGURE *of a young Mochic girl, this gold object has a removable hea and may have originally been used as a via*

A SACRIFICIAL KNIFE, *meant to be symbolic rather than real, is an elaborately wrought effigy of some unknown god or man.*

A NOBLE LADY, *this figure, found wrapped in the shroud of a nobleman, may once have been dressed in diminutive garments.*

A GOLDEN BIRD *is a decorative duplicate of the small clay vessels that are often found around the sites of Chimu villages.*

# GRAVEN IMAGES OF MAN

Colombia and Panama did not have splendid cities to match those of the Inca civilization in Peru, but they did have gold—often in abundance. "If there were people to extract it," wrote one Spanish explorer of the Colombian highlands, "there would be . . . enough to last forever." In Panama, the conquistadors were astonished and delighted when they were presented with a peace offering of some 500 pounds of gold jewelry by an Indian chief whose people lived in simple reed huts.

Within these local cultures, goldsmiths frequently worked in widely dissimilar styles—at times reducing the human body to pure geometry, at other times exaggerating its contours. Probably their greatest contribution was a method of casting gold over wax forms, which were then melted away.

A TOLIMA MAN, *arms and legs outspread, is pierced in a pattern of dots and lines. The figure was probably a chest ornament.*

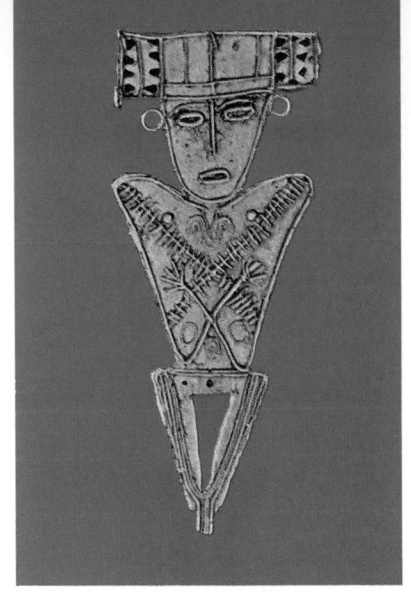

A MUISCA WARRIOR *was cast over a wax form; wax threads supplied his features.*

A HERO'S BREASTPLATE, *10 inches high, identified the bravest Coclé warriors; on its surface is an embossed alligator god.*

A HEROIC PORTRAIT *of a Quimbaya noble was cast from 1.37 pounds of gold.*

A GLITTERING BROOCH *inlaid with turquoise is a miniature version of a Mixtec ceremonial shield, with a fringe of gold bells along the bottom.*

# MEXICAN MAGNIFICENCE

"I have seen nothing in all my livelong days which so filled my heart with joy," wrote the great engraver Albrecht Dürer in 1520; he had just viewed an exhibit in Brussels of Middle American goldwork—the Aztec Moctezuma's gifts to his Spanish conquerors. Indeed, in the quality of their work the Mixtec and Aztec jewelers of Mexico rivaled the finest craftsmen in Europe. "They could cast a bird with a movable head, tongue, feet and hands, and in the hand put a toy so it appeared to dance with it," wrote a Franciscan missionary. After showing off their heathen treasures in the courts of Europe, the Spanish converted most of them into bullion.

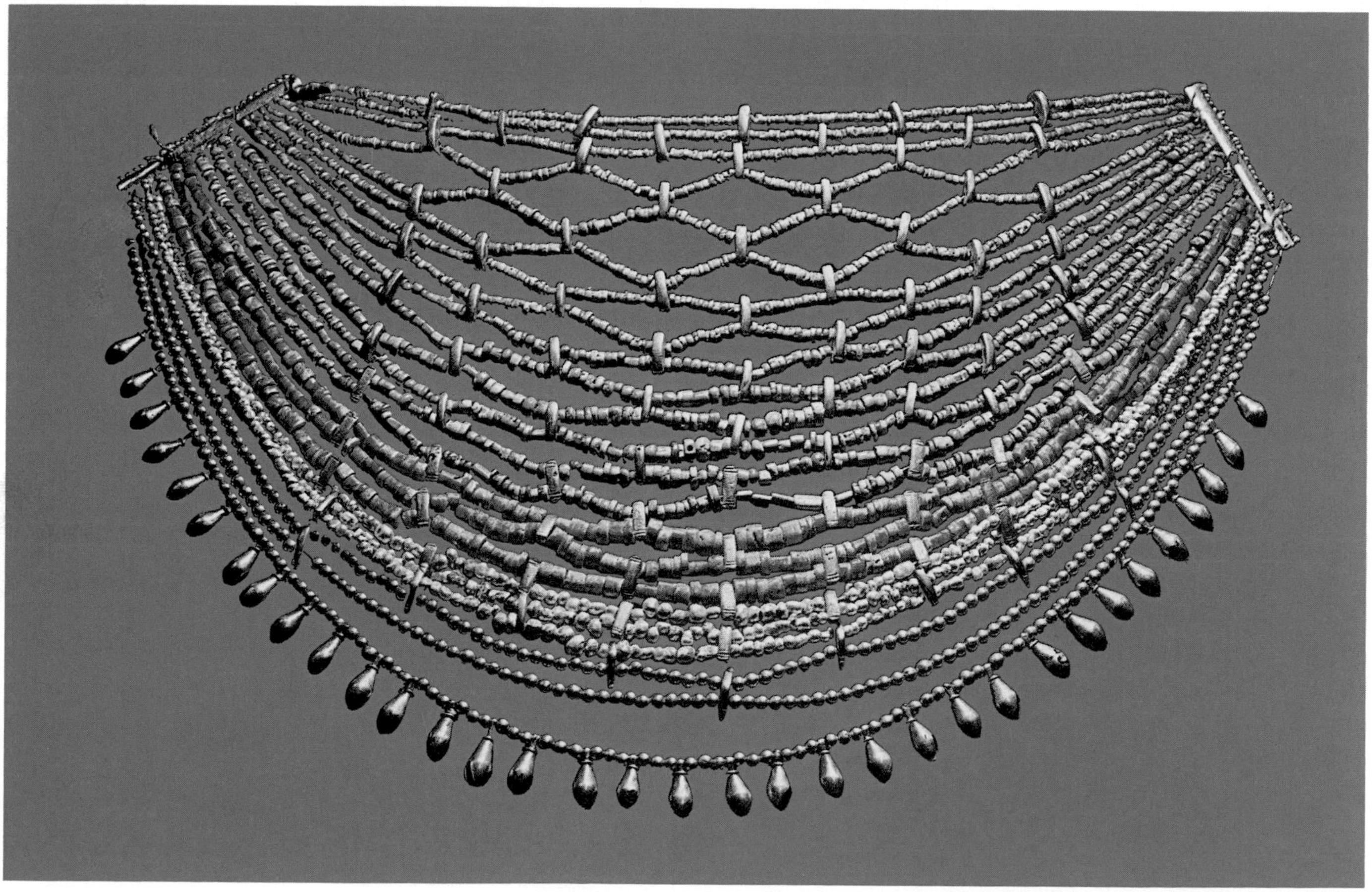

A LACY NECKLACE *of pearls, turquoise beads and tiny red shells is tied at intervals with loops of gold and is finished with a row of gold bells.*

A FORMIDABLE GOD, *this figure may represent the Mixtec lord of death and darkness; the symbols on his shoulders are calendrical notations.*

# 5

# GODS AND EMPIRES

How did the peoples of ancient America lead their lives? How did they govern themselves? To what degree did religion permeate their existence? There is no single set of answers to such questions because the numerous cultures of Middle and South America varied widely and underwent changes at different periods. Although little is known about many of them, a great deal is known about others. But even the civilizations that are best understood —the Aztec of Mexico and the Inca of Peru—have features so strikingly unusual to the modern mind that the motives and emotions of their originators can only be guessed at.

When first seen and described by the Spaniards, the highly organized Aztec and Inca states were alive and at the peak of their vigor. The conditions under which the conquerors viewed them, however, were anything but typical, and so the early Spanish accounts must be accepted with caution. The turmoil of conquest kept Indian society and government from functioning normally under European eyes, and since the Spaniards considered themselves crusaders against idolatry and were therefore prejudiced, they quickly destroyed Indian religions without fully comprehending them.

Nevertheless, some of the early chronicles, combined with the research of modern scholars, depict fairly accurately the structure of the Aztec Empire and the society that supported it. Tenochtitlán, the Aztec capital, was a city-state dominating other city-states in the rich Valley of Mexico and surrounding regions. In theory it was a democracy whose inhabitants elected their governing officers and served as citizen-soldiers. In practice it was an almost absolute monarchy whose chief of state and supreme commander, the semidivine emperor, was chosen from a single royal family by a council of leading noblemen.

The highest-ranking officials below the emperor, including the equivalent of a prime minister (who was known as the Snake Woman although he was a man) and other important administrative or military dignitaries, were also members of the royal house. Their positions were usually hereditary, but in some cases they were won by exceptional service in war. High priests of noble lineage headed the city's powerful priestly orders, some of which

*A ZAPOTEC DEITY, a maize god whose chest ornament is flanked by twin ears of corn, is portrayed on a clay urn. Prominent in his elaborate feathered and flowered headdress is the face of an open-mouthed bat, surmounted by a symbol of unknown significance which appears on many Zapotec objects.*

maintained schools for special religious training; there were also secular schools, where the youths of Tenochtitlán learned such mundane subjects as citizenship and military proficiency.

Underlying the ruling and religious strata was a large bureaucracy of officials composed of lesser nobles and able commoners, most of whom were appointed by the emperor and his advisors. There was also an important class of merchant-adventurers who combined politics with business; returning from trading expeditions to distant and dangerous lands, they reported to the emperor the discovery of towns whose wealth made them prospective conquests.

The bulk of Tenochtitlán's inhabitants were artisans and other common people without special position, and below them came the peasants who tilled the fields and were the backbone of the Aztecs' predominantly agricultural economy. Lowest on the social scale were a number of slaves, either prisoners captured in battle or men and women who had been sold into bondage.

With the exception of the slaves, all male civilians were potential soldiers. During a war many of them might be conscripted into the army, resuming their accustomed work when peace was declared. In addition, by the time the Spaniards arrived a considerable number of Aztec warriors were professionals who spent their active lives in the ranks.

Tenochtitlán as first viewed by its conquerors had the orderly aspect of a well-governed city. Its bureaucracy of judges and administrative officers settled disputes, meted out punishment, granted honors, operated a police force and other public services, and saw to the distribution of tribute from vanquished provinces.

One reflection of its efficient government was Tenochtitlán's tidiness, astonishing to Spaniards accustomed to the refuse-littered streets of 16th Century European towns and cities. They were particularly impressed with the neat and well-controlled Aztec markets, the most important of which was at the twin city of Tlaltelolco. Its enormous arcaded square was sometimes thronged with 60,000 buyers and sellers, but doing business there must have been a slow and complicated process. Since there was no money, most transactions were by barter. Buyers had to find sellers who possessed what they wanted and would accept the things that they offered in exchange. Certain commodities, including cacao (chocolate) beans and lengths of cloth, were in limited use as a kind of currency, and some Spanish chroniclers report that quills filled with gold dust served the same purpose. These clumsy media of exchange varied in quality and value, so even with their help all business transactions except the very simplest were cumbersome.

While the Aztecs ran their capital city remarkably well despite their inconvenient way of doing business, their Empire was maintained in a less orderly manner. Actually it was not an empire in the usual sense—a group of subject people acknowledging a strong central authority. It was only loosely held together: Tenochtitlán had long-standing but shaky alliances with some cities in the Valley of Mexico and it overawed others by superior power. But no sense of nationality had yet developed, and conquered states always hoped to stage successful revolts.

Almost no statesmanlike efforts were made by the Aztecs to consolidate their conquests. They created no effective machinery for the government of subject cities and performed no services that might have made them glad to stay in the Empire. Nor did they attempt that simplest of political moves: the establishment in a conquered province of a loyal ruling class. They governed by fear alone, periodically renewing the terror of their name by punitive forays.

In fact a peaceful and loyal empire would have

been impossible because of the religious convictions that were basic to Aztec civilization. The Aztecs believed that their gods were nourished on human hearts; without continual wars and revolts to be put down in the provinces, the supply of captives for sacrifice would have been reduced and the gods would have gone hungry. Then, according to Aztec thinking, Tenochtitlán would have certainly fallen from power, the sun itself might have ceased to rise and all life would have perished from the earth.

Fostering such beliefs was the Aztec warrior's attitude toward death, an attitude shared by the majority of his Mexican foes. The average Aztec did not look forward to anything like an enjoyable heaven, but soldiers anticipated a glorious afterlife. From childhood they had been trained to expect to be sacrificed if they were captured and they considered this fate an honor equal to death on the battlefield. Those who fell in combat or surrendered their lives on the altar of sacrifice had the assurance that the hot blood from their hearts would help to strengthen the sun for its daily battle against the night, and so they would become in a sense part of the sun. They would rise every morning in a joyous throng and accompany it until it reached the zenith, when the powers of death and night drew it down toward darkness.

To appreciate this reasoning, which was fundamental to the structure of the Aztec Empire, requires a look at the beginnings of ancient Mexico's religion and its long development culminating in the gods of Tenochtitlán.

Like most primitive people, the early inhabitants of Middle America appear to have worshiped simple nature deities, such as the sun and the moon and the gods of rain, springtime and fertility. They prayed to these gods, performed rituals before them, and made small offerings of grain, fruit and other food to win their favor. Sometimes mountains and trees were held sacred, and corn was the sacred plant; even today there are Mexican Indians who continue the age-old custom of addressing it reverently as "Your Lordship." Each small town also had its own special gods concerned primarily with the affairs of people in the vicinity, to be consulted and propitiated before planting a new field, building a new house, naming a child, setting out on a journey.

Such innocent rites and worship graded insensibly into sterner religious practices. During major crises such as a serious drought or attack by a formidable enemy, the Middle Americans sacrificed to the gods the most precious things that they possessed: human lives. In so doing they were not alone. Human sacrifice lurks in the background of nearly every people, including Europeans. It usually died out, however, with the advance of civilization, when oxen, sheep or other animals became domesticated and were offered for sacrifice instead of men. The people of Middle America never passed this critical turning point, perhaps because they had no domestic animals valuable or large enough to serve as impressive sacrifices.

Once begun, human sacrifice was never wholly absent from the Middle American scene. Even the comparatively gentle Maya knew it, but the Toltecs were the people who, in the 10th Century, made it dominant in Mexican religion. It was they who originated the belief that the sun fought a daily battle against the night and that to win these recurrent battles, on which the life of the world depended, the sun must be nourished with human hearts and blood. As often happens in the evolution of a religion, the Toltecs came to identify their own tribal war god, Tezcatlipoca, with the supreme sun, and worshiped both together with the same sacrificial rites.

The Aztecs, who came after the Toltecs, continued to worship Tezcatlipoca but added their own god, Huitzilopochtli, who was similar but more closely concerned with the political fortunes of Tenochtitlán. Gradually the conviction developed among them that the miraculous favors granted by Huitzilopochtli would be in proportion to the number of human hearts that he received.

Warriors taken in battle with independent states and rebellious subjects seized in the provinces were the main sources of Huitzilopochtli's nourishment. Sometimes, however, to avoid the economic cost of a real war the Aztecs organized what they called a "War of Flowers" with one of their neighbors. Equal numbers of warriors would meet at a specified place and fight until the requisite number had been captured. Then the battle would stop, and each side would lead its prisoners toward the altars of its insatiable gods.

Huitzilopochtli and Tezcatlipoca were not the only hungry gods of the Aztecs. The religion of Tenochtitlán was enthusiastically eclectic; it retained a great many ancient gods while adopting new ones. When the Aztec armies captured a city they often carried its idols home and set them up for worship—which usually meant more sacrifices. One authority estimates that by the advent of the Spaniards, Tenochtitlán's major gods numbered more than 40, and there were dozens of lesser ones.

Most Aztec victims intended for sacrifice were well treated up to the moment of their death. Because the majority actually welcomed death and union with the sun, they seldom tried to escape. A few are reported to have eluded their captors, but probably they came from a region where religious beliefs differed from those of people more closely related to the Aztecs.

Far more typical is a story that has been handed down of an enemy chieftain who was to be sacrificed in a kind of gladiatorial contest. He was tethered to a stone by a short length of rope, given dummy weapons edged with feathers and permitted to fight with five fully armed Aztec warriors.

When he defeated them all, he was not only freed but was offered the command of an Aztec army. He declined the honor, preferring to be sacrificed. Since he had been taken captive, he believed that he was destined for sacrifice and that if he continued to live he would be thwarting the will of the god who had ordained his death.

In spite of a religion emphasizing blood and death, there was much in Aztec life that was colorful and gay. All who could afford it dressed in bright-hued clothing, and the open squares of towns and cities were often the scenes of lively, pageantlike dances. Interspersed with grimmer ceremonies were such rituals as the midsummer "birth of flowers," when the people went into the country to gather blossoms with which to decorate the temples. On another occasion in celebration of the ripening of corn the emperor supplied food and drink for the entire population of Tenochtitlán, and feasting and dancing went on for seven or eight days.

Apparently no intellectuals or religious reformers ever challenged the power of Huitzilopochtli and the other barbaric gods of the Aztecs, but this does not mean that the frenzy of human sacrifice would have continued forever. When the Spanish conquerors arrived, the Aztec Empire was still in an expanding phase and captives were plentiful for the altars. Perhaps in a few more years, or generations, the gods would have learned to get along with less human blood and the Empire would have become stabilized. Indeed the widespread interest of both rulers and commoners in the rumored return of Quetzalcóatl, the ancient and beneficent god of civilization and knowledge, hints that some sort of religious reform may have been brewing. Ultimately, perhaps, it might have brought an era of peace and reason like Mexico's golden age of Teotihuacán, more than eight centuries earlier. But the Spaniards, who brought their own new era, ended that possibility forever.

BEDECKED WITH PLANTS, *a silver figure, probably of Inca origin, holds out an ear of corn. To the Peruvian Indians, whose economy depended largely on agriculture, fruits and vegetables were objects to be venerated and were frequently depicted in their art.*

The Inca Empire of Peru was much larger geographically than Aztec Mexico, and most of its area consisted of desert or precipitous mountains, with only small pockets of population between them. Its inhabitants followed hundreds of different customs and spoke many different languages. But the people of this difficult land had something that Aztec Mexico lacked: the ability to cooperate and keep the peace.

Although regional war was not uncommon in Peru during certain periods, a tendency toward cooperation and political unification must have developed in the character of the Andean Indian at an early date. Also, one of the principal sources of disorder that afflicted Middle America was absent in Peru: the land was not beset by invading waves of barbarian tribesmen like the Chichimecs who repeatedly overran the settled parts of Mexico. Until the coming of the Spaniards, the civilized Andes were never seriously threatened from outside. Peru was a world in itself, and its freedom from periodic disruption by predatory neighbors may have helped to make peace more habitual than war.

The practical value of cooperation was plainly seen once irrigation farming became established in Peru's coastal river valleys around the beginning of the Christian era. The valleys were narrow and steep, and in their natural condition only a small part of their water could be used to grow crops. More land became available for cultivation when canals were built to bring water from upstream down to dry regions that even flood waters never reached.

To build such an irrigation system called for cooperation, and operating it required respect for law. Farmers near a river mouth were at the mercy of those upstream who could damage the intakes of the canals or divert for their own use the entire flow of the river in the dry season. In very ancient times there may have been fighting between upstream and downstream farmers, but agreements for fair water distribution were soon accomplished.

Strong local governments existed in well-irrigated areas along Peru's desert coast as long ago as 1,500 years, and the example of their conspicuous prosperity must have affected the highlands. Little is known about highland society of that time except that it consisted of many different peoples who probably fought frequent, petty wars with one another. But seeing the advantages of cooperation, they too learned law and order. Consequently, most of Peru passed through the stage of small-scale nationalism at an early date. Aztec Mexico did not reach that stage until much later, and it never progressed beyond it.

Best illustrating Peru's trend toward unity is the speed and apparent ease with which the empire of Tiahuanaco, starting from centers in the high Andes, swept the country around 650 A.D. Besides a new god and art style, it brought the first centralized control, both political and religious, to the greater part of Peru. Even at that early period many Peruvians seem to have felt that peace and political union in the Andes might not be a bad thing.

The Inca Empire, which rose to power about eight hundred years later, gave Peru its second major experience with political unification. In some respects the extraordinary Inca system of government bears comparison with that of a 20th Century welfare state. It was, to be sure, a despotism ruled by a single dynastic family, but it was a remarkably benevolent despotism. Its essential elements had grown slowly; the easy acceptance of Inca unification by subject nations shows that cooperation and obedience to law and custom were by that time long-established habits in Peru.

On the lowest level of their government the Inca, who counted by tens as most modern people do, divided their citizens into groups of 10 or sometimes 50 families. The male head of one of the families was appointed foreman of his group, the lowest office in the overall system. Ten foremen reported to a higher official, usually a hereditary *curaca*, or chieftain, who was responsible for 100 families. Still higher-ranking curacas were in charge of 1,000 or 10,000 families. These officials were normally natives of the locality, and if their province had entered the Empire without too much resistance, they were chiefs who had ruled it before the Inca took over.

Above the highest-ranking curacas were Inca nobles who served as administrators in the provincial capitals and reported to the governors of the four quarters into which the Empire was divided. These exalted persons were close relatives of the emperor, or Inca, himself, the apex of the government, and they formed the supreme council of state in the imperial capital, Cuzco.

The numerical framework of the Inca system was not rigid; it was intended to be only a general guide. A man was not made head of an arbitrarily designated group, but was put in charge of a natural grouping, such as the inhabitants of a town or a valley, and given the rank and number of subordinates best suited to the number of families under his control. When possible the *ayllu*—the basic social unit of ancient Peru, which consisted of an enlarged family or several families claiming interrelationship—was preserved intact and fitted smoothly into the system. The count of families was kept up to date and each area's total was recorded decimally on knotted-string *quipus* and forwarded to the census office in Cuzco, where it formed one of the bases for the Empire's skillful economic planning.

Land was the other base, and the Inca planners, who were high officers with a good deal of initiative, made great efforts to match land to people. When a new province was brought into the Empire, they often had a three-dimensional clay model made to help them decide whether irrigation canals or other public works would make it more productive. If so, they counted on the new province to absorb surplus population from thickly settled regions.

Every year throughout the Empire Inca officials estimated the amount of cultivable land currently available. Then they set aside for the general population enough so that each family could raise sufficient food to keep itself comfortably fed, large families receiving more land than small ones. When everyone was provided for, the rest of the land—usually more than half—was either allotted to the state or was used for the support of religion.

The common people were required to cultivate the state and church lands before their own, and the start of such work was made a festive occasion. At the beginning of the planting season everyone worked the sacred fields together, including the highest officials and the Inca nobles, but these members of the upper ranks soon left to go about their other business. Even the Inca himself worked for a short time, breaking the ground with a golden, plowlike tool.

Crops harvested from the church's fields maintained the temples, procured materials for ceremonial robes, supplied offerings for the gods and fed the numerous priests. All other nonproducers—the nobles, officials, soldiers, skilled artisans, such specialists as architects and engineers and also widows, the old and the sick—were supported by crops grown on the state's lands. Part of the crop went into local storehouses against a time of crop failures, and part was sent to Cuzco and other administrative centers to sustain the large bureaucracy. After the commoners had tilled the lands of the state and church and later their own allotments, they were expected to labor for a specified number of days on roads, irrigation canals or other public works, or to serve in the army.

Money did not exist in the Peru of the Inca, nor was there any other medium of exchange comparable to the cacao bean or cloth sometimes used in Aztec Mexico. Trade was by barter supplemented by what amounted to a state credit system. Ordinary citizens made "deposits" of labor and could draw against this credit in food or other goods. Nobles, officials and others of superior rank got credits according to their stations. Trading was not extensive among the common people because there was seldom need for it. The farmers made most of their simple tools and implements, and their wives received an allowance of wool from state-owned llama and alpaca herds to spin and weave into clothes for the family.

Although the Inca state controlled and regulated the lives of its citizens and generally did so with benevolence, occasionally it displayed the callousness expected of an ancient despotism. For example, Inca officials periodically lined up all the young girls of a district who had reached the age of about 10 and selected the most intelligent and the most attractive. These girls, who became known as Chosen Women, were taken from their families and sent to conventlike schools in Cuzco and the pro-

vincial capitals for education in cooking, weaving, deportment, religion and other things that young girls should know. After a few years they were further classified. A few were assigned to lifelong celibacy as temple attendants or to other religious duties, but most of the Chosen Women were distributed as secondary wives or concubines to the Inca himself (whose primary wife was often his sister), or to nobles or high army officers.

When the remaining young people of a community reached marriageable age—about 20 for boys, 16 for girls—they were lined up in two rows facing each other and an official declared them engaged. This was not really the act of cold-hearted socialist tyranny that it seems. The boys and girls had already paired off; the official's main function was to settle disputes between rivals for a girl and to give the emperor's blessing to the unions. Later the marriage ceremonies were performed according to local custom. The couples were allotted land and became full members of the community.

Obviously the Inca government could have been unbearably oppressive; actually it was not. Inca agriculture, supervised by state-supported experts, was productive and was continually improved by irrigation works and by the construction of terraces to increase the cultivated area of steep-sided valleys. After all needs were met, including those of the court and the nobility, the remaining crops were sometimes so ample that the state granaries overflowed. Then the government distributed food dividends for public feasting.

It has often been suggested that the smooth working of the Inca state was its worst fault—that the well-cared-for commoners, leading lives of security, obedience, hard work and modest plenty, must have suffered from boredom. That may be. But above the common level life was far from dull. High officials lived in large houses, had several wives and numerous servants, wore fine and gaudy clothes and were exempt from physical labor. Their sons attended a formal school where they received a solid grounding in Inca history, language, religion, and where they learned to read the records of the knotted-string quipus. The highest officials, most of whom were related to the ruling family, dwelt amid elaborate luxury, and they enjoyed many privileges. These included the right to wear great earplugs of gold or silver (the Spanish conquerors called such officials *Orejones*, or "Big Ears"), to dress in a style similar to the emperor's, and to be in attendance at the Inca's splendid court in Cuzco.

Religion, while important, did not play the all-pervading role in Inca life that it did among the Aztecs of Mexico. The Inca Empire had in effect an established church that was part of the government and subordinate to it. Its base was probably the ancient folk religion of the Cuzco region. There was a creator god, Viracocha, who was theoretically supreme, but much more influential were the gods of the sun, moon, stars and thunder and ancient fertility gods like the Earth Mother, a favorite of farmers. All these were considered Viracocha's agents in charge of human affairs.

Dominant member of this practical pantheon was the sun, from which the Inca royal family was believed descended. The ruling Inca was therefore looked upon as a living god and was closely identified with the sun itself. As a god he could do no wrong, and all his wishes were law. By fostering this concept, the Inca dynasty neatly eliminated conflict between church and state.

Inca religion included some human sacrifice, but only on rare occasions. In case of a national emergency—a famine, the illness of an emperor or a similar crisis—one or more specially designated Chosen Women might be offered in sacrifice to the Inca gods. This sort of ritual killing, however, did not affect national policy as it did in Aztec Mexico.

The established church centered in Cuzco. Its impressive Temple of the Sun, once plated with gold and now mostly hidden beneath a Dominican monastery, dominated the heart of the city, and its gorgeous ceremonies were the outstanding events of the year. Although the sun cult was dominant in Inca religion, vast importance was also attached to ancestor worship. Reverence of the ancestral dead is common in some form all over the world, but the Incas went to incredible extremes. In Cuzco they preserved cloth-wrapped mummies who were said to be those of ruling Incas back to Manco Capac, who was the first. These mummies were housed in royal splendor as if they were still alive and were taken out periodically to witness ceremonies. Minor members of the ruling family and other important nobles also preserved their dead, and commoners throughout the Empire followed the custom according to their means.

One of Cuzco's most impressive ruins stands high above the city on a hill called Kenko. There, partly surrounding a rocky outcrop shot with caves and veined by fissures, is a semicircular wall of fine Inca stonework containing niches that resemble seats for spectators. Kenko was indeed a kind of theater, but for the honored dead. Students of Inca tradition believe that sacred mummy bundles were once brought up from the city and reverently placed in the niches.

At the focus of the semicircle a pinnacle of rock 20 feet high rises from a stone platform built around its base. The rock is undecorated and just as nature made it, and its pointed, jagged shape suggests the many precipitous peaks that loom about Cuzco. In that strangely beautiful place it is easy to imagine the mummies of long-dead Inca emperors being carried up from their glittering city to worship, as they must have done in life, the spirit of the mountains out of which their race is said to have come.

MASKED AS EARTH GODS, *actors begin their roles while trumpeters sound the ceremony's start. Among the deities, seen at the right, are the crocodile and the crab.*

# STAGING AN AWESOME PAGEANT

In 1946, Giles Healey, a young American photographer exploring a Maya site in southern Mexico, stumbled across a curious building hidden by jungle growth. Inside, on the walls of three vaulted rooms, he found a series of faded, half-obscured murals that apparently told a ceremonial narrative, beginning with a ritual procession and climaxing in a sacrificial dance. Healey's find turned out to be one of the greatest single discoveries in the history of Middle American archeology. A team of scholars and artists descended on the site, which was given the name of Bonampak, Maya for "painted walls." For months they painstakingly copied the 1,100-year-old murals, reconstructing them in their original vivid colors. The result is a rare portrait of a group of ancient Americans as they actually looked and lived—chatting with each other, dressing in magnificent costumes, and acting out a brilliant, often fantastic, pageant to propitiate their gods of the earth.

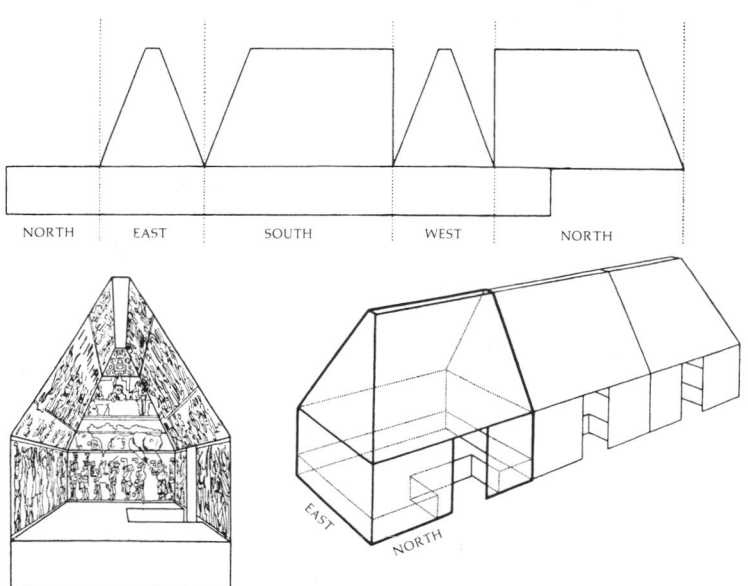

# THE SACRED CEREMONY BEGINS

THE MURAL SCHEME *on these pages is from Bonampak's "Room 1," outlined in black at right and seen with one end removed at left. In the copied murals, the two continuous scenes have been "unfolded" into individual panels (top).*

In the first of the three rooms in Bonampak's main building, a continuous mural around the sloping ceiling reveals a scene of bustling activity, as the Maya prepare for a ritual procession honoring their gods of fertility and the earth. In the two odd-shaped tall panels on this page, above, 14 white-robed aristocrats stand waiting in a row beneath the grotesque masks of a snake-headed rain god and other deities.

In the triangular panel to the right, the *halach uinic*, or head chief, sits in casual dress atop a massive stone table; he looks back to give orders to a servant holding a child—probably the chief's son, who is being allowed to watch the goings-on. Sharing the dais to the right of the chief is his wife; another highborn woman sits with them while a pair of servants attend below. In the panel at the far right other servants are seen dressing three of the chief's war captains, who stand on the low platform that runs through the scene. Already outfitted in splendid jaguar skins, heavy jade necklaces, earrings and wristlets, they are getting the finishing touches, including gorgeous hoops of sacred green quetzal feathers attached to their backs. In the long frieze covering the walls below, these same three captains take over the center of the stage as the colorful procession moves in from the sides.

PREPARATIONS FOR THE RITUAL *revolve about the head chief (triangular panel, this page), as lesser noblemen are dressed by servants or stand waiting for the ceremony to begin. Eight of these aristocrats are seen in the detail below. The small rectangles above them, made to receive the mysterious glyph writing seen elsewhere in the murals, are blank; apparently the artist could not record who they were or what was said.*

## A RAID FOR VICTIMS

Murals in Bonampak's second room reveal the next chapter of the narrative—as well as the Maya artists' stunning mastery of composition and movement. After their ceremonial procession to the gods, Bonampak's warriors staged a surprise raid on an enemy village to

capture prisoners for the all-important ritual of sacrifice. Waving clubs and blowing trumpets, they are seen here falling on their victims, whose lack of weapons show them to be totally unprepared. At the upper right is the chief, clutching a captive by the hair; his battle dress in-cludes his marks of rank: a jaguar headpiece, tunic and anklets, and a spear wrapped in jaguar skin. His three captains stand protectively nearby, spears at the ready; in this scene one wears a jaguar figure as a headpiece, an-other quetzal feathers and the third a crocodile head.

# THE JUDGMENT: DEATH

Back at Bonampak after the raid, the chief stands sternly atop the steps of a ceremonial platform and passes the expected sentence on his captives. As Maya noblemen dressed in weird animal heads assist in the rites, a naked prisoner at the chief's feet raises his arms in vain for some sign of mercy. Unlike the Maya themselves, who considered it an honor to be sacrificed for the good of all, these poor villagers seem thoroughly frightened.

Three prisoners at the lower left are bleeding from their fingers in what may have been a ritual wounding preliminary to their sacrifice; the hand of one at the far left is grasped by the hand of a partially obscured warrior, as if the latter had just pierced the captive's fingers to draw blood. (The two black circles, seen here and elsewhere in the murals, represent holes into which pairs of wooden roof beams were once fitted to help support the building's vaults.)

Directly beneath the chief's spear the figure of a victim sprawls with tragic grace across the steps, his eyes closed in death or in a faint brought on by terror. Other prisoners at right fearfully await their sentences—which may be symbolized by the disembodied head on the lower step, resting on a bed of ceremonial leaves.

# CELEBRATING THE FINAL RITES

Bonampak's story draws to a close in the murals of the third and last room. As the prisoners are led to their fate, the *halach uinic* seats himself on a ceremonial dais *(below)* and completes the long-hallowed ritual by pricking his tongue, adding his own blood to the offerings being made to the gods.

The scene is oddly similar to that of the same family group seen at the ceremony before the raid. The chief's wife sits stiffly at the left talking to a woman who stands behind the dais. Another woman kneels behind her, while a servant below her cradles the royal child. A male attendant kneeling at the right holds a second bloodletting implement for the chief's use. Meanwhile, atop the mural at right, four dignitaries attending the ceremonies sit crosslegged in animated conversation while they wait. Below them, as the gourds rattle and the trumpets sound, the final procession begins.

MUSICIANS AND ATTENDANTS, led by standard-bearers carrying devices of brightly colored feathers, march to the scene of sacrifice. Two members of the orchestra blow long wooden trumpets and two others await their cues, while other players shake gourdlike rattles.

THE CHIEF AND HIS LADIES, robed in long gowns of white cloth, sit on a large stone table for the bloodletting rite. A spiked ceremonial vessel lined with strips of bark paper awaits the contribution of the chief, who is seen pricking his tongue with a sharp thorn or bone.

# 6

# TRIUMPHS
# OF NATIVE GENIUS

The framework of technology that supported the peoples of ancient America was sophisticated in some respects, rudimentary in others. Obvious reasons for its deficiencies were the broad oceans that isolated the New World from the rest of mankind. Middle America and Peru could not borrow cultural advances from far-distant countries, in the way that Europe got paper, the mariner's compass, printing, gunpowder and other valuable inventions from China. The Americans could not learn from educated travelers how to write their language in a phonetic alphabet, as the Greeks traditionally learned from Cadmus of Miletus, or how to smelt iron ore, as the Egyptians learned from the Hittites. Since the American civilizations had to invent their technologies for themselves, exchanging only a little with one another, it was natural that in certain respects they should lag behind the civilizations of Europe and Asia, which over the centuries had pooled their technologies.

The most conspicuous weaknesses of the Indian cultures lay in their lack of helpful devices based upon the principle of the wheel, in their limited animal husbandry, in their ignorance of iron and steel and in the ineffectiveness of their written languages. These fundamental deficiencies caused other weaknesses.

The total absence of wheeled vehicles, or of wheels of any kind, was one of the first things the Spaniards noticed when they invaded Mexico and Peru. Archeologists have since unearthed in Mexico a small group of toylike animal figures mounted on wheels, proving that the wheel's principle was known to at least a few individuals in ancient America; but nowhere was practical advantage taken of it. Not only were there no carts or wagons for transport, there also were no pulleys or winches for hauling or hoisting heavy objects; nor was there a wheel to speed the potter's work.

Poverty in livestock was a serious hindrance to Indian agricultural technology before the arrival of the Spaniards. Domestic animals are not commonly thought of as agricultural machines, but in effect that is what many of them had been in the Old World since very remote antiquity. Grazing animals, such as cattle, sheep and goats, eat coarse vegetation unfit for man and convert it into meat

MAYA HIEROGLYPHS, *like these finely carved figures from a temple doorway at Palenque, Mexico, were the most sophisticated form of writing in ancient America. A system of dots, bars, faces and hands enabled scribes to record dates and events. The symbols have been only partially deciphered.*

TWO VALUED ANIMALS *of Peru are depicted in silver Inca figurines. The alpaca (left) supplied high-quality wool; the llama provided meat, coarser wool and pack transportation.*

and milk, the best of foods. Strong animals pull plows, enabling farmers to cultivate much more land than they could using only their own muscles. Lacking these "machines" in some regions and inadequately supplied with them in others, New World agriculture was seriously handicapped, and so were the societies it supported.

Middle America was more handicapped than Peru. It had no domestic animals except small dogs, turkeys, ducks and bees, kept for their honey. None of these could graze or pull a plow. All tilling of the fields had to be done by hand, and consequently land that did not repay this large investment in human labor remained unproductive. Population concentrated in places that were easily farmed, while many areas like the semiarid plains in northern Mexico, excellent rangeland, were sparsely inhabited for want of cattle and sheep to turn their rough fodder into food for man.

Partly compensating for these agricultural limitations, Mexican farmers developed the very effective method of *chinampa* gardening on lush, artificial islands built in the shallow lakes of the Valley of Mexico. Canal irrigation was also practiced in some parts of Middle America, but the highly cultured Maya and their neighbors never progressed beyond primitive slash-and-burn farming.

Peru had better domestic animals than Middle America. None of them was strong enough to help in farming, so Peruvian agriculture was also dependent on hand cultivation, but its animals were valuable in other important ways.

As early as 1500 B.C. the small, humpless cameloid of the Andes, the guanaco, had been tamed, and by skillful breeding and selection the Peruvians developed it into the domestic llama and alpaca. These animals grazed on the otherwise useless bunch grass that grows on the cold highlands and converted it into meat and wool. The comparatively small alpacas were raised chiefly for their silky wool, as

they are today. The larger llamas had coarser wool but they gave more meat, and although each could carry a load of only about 100 pounds, they were valuable as pack animals. They are still used in the high Andes, where other beasts of burden suffer from the altitude.

In Inca times the government-owned herds of llamas and alpacas played a major role in Peru's economy. Both were sources of wool and meat, and trains of several hundred llamas trooped along the Inca roads, covering up to 12 miles a day and carrying the supplies of the Empire. The Inca armies depended largely on llama transport, and this was one of the reasons why the Empire could conquer and hold distant provinces. Pack llamas gave the armies mobility—and they had two distinct advantages over the human porters that the Aztec armies of Mexico were forced to use: they fed themselves at roadside pastures and they could be eaten if necessary.

Besides having better domestic animals than the peoples of Middle America, the Peruvians were generally better farmers. Their farming implements were simple—principally a bronze-bladed hoe and a digging stick with a stirruplike attachment for forcing it into the ground by foot like a spade. But Peru's farmers, helped by their hydraulic engineers, achieved agricultural wonders.

Peru's coastal valleys are almost rainless, but where enough water came down their rivers, every inch of available land was used for cultivation, including the river deltas near the sea and the narrow flood plains leading into the Andean foothills. Villages were built where they would not intrude on cropland; even the large homes of local chiefs and Inca administrators were often perched on rocky elevations.

In these intensely cultivated valleys farmers usually raised two or more crops a year, a degree of production made possible by the close network of large and small irrigation canals that men first built there about 2,000 years ago. Often the canals were stone-lined, with stone sluice gates to regulate their flow of water from the rivers. As population increased and engineering skill improved, the canals climbed higher and higher up the sides of the valleys, following their contours for as much as 50 or 75 miles and sometimes crossing divides to bring water to valleys with no rivers of their own. Many of these ancient canals are still in use. Others have been abandoned, but traces of them can still be seen winding along steep slopes far above the level of modern cultivation.

Water flowing through the canals served a double purpose. In addition to irrigating the fields, it enriched their soil with silt and dissolved plant nutrients carried from the rivers, especially during flood seasons. As a result the soil of the valleys was not exhausted as quickly as that of the fields of Middle America's slash-and-burn farmers. Peruvian farmers also had the advantage of an excellent, concentrated fertilizer, *guano*, the droppings of sea birds that nest by the millions on rocky islands off the coast. Even in pre-Inca days guano was carried far up the valleys to be spread on fields near the rivers' sources. The Inca government protected these valuable birds, as the Peruvian government does today, to keep them working for human benefit.

Although canal irrigation was used in the high-lands of Peru as well as in the valleys, it was less necessary there since the rainfall was usually sufficient to produce at least one crop a year. The most serious problem facing farmers in the mountains was the scarcity of level land for cultivation. Steep land can be farmed, but unless precautions are taken it erodes quickly: once its natural covering of vegetation is disturbed, the soil washes down to the valley floor, leaving little but rocks.

The Inca well understood this problem, and as soon as they had established peace in a newly acquired province they put the population to work constructing the *andanes*, or terraces, that transformed the mountain slopes into arable land that did not erode. Behind sturdy retaining walls made of stones, other stones were piled to act as fill and to ensure good drainage. First soil and then topsoil carried up from the valley below was placed over the fill and tamped down. The result was a narrow but level and extremely productive field which was sometimes irrigated. Ancient andanes, rising tier on tier like gigantic stairs, and often as sound today as when they were built, can be seen on many Peruvian hillsides, and some of them are still thickly set with crops in season.

Inca engineers had specialties in addition to building irrigation works and agricultural terraces. One of them was road- and bridge-construction. They carried their roads over narrow, shallow rivers on masonry piers upon which rested a pavement of rectangular stone slabs. Wide, deep and slow-running rivers were crossed on bridges of boats or rafts lashed together with fiber cables. Rivers flowing swiftly and turbulently in steep-walled canyons called for more elaborate treatment. The engineers conquered such obstacles by building massive stone piers on each side of a canyon and slinging between them five great cables of twisted or braided fiber, three of which supported a roadway of wooden crosspieces while the remaining two served as guard rails. These suspension bridges sagged and swayed alarmingly and crossing one of them must have been a worrisome experience, but they spanned formidable gorges as wide as 200 feet.

Engineering projects connected with agriculture do not seem to have enjoyed the same high level of attention in Middle America that they received in Peru, and apparently most bridges were fairly simple affairs of logs or wooden beams. But the Middle Americans—especially the Aztecs—had skillful engineers for other jobs. Among their most impressive feats was their solution of Tenochtitlán's difficult water problems by means of projects whose planning and execution required expert knowledge of hydrology.

The Aztec capital stood on a low island in Lake Texcoco, one of several connected lakes that had no outlet beyond the Valley of Mexico. Water level in the lakes therefore depended on the amount of rainfall and evaporation. In exceptionally rainy years Lake Texcoco rose and flooded the city. To make matters worse, the water was so full of salt dissolved from the surrounding mainland that it damaged crops on the chinampas, the city's principal food supply. Also, as population increased around the lake, the water became polluted.

One step taken to control the troublesome water was the 10-mile dike built across the lake by Nezahualcoyotl, the philosopher-poet-engineer king of the city of Texcoco, on behalf of his ally, Tenochtitlán. The dike cut the Aztec capital off from the main body of the salty lake and sheltered it in an enclosed bay whose water soon became fresh because of the good-sized rivers flowing into it. The chinampas were no longer poisoned by salt, and the level of the bay could be controlled to some extent by opening or closing gates in the dike.

The lake water never became fit for drinking, but the engineers of Tenochtitlán solved this problem by constructing an aqueduct three miles long to springs on the mainland. Each of the structure's two earthenware channels was about two feet wide and while one was in use the other was being cleaned. Another aqueduct of masonry was later built along one of the three manmade causeways linking the island capital to the lake shore. Water from both aqueducts was carried across the canals that laced the city on what the Spanish conquerors called "hollow bridges." Few European cities of the time, perhaps none, had as good a supply of clean, pure water as Tenochtitlán.

When the Spaniards invaded Aztec Mexico and Inca Peru, they were lost in admiration of their magnificent temples, palaces and carved monuments of stone. Earlier Indian peoples, including the Maya of Middle America and the Tiahuanacans on their bleak Andean plateau, had also raised splendid stone structures by the hundreds. Incredible as it seems, all of these works had been created without benefit of the iron and steel stonecutting tools on which Old World builders had depended since long before the birth of Christ.

The technique of iron smelting was never discovered in the Americas. The Peruvians knew copper as early as the beginning of the Christian era, and since it is not found in the Andes in the metallic state, they had to extract it from its ores by smelting in furnaces, which they often located in places where the winds would fan their fires. Bronze, a hard alloy of copper and tin, probably came into use in Peru and Bolivia some five centuries later, but it was not widely used until Inca times. Copper and bronze played important roles in Peruvian technology—in knives and weapons, in the blades of various agricultural tools and for making ornaments—but neither metal was hard enough to work stone effectively. The art of smelting copper and forming it into implements reached Middle

America about 900 A.D. by slow cultural diffusion from Peru, but the metal did not come into general use in the Aztec Empire until shortly before the Spanish conquest.

Although they lacked efficient metal tools for stoneworking, ancient America's masons and sculptors were abundantly supplied with patience and muscle. In both Peru and Middle America all stone for buildings and statuary had to be shaped by hammering, chiseling or grinding with implements of harder stone; sand was often used as an abrasive for smoothing surfaces. These methods were time-consuming and required enormous effort; when a stonecutter finished a single rectangular building block of moderate size he must have enjoyed a considerable sense of accomplishment.

Wherever possible, short cuts were taken to avoid such heavy labor. The Maya, for example, built their elaborate temples out of a kind of limestone that was soft when quarried but became hard after exposure to the air. They and most other Middle American peoples not only used stucco or plaster extensively as finishes for their structures, but they also covered some roughly carved stone decorations with a layer of plaster.

The master builders in stone were the Inca, and examples of their masonry still standing in the highlands of Peru rival in quality the best of ancient Greece and Egypt. So stable is this stonework that Peru's violent earthquakes seldom damage it. The terrible quake that rocked Cuzco in 1950 wrecked many Spanish structures of colonial times, revealing the Inca foundations on which some of them rested, but it had little effect on anything built by the Inca.

Lime was available to the Peruvians and could have been used as mortar to join stones or to cover rough walls, as in Middle America, but the Inca disdained such compromises. For their finest work they shaped, finished and fitted massive blocks with such amazing accuracy that the joint between any two of them can be seen as a hairline but cannot be felt with a fingertip. Some of their walls consist of stones laid in even courses, although this is not the way the Inca architects usually preferred to design them. Their most charming masonry owes its effect to its artistically planned irregularity; the stones have slightly convex faces and are of varying sizes, producing attractive shadow patterns, and they are often laid in gently curving courses. Apparently the Inca admired stones for their own sake. In their capital city of Cuzco they set large, smooth green stones into the corners of prominent buildings to contrast conspicuously with the commoner stones around them.

An impressive Inca achievement in stone is the enormous citadel of Sacsahuamán on a plateau above Cuzco. It was begun by the great emperor-conqueror Pachacuti as part of his plan to rebuild and beautify the entire capital in the latter half of the 15th Century. The triple walls of the fortress, arranged one above another on terraces and enclosing towers and buildings, rise to a total height of about 60 feet and extend for more than a third of a mile. Some of their precision-cut stones are nearly 20 feet high and weigh over 100 tons. Transporting such a block on wooden rollers or runners from the quarries, and then hauling it into position up earthen ramps must have necessitated the coordinated efforts of hundreds of laborers.

No stone construction in Middle America matches in sophistication that of the Inca builders. The Middle Americans, however, surpassed the Inca in another stonecutting technique—the carving of hard, decorative stones, such as jade, an art that was already well advanced by 800 B.C. among the Olmecs of Mexico's Gulf Coast.

Jade is extremely difficult to work, and to transform a block of it into a figurine the Olmecs and later Indian lapidaries patiently ground it against harder stones until it approached the desired shape. With a tough cord coated with fine wet sand or thin saws of wood or stone whose edges were also charged with sand, they cut slots in the roughed-out form to approximate the features, or sank holes into it with bone or bamboo drills. Then the jade between the slots or holes was chipped away with slim stone chisels and the figure was completed by extensive rubbing with abrasives. Though the work must have been extraordinarily tedious, it produced figurines that are as beautifully designed and finished as anything made by present-day lapidaries. Some of the feats performed by the ancient artisans with their simple tools were truly remarkable. Jade cylinders a half inch in diameter and four or five inches long were carefully drilled to form tubular beads. The brittle volcanic glass, obsidian, was ground into translucent spool-shaped ear ornaments as thin as cardboard. Delicately fashioned stone objects such as these were the most precious treasures of the Middle Americans, and they held them in higher esteem than gold.

Indeed, throughout ancient America the gold that inflamed the avarice of the Spaniards was valued simply as a decorative or utilitarian material, to be hammered or cast into jewelry or other ornaments, to plate the walls of temples and palaces, or to make such necessities as pins and tweezers for the nobility. Both the Middle Americans and the Peruvians, as well as several peoples of the intervening regions, excelled in goldworking, and the Mixtec and Aztec goldsmiths of Mexico especially reached heights of great artistry. A number of their creations have been preserved, and many of them are astonishingly intricate and elegant. One Aztec labret, or lip plug, for instance, is in the form of a gracefully rearing serpent whose articulated tongue moves freely in its mouth. A pair of Mixtec ear ornaments represent golden

hummingbirds, their bodies, wings and tails suggested by fine wires, and from each slender beak dangles a butterflylike plaque supporting three small bells. Sometimes the ancient craftsmen set into golden ornaments such materials as turquoise, rock crystal or mother-of-pearl to heighten their effect.

In the arts and crafts the great marvels of Peru were its textiles, the most skillfully woven of which have seldom, if ever, been equaled anywhere or at any time. Plentiful examples are known, almost all of them from the bone-dry graves along the seacoast, but the highland Inca also had enormous stocks of fine decorated fabrics that were prominently featured in their ceremonial and artistic life.

Three main factors contributed to the rise of Peru's textile tradition. To begin with, the climate in most parts of the country made warm clothing desirable. Secondly, in addition to having excellent cotton to be spun into thread or yarn, the Peruvians were unique among ancient Indian peoples in their possession of domesticated animals—the llama and the alpaca—that yielded wool. And finally, their advanced agriculture afforded them leisure time from work in the fields to develop and refine their weaving techniques, many of which were exceedingly involved.

But though the techniques were complicated, the equipment used was simple. Thread was spun by a woman who held under one arm a stick carrying a bunch of combed and fluffed cotton or wool fibers. From this bunch she pulled a length of loose fibers and attached it to a spindle, which was merely another stick that was generally weighted at one end. She let the spindle hang, set it twirling, and this motion twisted the fibers into thread. In Andean cities and villages Indian women still spin thread in this time-honored way, often while walking to market with a load of produce, and perhaps

a baby as well, slung in a cloth fastened around their shoulders.

Nearly all weaving was done on looms consisting of two wooden bars between which threads were kept at proper tension by the weaver leaning against a strap around her back. On such primitive devices were created gorgeous brocades, tapestries and airy gauzes, and complicated double cloths—two layers of fabric of contrasting colors interlocked so that the design on one side appears on the reverse in the opposite color. Experts assert that ancient Peruvian women knew practically every weave and method of textile decoration used today as well as some that are too intricate to be handled on mechanical looms. Their finest work is incredibly close-textured. Ordinary modern shirting has about 60 cross threads per inch; the Peruvians often crowded 250, occasionally 500, threads into that space.

Perhaps the most notable accomplishment of the ancient Americans was the way in which they built their elaborate civilizations with scant assistance from written language. Among the oldest of the Old World civilizations, those of Mesopotamia and Egypt, effective systems of writing appeared at a very early date and quickly became of prime importance for communication and storing information. Written records were the collective memory of all the Old World cultures, and they could not have functioned without them.

The American civilizations had nothing comparable. The Inca and earlier civilized peoples of Peru, since they lacked any sort of writing, were dependent on the *quipus* whose knotted strings were capable of little more than recording numbers and telling what objects the numbers referred to. When Inca engineers used models or diagrams in planning their buildings or irrigation works, they could not label their parts, nor could they consult handbooks to determine how thick the cables of a suspension bridge should be. All such details had to be passed from memory to memory. The Inca general who wanted to send instructions from his headquarters to the commander of a distant army had to rely on the memories of hundreds of *chasquis*, the fleet-footed relay messengers stationed along the principal roads of the Empire. A single mistake in repeating one of these messages could result in disaster.

The Aztecs were somewhat better off. They had an embryonic kind of writing that combined pictures with a few glyphs carrying simple meanings. This system, similar to that used by the Mixtecs, was sufficient for recording straightforward information, such as lists of tribute paid by conquered Mexican states, and it could indicate numbers by an awkward arrangement of dots, flags and other symbols. It could also tell the names of peoples and places and recount history in a vague sort of way. Some scholars believe that the Aztec system was in the process of evolving into a phonetic writing that would record all the thoughts and shades of meaning expressed in Aztec speech, but at the time of the Spanish conquest it was far from that goal. Consequently the Aztecs' written literature was limited almost entirely to crude chronicles and horoscopes, and like the Inca they relied heavily on the perishable and fallible human memory as a storehouse for much of their cultural tradition.

Maya writing was ancient America's most advanced. It was probably based on that originated by the Olmecs or by converts to their cult of the jaguar god. The Maya had a great many glyphs, only about one fourth of which have been deciphered, and they carved these grotesque characters on temple walls and monuments, incised them in jade or shell objects, painted them on pottery and drew them in books. Some are elements in a complex dating system, others proclaim the names of gods or cities, and in the opinion of at least one expert they combine simple phonetic and ideographic principles. Still other glyphs represent numbers in the Maya's mathematical system which, together with their remarkably accurate calendar, was a major intellectual triumph. Ancient Maya scholars knew all the essential components of present-day arithmetic; almost a millennium before that concept filtered through to Western Europe from the East, their mathematics involved the use of the abstract quantity of zero.

But even after a thousand years of development the glyphs of the Maya did not give rise to a handwritten language for general use. One reason may have been that the glyphs were extremely clumsy to use. Because many of them were similar and easy to confuse they had to be portrayed with a high degree of accuracy, and it is likely that only the priests understood them.

Only three examples of books written by the Maya have survived. Their glyphs, accompanied by pictures, are drawn on pages made of the bark of a wild fig tree and joined together like the sections of a folding screen. None of the books has been fully deciphered. Even if they could be read, it is doubtful that they would shed great light on Maya civilization and history. One manuscript is apparently concerned with astronomical observations used by Maya priests in maintaining their calendar; the others deal with religious rituals.

When the Spanish conquerors arrived, the Maya were culturally decadent, but they possessed quantities of books handed down to them from their great days. These might have told the world many things about Maya sciences and other intellectual pursuits, but they never got the chance. Bishop Diego de Landa, one of the Spanish missionaries who followed hard on the heels of the conquerors, tells in his memoirs exactly what happened.

"These people," wrote the zealous Bishop, ". . . made use of certain characters or letters, with which they wrote in their books their ancient matters and their sciences . . . We found a large number of books in these characters, and, as they contained nothing in which there were not to be seen superstition and lies of the devil, we burned them all."

STONE WALLS *frame a view of terraces, stairways and houses in the 6,750-foot-high Inca city of Machu Picchu.*

# THE INDIAN ENGINEERS

Despite an almost total lack of the implements and materials considered essential to modern engineering, the builders of ancient Peru constructed works of extraordinary scope. To conquer their parched deserts and craggy mountains, they created aqueducts and irrigation systems, accomplished complex surveying jobs and traversed rough terrain with roadways and ingenious suspension bridges. To consolidate their empires they also raised hilltop fortresses of advanced military design, and even perched cities (above) atop precipitous mountain ridges.

SLIM TRIANGLES *extend for nearly a mile along a flat-topped ridge. Preserved for over a thousand years in a dry area of southern Peru, the patterns were found only when pilots began flying over them.*

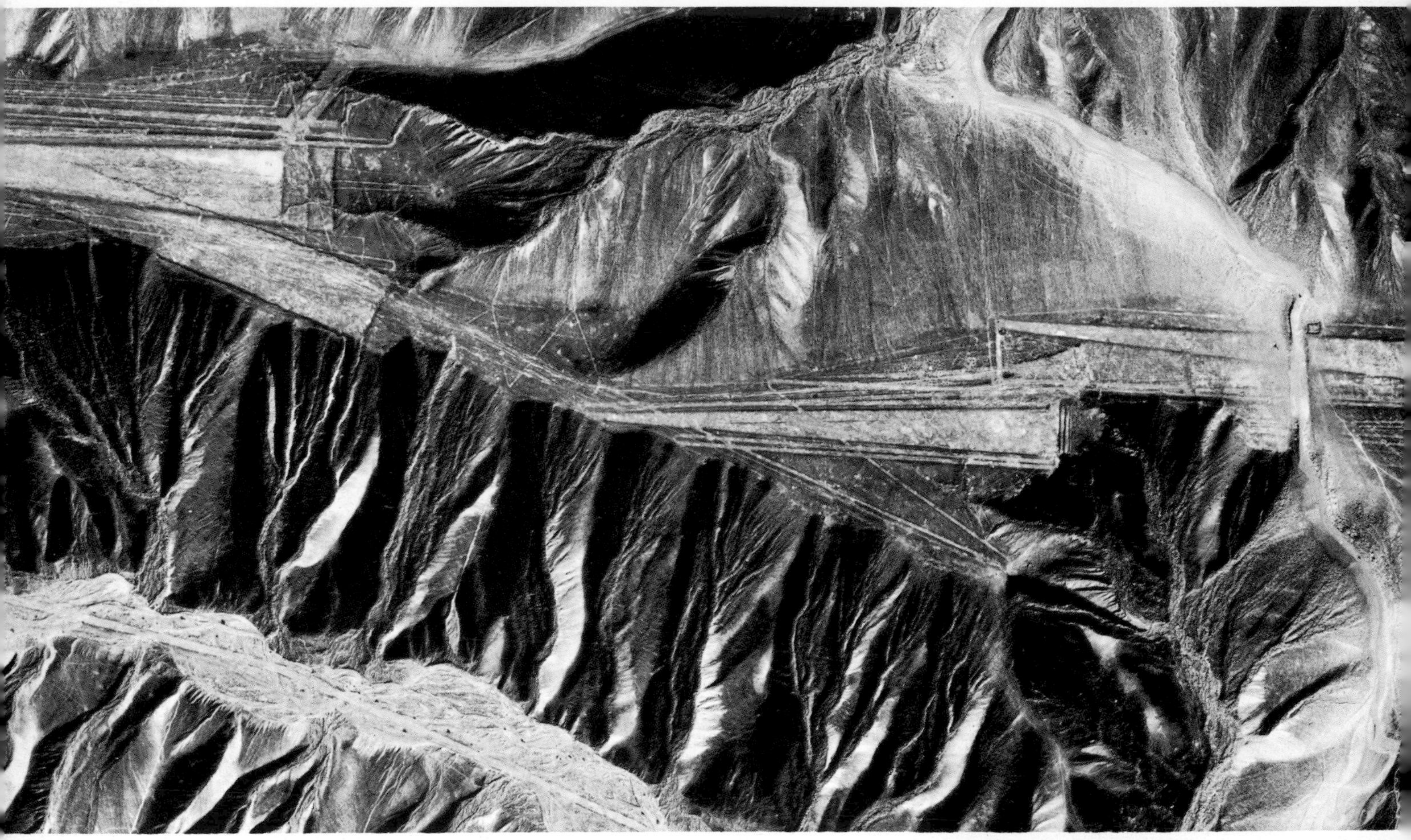

# RIDDLES OF THE DESERT

Some of ancient Peru's earliest engineering works are also its most baffling. Visible only from high in the air, the strange patterns seen here were etched before 800 A.D. by Nazca Valley Indians on desert plateaus above their irrigated settlements. Many are huge geometrical figures whose ruler-straight lines and angles could hardly be bettered with modern surveying instruments. Since some of the lines relate to summer and winter solstices, scholars think they may have served the Nazcas as vast astronomical calendars to help determine dates for planting crops and readying irrigation ditches to catch the flow of seasonal rivers. The spirals and animal shapes scattered over the desert are harder to explain. One theory is that they were drawn as offerings, meant to be seen only by the Peruvians' sky-dwelling gods.

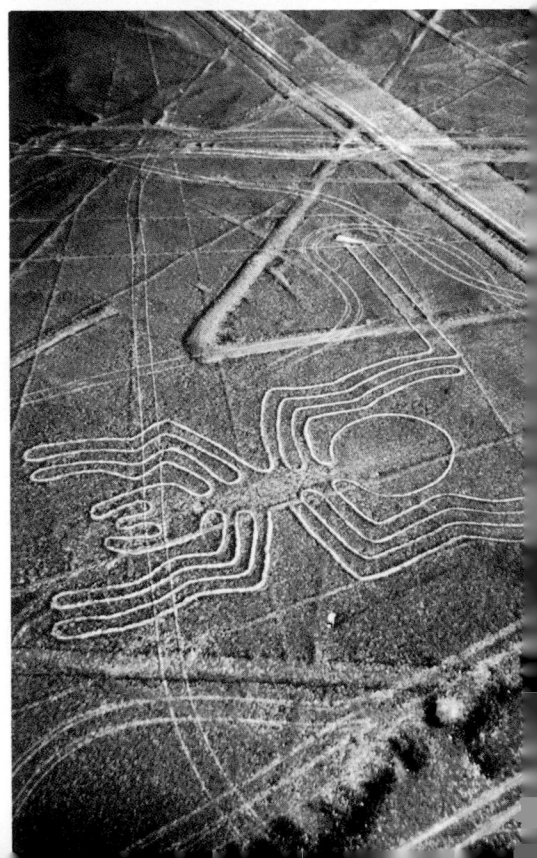

STRANGE ANIMAL SHAPES *are inter-spersed among the Nazcas' rectilinear patterns. The figure seen at left, which stretches 150 feet in length, resembles an eight-legged spider, and the one at right appears to be a long-billed hummingbird; their precise significance, however, is not known. To execute such designs, the Nazcas scraped the ground clear of a thin layer of dark, weathered gravel, uncovering lighter gravel underneath. The looping lines suggest that these patterns were laid out first by stretching long, measured lengths of rope along the ground.*

# NETWORKS OF ROADS AND BRIDGES

Early Peruvian kingdoms linked valley to valley with good roads; the later Inca, bent on expanding their realm, raised such highway building to a fine art. Like Roman highways, Peruvian road systems were designed more for conquest and administration than for trade; the Inca built theirs to keep order in an empire that stretched for more than 2,500 miles from end to end. Trained relay runners used the roads to carry word of distant uprisings, which could be quickly suppressed by dispatching large armies back along the road. To keep the routes free for official traffic, common people were allowed to use them only on rare occasions.

Where their highways had to cross rivers and deep mountain ravines, Peruvian engineers devised the first true suspension bridges in the New World. Hung by vine ropes, their basket-sided pathways swung in the wind and trembled under heavy loads. Yet even the Spanish conquistadors, who at first were terrified of their flimsy-looking construction, were unable to improve upon their design.

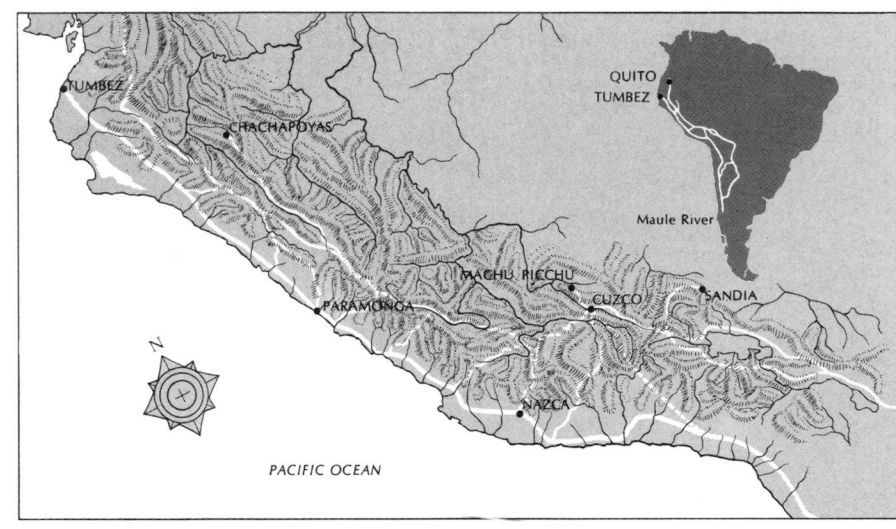

THE INCA HIGHWAY SYSTEM *crisscrossed Peru's coast from Colombia to Chile with 7,000 miles of roads. Two main arteries, one in the highlands and the other along the coast, were linked by lateral routes. Designed only for llama and foot traffic, the roads varied in width according to terrain. In the mountains they were carved out of cliff sides; in the coastal plains (below) they ran arrow-straight through desert and scrub.*

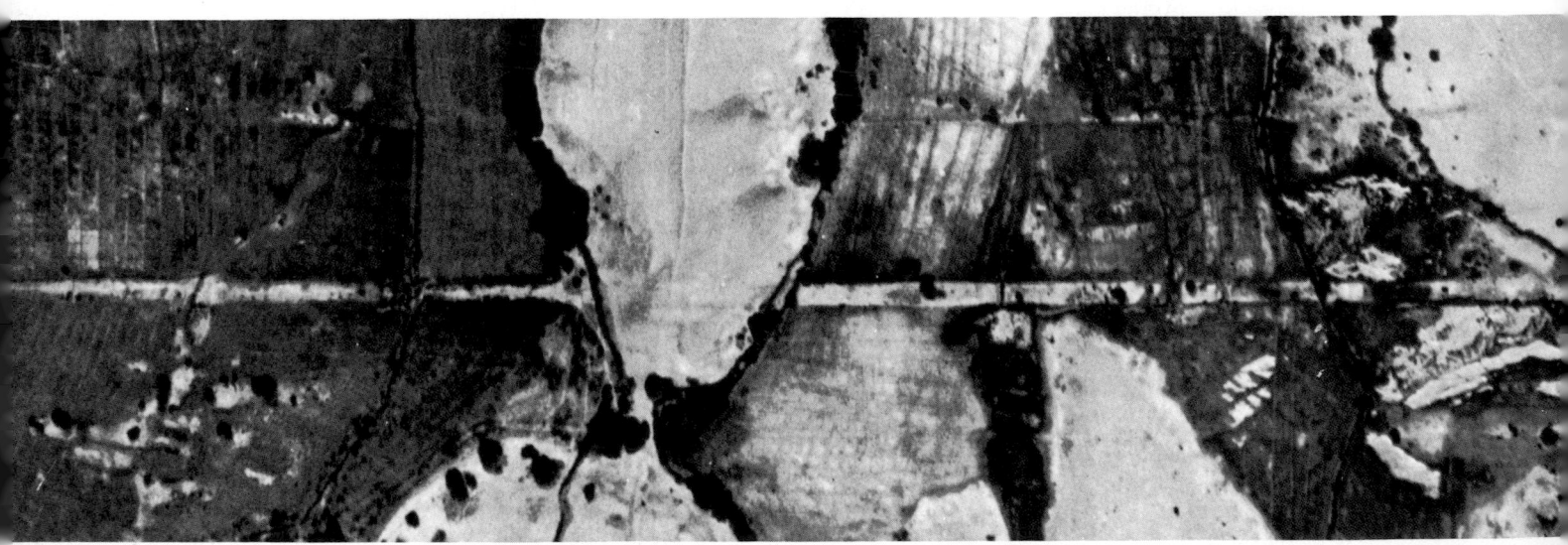

STONE BRIDGE PIERS (left) flank the gorge of the Cara-baya River. As the sketch below shows, the piers were raised on stone embankments and once supported a roadway hung from thick cables braided out of vines and pliable twigs. As a safety precaution, these cables were replaced with new ones every year by local villagers, who in return for this duty were spared all taxes.

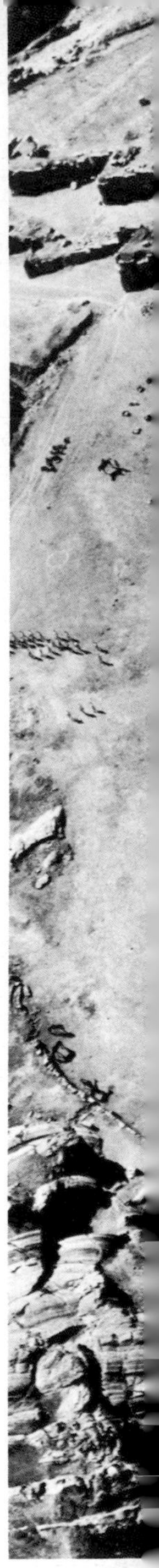

PARAMONGA CITADEL *housed a large garrison to protect Chimu valley dwellers near the Inca border, until it was outflanked by a huge Inca army of invasion. Situated on top of a strategically located hill (above), Paramonga's tiers of walls and buildings were built of sun-dried adobe blocks, the most common building material in Peru's coastal regions. Bastions projected from each of the fortress' four corners (right), giving defenders vantage points from which to fling missiles at anyone attempting to scale the walls.*

MASSIVE TRIPLE WALLS *guard Cuzco's Sacsahuamán citadel, whose ruined foundations are visible at top right. Circular walls mark the site of a tower.*

# FORMIDABLE LINES
# OF DEFENSE

With the rise of aggressive peoples like the Inca, Peru's engineers turned increasingly to the task of building fortresses. To the north, the Chimu Empire tried to stem the Inca tide by constructing a veritable Maginot Line of adobe citadels, some of which bear a striking resemblance to later European fortifications. The Inca themselves designed impressively fortified citadels. To defend their capital at Cuzco —and to provide an emergency refuge for the city's entire population —Inca engineers constructed Sacsahuamán fortress, whose huge, zigzagging stone walls were broken into 66 sharply projecting angles so that defending spearmen could catch attackers in a withering crossfire.

A TWELVE-SIDED STONE *fits tightly into the wall of an Inca palace in Cuzco. The stone, which measures some five feet across, shows the beveled joints which create intriguing patterns of light and shadow on Inca walls.*

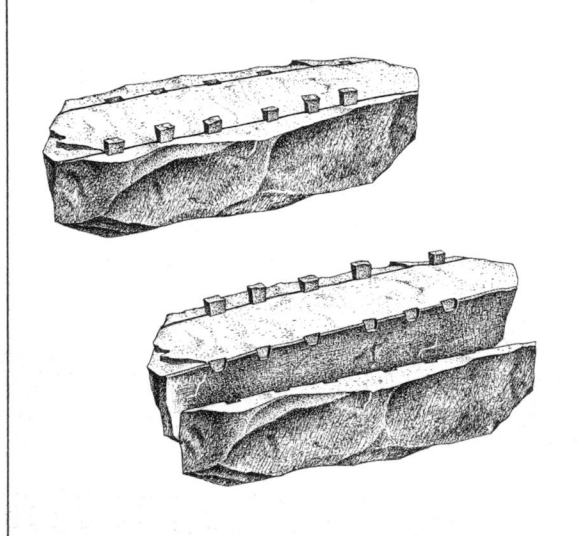

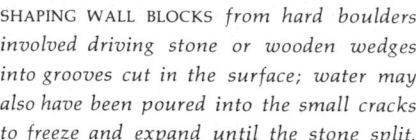

SHAPING WALL BLOCKS *from hard boulders involved driving stone or wooden wedges into grooves cut in the surface; water may also have been poured into the small cracks to freeze and expand until the stone split.*

GIGANTIC BULWARKS *guard Cuzco's Sacsahuamán citadel. Most of the stone was quarried on the spot, but the project, for which 20,000 workers were conscripted from the provinces, still took some 90 years to finish.*

# MASSIVE WALLS OF INTERLOCKING STONES

"The work is strange and wonderful," exclaimed a Spanish priest who studied the ponderous masonry of Inca buildings. Made up of huge, multisided stones, many walls were assembled so carefully that a knife blade cannot be forced into their joints. How Inca engineers achieved this precision still astonishes archeologists. They had only stone tools to use in shaping hard Andean granite, porphyry and limestone, and neither strong draft animals nor wheeled vehicles to transport the boulders they used—some of which weighed over 100 tons.

Inca architects evidently admired complex jigsaw shapes in stonework (left). To construct such walls took months of elaborate fitting for each stone. Yet these interlocking patterns are highly functional as well as beautiful. In a country where earthquakes still tumble conventional masonry, much Inca stonework has survived for centuries.

THE "LOST CITY" OF THE INCA, *the ancient stronghold of Machu Picchu sprawls along a razorback ridge in the Andes Mountains. Its steeply gabled stone hous*

## CITY ON A MOUNTAINTOP

High in the Andes the Inca erected what is probably the most spectacular work of engineering in all of ancient America. Straddling a narrow ridge between two mountain peaks, the fabled city of Machu Picchu rises 2,000 feet above the valley of the Urubamba River. The only access to the city, whose history and function are unknown, was a narrow road that winds along the tops of the Andes themselves.

Machu Picchu's architecture testifies to the ingenuity of its

*re once roofed with grass thatch and connected with rows of narrow terraces used for farming. A lookout station was built on top of the high peak at right.*

builders. Stoneworkers quarried hard granite blocks from the mountaintop for the city's more than 100 acres of buildings, walls and plazas, cut level foundations into the rock and raised huge masses of close-fitting stones. Stairways were carved into the mountain face to connect palaces, temples, military barracks and homes; fountains fed by aqueducts supplied the inhabitants with water. To make the city as self-sufficient as possible, the steep slopes below it were banked with rows of narrow agricultural terraces, whose retaining walls also formed multiple defense lines against attack.

The attack apparently never came. Abandoned some time after the Spanish conquest, Machu Picchu was never mentioned in official records and vanished from memory for four centuries. Then in 1911 the U.S. archeologist Hiram Bingham rediscovered the mountaintop stronghold, and brought to light the most completely preserved Inca city left in Peru.

# 7

# HORSEMEN FROM THE SEA

In 1519 Moctezuma II, the Aztec Emperor, was about 40 years old and had ruled with a firm and skillful hand for 17 years. But recently his personality had changed. Gone was his former ability in war and diplomacy; in its place was uncertainty accompanied by spells of brooding. He seldom appeared in public but kept to the guarded interior of his enormous palace, consulting with priests and soothsayers or meditating alone.

The people of his capital, Tenochtitlán, were deeply worried too. For years the omens had been bad. Strange lights had shone in the sky. Temples had caught fire and burned uncontrollably. At night a mysterious woman was often heard in the streets crying: "O my beloved sons, now we are about to go." And fishermen brought to Moctezuma a fantastic bird with a mirror on its head. When the Emperor looked in the mirror he saw armed warriors with the triumphant air of conquerors, riding on the backs of monsters resembling deer.

What did these portents mean? Many Mexicans, including Moctezuma, suspected that they foreshadowed the second coming of Quetzalcóatl, the legendary god-king of the Toltecs who had gone into exile over five centuries before and had promised to return from the direction of the rising sun. The scheduled time for his return was now approaching, and rumors flew that he or his emissaries had actually been sighted. They were heavily bearded, as Quetzalcóatl was believed to have been, and their weapons were thunder and lightning.

These rumors were distortions of even more menacing truths. Ever since the first voyage of Columbus 27 years before, the Spaniards had been drawing closer to Mexico, preceded by dreadful reports. They had occupied Cuba, slaughtering or enslaving its inhabitants, and probed westward in their "floating houses." Now the strangers had arrived, led by an extraordinary man whose intelligence, forcefulness and audacity made him appear as much like a demigod as any soldier in history.

Hernán Cortés, conqueror of Mexico, then 34, had been an adventurer almost from childhood. The son of a minor Spanish nobleman, he arrived in the West Indies when he was 19. He took part in the conquest of Cuba and became influential with Diego Velásquez, governor of the island. But like

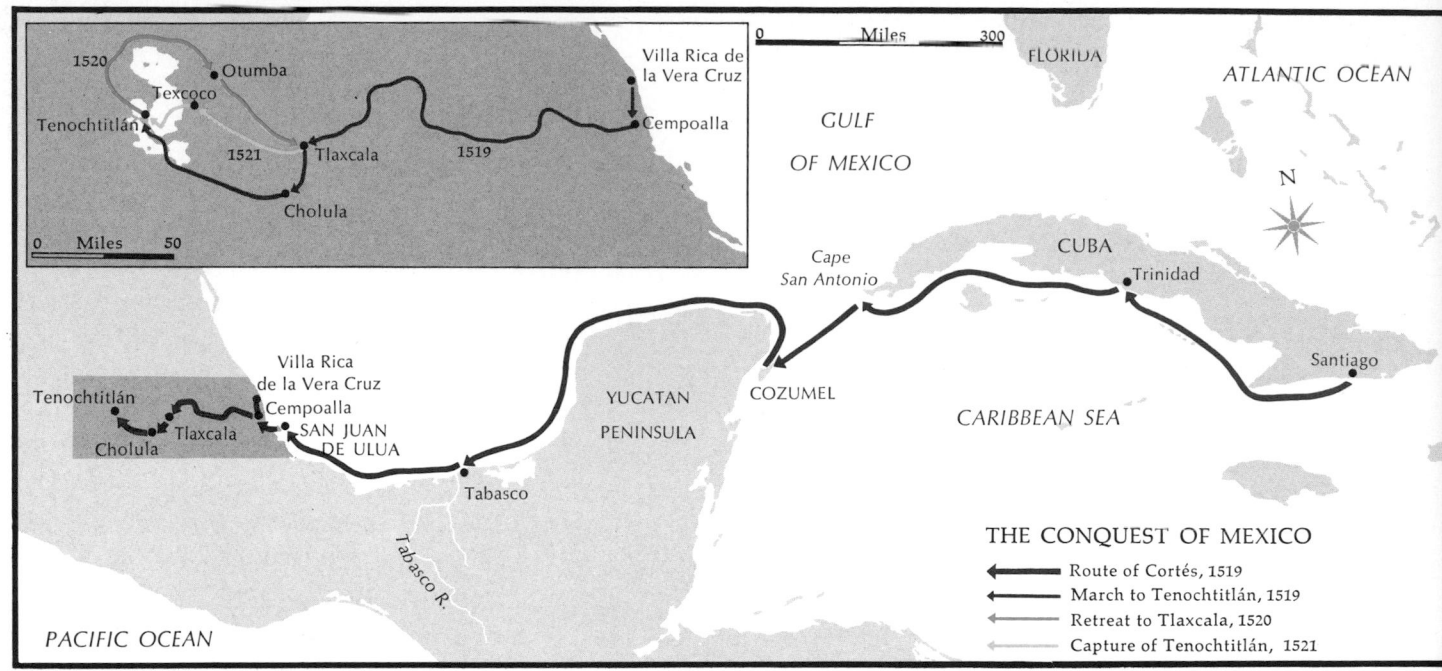

THE CONQUEST OF MEXICO *was launched by Hernán Cortés from Cuba, where he had assembled 553 men. He first explored the coast of Yucatán, then visited Indian villages at San Juan de Ulúa and Cempoalla, and finally established a base at Villa Rica* de la Vera Cruz *(modern Veracruz is located near San Juan de Ulúa). From there he advanced to the Aztec capital, Tenochtitlán, in 1519. In 1520 an Aztec revolt forced him back to Tlaxcala (inset), but the next year he returned to complete the conquest.*

most Spaniards he was looking for gold, and Cuba had little. When Velásquez organized an expedition to trade with the recently discovered Aztecs in Mexico, he appointed Cortés its leader. Almost at once the Governor regretted this choice. The magnetism of Cortés inspired a burst of enthusiasm among Cuba's gold-hungry malcontents. The expedition grew as wild adventurers flocked to his standard. He raised money and acquired ships in addition to those authorized by Velásquez; obviously he was planning more than a simple trading venture. But before the Governor could relieve him of the command, Cortés' fleet of 11 ships, bearing 553 men and 16 horses, had sailed for the West, bound for gold and glory.

On his way to central Mexico, Cortés stopped along the coast of Tabasco and acquired what was to prove an invaluable asset: an extremely intelligent Indian girl who knew not only the local dialects but the Aztec language as well, and who learned Spanish so easily that she soon became a proficient interpreter. She was also uncommonly attractive, and Cortés made her his mistress and closest adviser. Under the name of Marina she became a Christian and wholly loyal to Cortés.

Without Doña Marina's knowledge of Indian politics and ways of thinking, Cortés might not have conquered Mexico. Through her he learned the fatal weakness of the Aztec Empire: that its provinces were burning with hatred and eager to revolt. From her he also heard about the rumored return of Quetzalcóatl. The moment when he learned that he himself was being mistaken for the exiled god must have been an astonishing one even in the life of this astonishing man.

When the expedition landed in Aztec territory, near the site of modern Veracruz, the local Indians were friendly, and an Aztec official appeared to make the strangers formally welcome. This gentle reception did not conform to what Cortés had heard about the fierce and arrogant Aztecs. He kept his men under arms, always alert for trouble, and dispatched a message to Moctezuma asking permission to visit his capital.

A week or so later a great troop of laden porters streamed into the Spanish camp led by Aztec nobles, gorgeously arrayed. Cortés received the haughty Aztecs with dignity as lofty as their own and watched while the porters unpacked splendid gifts sent by Moctezuma. Among these were fine robes of cotton interwoven with brilliant feathers, but the Spaniards were most impressed by the articles of gold. According to Bernal Díaz, a soldier who wrote his memories of the conquest: "The first article presented was a wheel like a sun, as big as a cartwheel, with many sorts of pictures on it, the whole of fine gold and a wonderful thing to behold. . . . Then were brought twenty golden ducks, beautifully worked and very natural looking, and many articles of gold in the shape of tigers and lions and monkeys . . . all in beautiful hollow work of fine gold."

Cortés was dazzled by the gifts, but when the Aztec ambassadors politely asked him to leave Mexico, he replied that the King of Spain had commanded him to visit Moctezuma, and he was determined to do so. He interpreted the gifts as signs of weakness, and an incredibly audacious plan to conquer the whole Aztec Empire began to take shape in his mind.

Soon after there came an event that Cortés, advised by Marina, had doubtless been expecting. Five important-looking Indians, dressed differently from Aztecs, arrived in camp, explaining that they were Totonacs, members of a nation recently conquered by the Aztecs and sorely oppressed by them. They had heard of the Spaniards' prowess and weapons, and they begged the wonderful strangers to visit their nearby capital, Cempoalla. Cortés must have tensed with excitement. Here was the proof of the soundness of his plan. He well knew that with only his small band of Spaniards he could not conquer the Aztec Empire, which had perhaps 11 million inhabitants. What he intended to do was to overthrow the Aztecs with the help of other Indians. The Totonacs, he hoped, would be the first of many allies.

Cortés' visit to Cempoalla was a diplomatic triumph. He convinced the Totonacs that by pledging him allegiance they could successfully revolt against their oppressors, and he left the city at the head of some 1,500 Totonac warriors. Before marching on Tenochtitlán he gave orders to destroy his ships, to keep any fainthearted Spaniards from deserting and returning to Cuba. Then he marched inland toward the Valley of Mexico to face the dreaded Aztecs in their mountain-girt stronghold.

On the advice of the Totonacs he headed first for Tlaxcala, domain of the fiercely independent mountaineers who were the Aztecs' bitterest enemies. Both Spaniards and Totonacs marched in battle array, and when no attacks came Cortés began to feel that perhaps Moctezuma really did believe that he was Quetzalcóatl returning.

For Moctezuma in Tenochtitlán a long nightmare of superstitious dread had started the moment Cortés landed in Mexico. Couriers had streamed up from the coast to describe the strangers to him; his artists drew pictures of them and of their horses, animals much bigger than any the Mexicans had seen. Were these people gods? the Emperor asked. Was their blackbearded leader indeed Quetzalcóatl?

It is hard for a modern mind to understand the vacillation and apparent cowardice of Moctezuma, but his mind was saturated with a religion that blurred the distinction between gods and men. To him the appearance of gods marching on earth like men seemed not beyond the bounds of credibility, and he felt that it would be impious for his armies to attack the invading Spaniards. So he wavered and hoped. Perhaps the warlike mountaineers of Tlaxcala would destroy them for him.

The news Moctezuma received from Tlaxcala was not encouraging. The Spaniards and their Totonac allies had been heavily attacked by 30,000 plumed and painted Tlaxcalan warriors, hurling spears, swinging obsidian-edged swords and screaming their ear-piercing war cry. But the Indians had never faced such deadly things as the steel swords, crossbows, harquebuses and light artillery of the helmeted Spaniards, and these superior weapons had had a devastating and demoralizing effect on them. So had the tiny squadron of 16 cavalrymen: the Tlaxcalans, believing that each horse and rider were one creature, had been terrified.

Even more advantageous for the Spaniards than their arms and cavalry was the Indian concept of warfare. Since the Tlaxcalans and other Mexicans fought not to kill but to capture living victims for sacrifice to their gods, they tried merely to stun a Spaniard or drag him away. Other Spaniards then came to his rescue, usually killing his assailants. Another weakness of the Indians was their inability to marshal their forces effectively. Though they greatly outnumbered the Spaniards, many of their soldiers never got into the fight.

In Tlaxcala the Spaniards triumphed with difficulty, but they found they had won more than a simple victory. In post-battle negotiations, during which Doña Marina distinguished herself as a diplomat, the Tlaxcalans not only surrendered to Cortés but also offered to join him in the alliance against the hated Aztecs. His plan to conquer Mexico was working magnificently.

For Moctezuma this latest report was alarming. Cortés was now allied with his most vindictive enemies, and envoys from other Aztec subject states were offering their support. Still the Emperor could not bring himself to attack the men who might be gods. Instead he surprised the Spaniards by inviting them to visit him at Tenochtitlán.

Loudly the Tlaxcalans warned Cortés not to accept the invitation. They described the overwhelming strength of the imperial city, the great armies that it could muster, its impregnable position in Lake Texcoco where it could be reached only by three causeways, each with bridges that could be raised to trap intruders.

Cortés rejected their warnings. Replacing his battle-weary Totonacs with 5,000 picked Tlaxcalan troops he proceeded toward Tenochtitlán. On the way he almost destroyed the ancient cultural center of Cholula, a city loyal to Moctezuma and whose chiefs had plotted to wipe out the invaders. When this terrible news reached the Emperor he fell into a panic. Surely these men from the sea were gods and invincible in war. His great armies would have fought valiantly against men or gods, but even now he dared not order them into battle. Instead he sent presents to Cortés and disclaimed all connection with the hostility of Cholula.

Cortés was now convinced that Moctezuma feared him and would permit him to enter Tenochtitlán unharmed. He marched out of Cholula in a proud parade, his force constantly growing as warriors from far and near came to join him. In the mountains encircling the Aztec homeland the air was cold and thin, and snow powdered the ground; then the road dipped down again and soon the Spaniards saw the fabled Valley of Mexico with its cluster of lakes surrounded by elegant cities and fringed by fertile "floating gardens." At last came their first glimpse of Tenochtitlán itself, the great island city gleaming white in the sun. "We were amazed," wrote the soldier-chronicler Bernal Díaz, "on account of the great towers and buildings rising from the water, and all built of masonry. And some of our soldiers even asked whether the things that we saw were not a dream."

After halting for the night, the Spaniards and their allies marched toward the city over one of its wide causeways. Wrote Díaz: "Gazing on such wonderful sights, we did not know what to say, or whether what appeared before us was real, for on one side, on the land, there were great cities, and in the lake ever so many more, and the lake itself was crowded with canoes . . . and in front of us stood the great City of Mexico, and we—we did not even number four hundred soldiers!"

Along the causeway to meet the Spaniards came

HERNAN CORTES, *the conqueror of Mexico, was portrayed by an anonymous 17th Century artist wearing elaborate armor and holding a baton, as emblem of his command.*

lived in vast magnificence with hordes of courtiers and a thousand wives and concubines. He also arranged for Cortés a tour of the city and its grisly temples. Bernal Díaz was on this tour and vividly described what he saw in one of the twin temples on the top of the tallest pyramid. "On each altar," he wrote, "were two figures, like giants with very tall bodies and very fat, and the first, they said, was their god of war; it had a broad face and monstrous and terrible eyes, and the body was girdled by great snakes made of gold and precious stones. . . . all the walls of the oratory were so splashed and encrusted with blood that they were black."

Through the charming lips of Doña Marina, Cortés and Moctezuma discussed their respective countries, and Cortés tried without success to convert the Emperor to Christianity. Around them the life of the city seemed to proceed normally, but Cortés was growing uneasy. He suspected that the unpredictable Moctezuma might be plotting to destroy him. Even more he feared that his rough Spanish soldiers or the wild Tlaxcalans might commit some outrage that would turn the Emperor against him.

After careful preparation he took the final, audacious step in his scheme for conquest. Entering Moctezuma's palace with 30 armed Spaniards, he took the Emperor prisoner and had him carried to the Spanish quarters in his own imperial litter. Moctezuma made no resistance; he was completely irresolute, almost as if in a trance. As the royal cortege moved through the streets, the people stood watching silently, paralyzed by their belief in the legend of Quetzalcóatl. The ancient god had returned, they told one another, to rule over their nation in the guise of the blackbearded Spaniards.

Cortés was now in complete control of the Aztec capital, but soon he had to hurry back to the coast to deal with a Spanish army of 900 men sent by Governor Velásquez of Cuba, who had heard of Cortés' growing power and was determined to

Moctezuma, borne in a rich litter and accompanied by his nobles. The Emperor was tall and rather thin with a sparse black beard, and on his head he wore a plume of long green feathers that floated down his back. He greeted Cortés and conversed with him politely through Doña Marina. No one would have judged from his dignified demeanor that the night before he had shut himself in his palace in panic and despair, praying to his gods and offering sacrifices. The gods had given no reassurance. "Of what use is resistance," Moctezuma asked his council of noble advisers, "when the gods themselves have declared against us?"

Now inside the city, the Spaniards were quartered in a commodious palace (their Indian allies camped in its courtyard) and were fed and attended by a great number of slaves. A relationship resembling friendship developed between Moctezuma and Cortés. The Emperor came to call on the Spaniard and invited him to his own palace, where he curb it. The leader of the army was captured and its troops accepted Cortés as commander.

Before Cortés and his greatly enlarged forces could get back to Tenochtitlán, there came the startling news that the city was in full revolt. Pedro de Alvarado, the officer he had left in charge, had invited 600 of the highest Aztec nobles into a temple enclosure to celebrate one of their religious festivals. While they were engaged in a ritual dance, his soldiers had slaughtered all of them and stripped their bodies of their golden ornaments.

When this atrocity became known, the city rose in arms and a sea of furious Aztecs surged around the Spaniards. They would have been overwhelmed if Moctezuma had not partially calmed his people. Then the assault subsided to a sullen siege.

When Cortés arrived at the head of his new army, his march to the Spanish quarters was through a silent and apparently empty city. Not daring to leave the palace even though active hostilities had ceased, Alvarado's soldiers and Tlaxcalans were close to starvation and reduced to drinking brackish water from wells dug in the palace grounds. Cortés upbraided Alvarado for his greedy savagery and through Moctezuma tried unsuccessfully to get the city under control. He sent the Emperor's brother, Cuitlahua, as a peace envoy to the hostile chiefs. This was one of his few serious mistakes. Since Moctezuma was powerless to govern, Cuitlahua was heir to the throne under the Aztec system of succession. He presently declared himself Emperor, providing the Aztecs with a leader who had no religious scruples about how to deal with the invaders.

Now that they had a leader, there was nothing hesitant about the Aztecs. The next day hordes of warriors gathered to assault their defenses and rained arrows and other missiles on them. Several bloody sallies were made against the attackers, and Bernal Díaz, who took part in them, wrote: "We noted their tenacity in fighting, but I declare that

I do not know how to describe it, for neither cannon nor muskets nor crossbows availed, nor hand-to-hand fighting, nor killing thirty or forty of them every time we charged, for they still fought with more energy than in the beginning."

Moctezuma mounted the roof of the Spaniards' quarters and once more attempted to pacify his people. The furious attackers fell silent when they saw him and permitted him to speak. Then the Indians discharged a shower of stones and arrows, and Moctezuma fell, seriously wounded. He refused to be tended, and soon he died.

With Moctezuma dead the Spaniards were only a handful of foreigners in a hostile city, with no magic armor to protect them from the enraged inhabitants. Cortés realized that he must evacuate Tenochtitlán. Calmly he made his plans. He knew that escape would not be easy, for the Aztecs had removed the bridges from the causeways, leaving gaps that must somehow be crossed. While battle raged around them, the Spaniards with desperate haste constructed a portable wooden bridge strong enough to bear the weight of mounted men. After darkness fell and the Aztec attack had temporarily slackened, Cortés gave the order to march. All went well as far as the first of three gaps in the causeway that he had chosen, but then Aztec sentries cried the alarm. An enormous drum on Tenochtitlán's tallest pyramid boomed a deep, melancholy note; a great fleet of canoes swept close to the causeway and the warriors in them showered arrows and stones on the slow-moving column.

At the first of the gaps the portable bridge did its work, but when the Spaniards tried to carry it forward to use it again, it stuck fast between the abutments. With cries of despair the soldiers of Cortés rushed to the second gap. Those in advance were pushed into the water by the press behind them, and many of them sank, weighted down by their own armor or by the Aztec gold that they carried. While the great drum boomed and fires flared on the pyramids, more canoes full of screaming Aztecs surged out of the darkness, and the bodies of Spaniards and Indians alike piled up in the gap, along with toppled cannon, ammunition wagons and chests of golden treasure. At last the mound of flesh and wreckage was high enough for the rest of the army to cross. The third gap was passed in the same gory way, though the Spaniards and Tlaxcalans were fewer now.

This was the *Noche Triste*, the "Sad Night" of Mexican history. When dawn came, the remnants of the army gathered on the mainland near a great cypress tree, *El Arbol de la Noche Triste*, which still stands in Mexico City. All artillery had been lost; all muskets and many other weapons had been thrown away. It is probable that two thirds of the Spaniards had been killed or dragged off for sacrifice, and all those who remained were wounded.

If Cortés felt despondent, that man of iron did not show it. He marched the survivors away from the lake and after a good deal of skirmishing with Aztec forces finally reached Tlaxcala, where he was welcomed. The Tlaxcalans did not seem in the least dismayed by the Spanish setback or by the loss of so many of their own warriors.

Despite crippling losses in men and equipment, Cortés was not forced to abandon his original plan to conquer Mexico by setting Indians against Indians. When the new Aztec emperor, Cuitlahua, urged the Tlaxcalans to make common cause with him against the invaders, they refused, and so did many provinces of the Empire. From his base in Tlaxcala, Cortés encouraged every revolt, helped cities expel their Aztec garrisons, and trained his Indian allies in Spanish military tactics.

The lesson of the *Noche Triste* made it very plain that to attack Tenochtitlán across the exposed causeways would be imprudent. Deciding that the water-walled city could not be taken without controlling the lake in which it stood, Cortés conceived the bold idea of constructing a demountable fleet that could be carried piece by piece to the Valley of Mexico and reassembled. The metal parts of the ships that he had ordered destroyed at Veracruz were still in storage there, and he now had them brought to Tlaxcala. Luckily he had with him a skilled shipbuilder, Martín Lopez, whom he put to work with a host of Indian helpers. About this time he also received unexpected reinforcements in men, arms and horses from several ships that put into Veracruz.

Additional help came from another ally, dreadful and unexpected. Smallpox, starting at Veracruz, swept through the country, killing friend and foe alike. The disease was unknown in Mexico, and the Indians, who had no resistance to it, died by hundreds of thousands. Among the victims was the Emperor Cuitlahua, who had so valiantly rallied his people. His death reduced the strength of Tenochtitlán while the raging pestilence further disrupted its empire.

On December 28, 1520, Cortés set out from Tlaxcala for his second march on the now weakened Aztec capital. With him marched an army of 600 well-armed Spaniards, including about 40 cavalrymen, and the flower of Tlaxcala's warriors. En route his force grew to more than 100,000, swelled by Indian recruits seeking revenge against their Aztec oppressors. Tenochtitlán was almost alone.

Cortés set up headquarters in Texcoco, where a pro-Spanish Indian faction had taken control. The demountable navy—13 small sailing vessels called brigantines—was now completed and had been carried across the mountains in pieces. While it was being assembled, the Spaniards and their Indian allies harried beleaguered Tenochtitlán. They cut the aqueducts that brought fresh water to the city and laid waste the lakeshore so that foraging parties would find no food.

Hearing that pestilence and famine raged in Tenochtitlán, Cortés allowed himself to be persuaded to try an attack across one of the causeways, but the Aztecs showed undiminished spirit and beat back the assault with heavy losses. The city now had a new emperor, Cuauhtemoc, a 25-year-old nephew of Moctezuma, and he swore that he would fight until every Aztec warrior had been killed.

At last the brigantines were ready. They sailed out on the lake where a great flotilla of Aztec canoes was waiting for them. The unequal engagement that followed foreshadowed the end of Tenochtitlán. Maneuvering back and forth, the brigantines ran down the canoes, smashing them like eggshells. With the waters of the lake controlled by the invaders and with hostile armies lining its shores, the imperial city was cut off from all support.

The Aztecs, weakened by hunger and disease, no longer had strength enough to halt the besiegers. The cannon of the brigantines swept the causeways clear of defenders, and an army of porters brought stone and earth from the mainland to fill the gaps once spanned by bridges. When the first Spaniards reached the city the Aztecs, exhausted though they were, rallied under the young Emperor and ferociously contested every inch of the way. Their corpses piled up in the streets and floated thickly in canals.

Still Cuauhtemoc would not surrender or even exchange messages with the attackers. When Cortés ordered a final assault, the starving and tattered Aztecs fought as fiercely as ever while three large canoes pushed out of the city and tried to cross to the mainland. They were intercepted by the brigantines. In one canoe was Cuauhtemoc. As news of his capture spread, the few remaining Aztecs stopped fighting; they had only been trying to cover their leader's escape.

That was the end of Tenochtitlán. The remnants of its people were allowed to seek on the mainland such refuge as they could find. The Aztec Empire quickly broke into fragments, but the Indian allies who enabled Cortés to conquer it did not enjoy their newly won independence for long. The next stage of Mexican history was to be one of melancholy decline as disease and disorganization took their toll of the Indians, while Spanish soldiers of fortune swarmed into the conquered country to exploit it without mercy.

Cortés' conquest of the Aztec Empire ranks among history's boldest exploits. But within 14 years this feat was surpassed by that of another Spanish adventurer who toppled a bigger and better organized empire with an army half as large, and did it when he was more than 60 years old.

Francisco Pizarro, conqueror of Peru, was born about 1471. He was an illegitimate child abandoned as an infant at the door of a church, and since no human wet-nurse was handy he was reportedly suckled by a sow. Unlike the elegant and educated Cortés, Pizarro never learned to read or write. After working as a swineherd in Spain, he became a soldier and drifted to the West Indies.

When Vasco Nuñez de Balboa crossed the Isthmus of Panama in 1513 and discovered the Pacific Ocean, Pizarro was with him, and heard an Indian tell of a wonderful land of gold far to the south. At the time he was not free to follow up this lead, but in 1524 he joined another grizzled veteran of the Indies, Diego de Almagro, in organizing a shoestring expedition of two small ships that set out from the Spanish colony at Panama to explore the wild jungles along the Pacific coast of Colombia.

The first expedition ended as a costly failure, but two years later Pizarro and Almagro tried again. After the hostile jungles were left behind, Almagro turned back to Panama for supplies, but Pizarro sailed on across the Bay of Guayaquil in

THE CONQUEST OF PERU *by Pizarro required three expeditions over nine years.
The first (green line) was halted by storms,
the second (blue line) was recalled by Spanish officials. On the third (red line) Pizarro
captured the Inca emperor and the capital.*

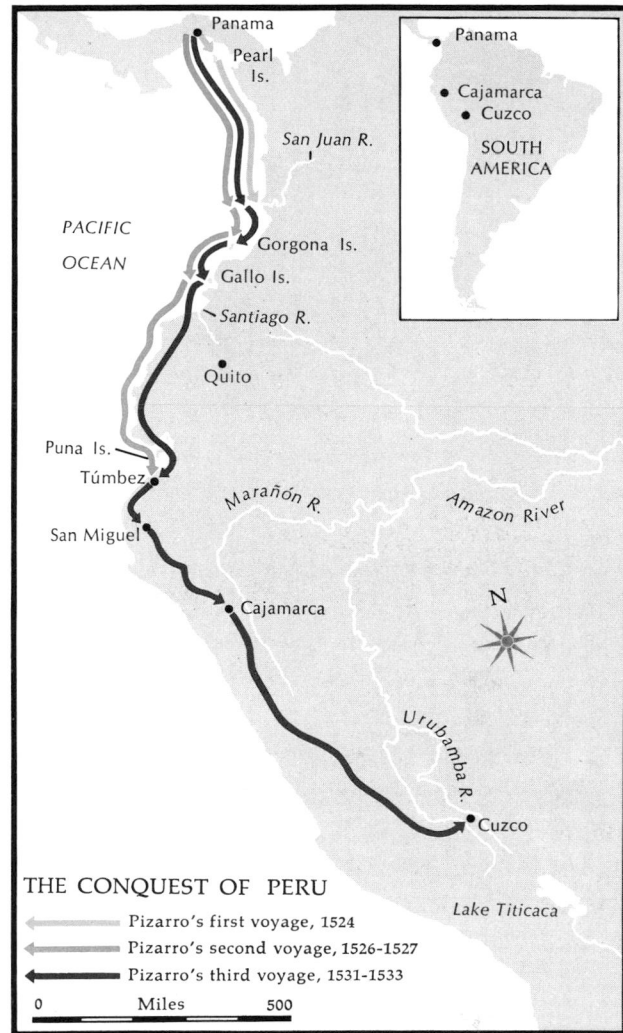

THE CONQUEST OF PERU

Pizarro's first voyage, 1524
Pizarro's second voyage, 1526-1527
Pizarro's third voyage, 1531-1533

0    Miles    500

Ecuador and found himself in another world. On the shore was the pleasant Peruvian city of Túmbez set in a green oasis of irrigated fields. Its hospitable people welcomed the Spaniards and showed them their temple, which was decorated with gleaming sheets of gold. Under the strict command of Pizarro, the Spaniards pretended not to notice the gold, and they treated the Peruvians with consideration. The time for plunder had not come.

Pizarro had had a tempting glimpse of the Inca Empire at the peak of its order and prosperity. The Inca Huayna Capac had recently died but civil war between his sons had not yet begun. If the Spaniards had attacked at that time, they would have met organized and determined resistance. It was Pizarro's great good fortune that the weakness of his forces compelled him to delay the assault until Peru had been distracted by internal war.

Embarking for Spain in the spring of 1528, Pizarro visited King Charles V and showed him golden drinking vessels acquired at Túmbez as well as a live llama and two young Peruvians whom he was training as interpreters. The King was sufficiently impressed to give him a royal charter to conquer the land of gold, and the title of Governor and Captain-General of the lands he had yet to win.

Not until early in 1530 did a small, ill-equipped expedition start to straggle across the Atlantic to gather at Panama. In January of 1531, after more delays at Panama, Pizarro set sail for the south with three ships, about 180 men and 27 horses. His partner, Almagro, was to follow later with reinforcements.

Instead of heading directly for Túmbez, Pizarro landed well to the north, where he plundered helpless coastal towns. None of those piratical raids met serious resistance. The Inca Empire had apparently abandoned its frontiers, and through his interpreters Pizarro soon learned why. At his death, Huayna Capac had divided his domain. Huascar,

his son by his sister-wife, received the greater part of it, including the capital of Cuzco. The Kingdom of Quito in what is now Ecuador went to Atahuallpa, his son by a favorite concubine. Soon the half-brothers were at war. Atahuallpa, the abler man, had with him in the north the bulk of his father's veteran soldiers. Not long before the Spaniards landed, his armies had taken Huascar prisoner and captured Cuzco.

Pizarro was familiar with the exploits of Cortés in Mexico and thought he saw in the disarray of the Inca Empire an opportunity to use Indians to conquer other Indians, as Cortés had done. In this hope he was wrong. No Peruvians offered to help him attack. Pizarro was to be successful because of a fundamental weakness of the Inca Empire—its exclusively vertical political organization, at the top of which was the omnipotent Inca, the one man upon whom the strength of the Empire de-

147

pended and without whose leadership its lesser officials could not function.

Before the Spaniards reached Túmbez they were reinforced by about 130 men and additional horses from Panama. When they entered the city they found it almost deserted and largely destroyed. As they marched down the coast they saw other signs of the recent conflict. Whole valleys lacked men of military age, all of them conscripted by Atahuallpa's armies.

Learning that Atahuallpa was encamped near Cajamarca in the Andes, Pizarro left a garrison on the coast and turned eastward into the mountains, following a narrow but well-paved road. No one opposed him; the fortresses that watched the road were empty and silent, the bridges across mountain chasms undestroyed, the narrow passes unguarded. Nine of his followers proved fainthearted and turned back. That left him with less than 200 men to face an empire of perhaps six million inhabitants.

Up and up led the road, in some places giving way to steep stairways carved in the mountainsides, where the horses had to be led. When the army was deep in the mountains it was met by a high-ranking Inca noble, an envoy from Atahuallpa, who gravely announced that the Inca wanted to be friends with the Spaniards and was awaiting them in peace at Cajamarca.

Several weeks later the Spaniards crossed a high ridge in the Andes. Below them lay an oval valley about 15 miles long and green with cultivated fields, with the charming small city of Cajamarca at one end. A few miles from the city arose clouds of vapor marking the position of hot springs, a favorite health resort, where the Inca was encamped. Pizarro marched into the city, which was silent and empty. The old soldier surveyed the deserted streets with narrow-eyed suspicion. Perhaps this was a trap prepared for him and his men. Resolv-

ing to make a good fight if fighting became necessary, he fortified a large triangular plaza in the heart of the city and posted strong guards at strategic points in the surrounding buildings.

The hot springs where Atahuallpa and his retinue were relaxing when Pizarro arrived are still in use. Visitors are shown a large tank of ancient stonework said to be the Bath of the Inca. It has two adjustable inlets, one for the hot water that bubbles out of the ground nearby, the other for cold water from a nonthermal spring. Today anyone can bathe in the tank for a small fee, but in Atahuallpa's time it was reserved for the Inca and his concubines. A broad causeway, which now carries a highway called the Avenue of the Inca, led over marshy ground to this place of pleasure.

As soon as Pizarro had disposed his forces, he sent Hernando de Soto, later the discoverer of the Mississippi River, with 15 horsemen to visit the Inca. A battalion of Indian soldiers stood massed before the imperial headquarters, and the building's courtyard was thronged with Inca noblemen and their women, all adorned with gleaming golden ornaments. In the center of this brilliant assembly sat Atahuallpa on a low stool. His face was grave and calm, and although he had never seen a horse or the bright steel armor that the strangers wore, he gave no hint that he was impressed.

The Spaniards rode up to him, bowed politely without dismounting and announced through an interpreter that their commander cordially invited the Inca to visit him in his quarters. At first Atahuallpa did not reply; then he smiled. "Tell your commander," he said, "that I am keeping a fast that will end tomorrow. Then I will visit him with my chieftains."

De Soto noticed that the Inca was looking with interest at his horse. Digging his spurs into the animal's flanks he gave a brilliant display of horsemanship, dashing away at a gallop, rearing, wheel-

FRANCISCO PIZARRO, *conqueror of Peru, is depicted in full military gear. A tough adventurer, he rose from peasant to master of the Inca Empire before being murdered by jealous subordinates.*

ing. Then he rode full speed at Atahuallpa, checking the horse so close to him that flecks of foam fell on the Inca's clothing. Not a tremor of expression crossed Atahuallpa's face.

Deeply affected by this display of fortitude, and also by the sight of the Inca's numerous and well-disciplined soldiers, the Spaniards rode back to Cajamarca in low spirits. Atahuallpa was obviously no weakling like Moctezuma, whose will had been paralyzed by religious doubts and fears. Following De Soto's report something approaching panic ran through the Spanish camp, but instead of sharing the dismay of his companions, Pizarro was pleased by their black mood, for only desperate men would be willing to risk the bold scheme he now proposed. Calling his officers together that night, he convinced them that their sole hope of survival in this hostile land lay in capturing the Inca himself within sight of his powerful army. Any less drastic move, he pointed out, would ultimately lead to death for the little band of Spaniards.

When dawn came, Pizarro prepared for Atahuallpa's visit by concealing his soldiers in the public buildings that opened on the plaza occupied by the Spaniards and told them to wait silently until the Inca entered. Then at a signal—the firing of a gun—they were to sally out, slaughter the Inca's followers and seize his person. When all arrangements were complete, the priests who accompanied the expedition said Solemn Mass and asked the help of God for these soldiers of the Cross who would soon be fighting to extend the blessings of Christianity.

Shortly after midday strong contingents of Indian troops advanced toward the city and occupied the meadows on either side of the causeway leading from the Inca's headquarters. Then a brilliant procession moved slowly along the avenue. First came attendants to sweep the ground, followed by a crowd of gorgeously dressed nobles whose golden jewelry blazed in the sun. Above them all rode Atahuallpa in a golden litter carried on the shoulders of his highest-ranking noblemen. Half a mile from the city the procession stopped while messages passed back and forth between Pizarro and Atahuallpa. The Spanish leader informed the Emperor that he had provided entertainment for him and expected to enjoy his company at supper. The Inca replied that he accepted the invitation and also sent the startling news that he would leave most of his warriors behind, and those that entered the city with him would be unarmed. Pizarro could hardly believe his ears. Surely this was a sign that Heaven was on his side.

Why Atahuallpa acted in such an incautious way is not clear. The history of his brief reign shows that he was often suspicious and could be crafty on occasion. He probably visited the Spaniards because he wanted to display the pomp and glitter of his entourage; such ceremonial visits were part of the Peruvian technique of government. It may not have occurred to him that the Spaniards might attack him. The power of an Inca was so absolute that any such action was unthinkable.

Slowly the royal procession began to move again.

149

Surrounded by thousands of glittering retainers, Atahuallpa entered the great plaza. No Spaniard was in sight. The Inca gave the sign to stop and asked: "Where are the strangers?" Father Vicente de Valverde, Pizarro's chaplain, then came forward and through one of the Indian interpreters explained to Atahuallpa that the Spaniards had come to bring Christianity to Peru. The Inca did not follow Father Valverde's long, involved account of Christian doctrine, but when he was told that the upshot of the discourse was that he must change his religion and become a vassal of Charles V of Spain, he showed annoyance. "I will be no man's vassal," he said to the priest. "I am greater than any prince on earth. As for my religion, I will not change it. You say your God was put to death, but mine"—he pointed to the sun—"still lives."

Father Valverde handed his breviary up to the Inca. Atahuallpa examined it and threw it down. The priest ran to Pizarro. "Don't you see what is happening?" he cried angrily. "While we are arguing with this arrogant dog the fields are filling with Indians. Set on him! I absolve you."

Pizarro waved a white scarf, the awaited signal. A gun thundered, and the massacre began. The Spaniards rushed out of hiding and fell on the unarmed Indians. Their cavalry charged through the densely packed throng, trampling helpless bodies under the horses' hooves. Desperately Atahuallpa's retainers crowded around the royal litter to protect their ruler. They had no weapons, but they made a barrier of their flesh and clung to the horses until the Spaniards cut them away with their swords. Fearing that Atahuallpa might be injured, Pizarro plunged into the melee, shouting that any soldier who harmed the Inca would be put to death. He was slightly cut on the hand by one of his own men and was the only Spaniard wounded that day.

Its bearers slaughtered, the litter toppled sideways, and Atahuallpa might have been killed if Pizarro and his officers had not caught him in their arms and dragged him to safety in a nearby building. With the Inca out of sight, the Peruvians ceased all resistance. The survivors escaped from the plaza and surged into the open, spreading panic among the troops stationed outside the city. Not knowing what had happened and with no one to command them, the Indian soldiers turned and fled.

The massacre had lasted little more than half an hour, but at least 2,000—some reports say 10,000—Peruvians were killed, including the flower of Inca nobility, which constituted the administrative core of the Empire. When all was quiet Pizarro invited Atahuallpa to supper, as he had promised to do. The banquet was held in one of the buildings facing the plaza, still carpeted with the dead. Pizarro sat beside his captive, who showed remarkable composure. "It is the way of war," the Inca remarked with dignity, "to conquer or be conquered."

With Atahuallpa in his custody, Pizarro found himself in an extraordinary position of power. He brought into Cajamarca a large part of the Inca's court, including his favorite concubines, his cooks and other servants, among them the young girls who waited on him hand and foot. The Inca lived in state, dining as usual off golden plates; but he was a prisoner nevertheless, and the orders given in his name were those of Pizarro. The people of the Empire, accustomed to obeying the Inca's every wish, did not question the stranger through whom they believed their ruler was speaking.

For the next nine months the conquerer and the Inca lived together in taut watchfulness. Pizarro was waiting for reinforcements, and Atahuallpa was doubtless hoping to regain his freedom and take full revenge on his captors. He had noticed the extraordinary effect which gold had on the Spaniards and this suggested a way to escape captivity. To Atahuallpa gold was chiefly a decorative material; since Peru used no money of any kind, he could not comprehend its importance as a medium of exchange, but he saw that the Spaniards craved it above all else. One day when he and Pizarro were in a building near the plaza of Cajamarca, he offered to cover with gold the floor of the room in which they stood if Pizarro would set him free. The Spaniards present were struck silent by this amazing proposal, and when no one spoke immediately, he increased the offer. He would fill the room with gold as high as he could reach. Pizarro accepted. The Inca reached as high as he could, standing on tiptoe, and Pizarro drew a red line at the height of his fingertips.

The stone-walled room where the offer was made is still to be seen in Cajamarca. It measures about 22 by 17 feet, and the red line, which has since been renewed, is about four inches below the level that a six-foot man can reach.

The Inca at once sent orders to all main centers of the Empire, and soon the gold began to arrive and pile up on the floor of the ransom room. The Spaniards watched with eager greed but also with concern. They wondered what they would do when Atahuallpa had finally filled the room with gold and demanded his freedom. Perhaps he was already plotting against them. Perhaps as soon as he was freed the Empire would rise and kill every Spaniard. These worries were heightened when Pizarro learned that Huascar, the legitimate heir to the Inca throne, had been murdered on Atahuallpa's secret orders, probably to keep the Spaniards from making use of him as a puppet ruler.

Since rumors had already been heard of a brewing uprising among the Peruvians, Pizarro dispatched exploring parties to find out what was really happening in the Empire. Three Spaniards went all the way to Cuzco, 600 miles distant. Traveling on the authority of Atahuallpa, who wished to prove that the rumors were unfounded, they were carried in litters by troops of bearers, and during their journey they were greeted with reverence instead of hostility. In the populous regions through which they passed, the life of Peru was proceeding with all its accustomed order. They saw Cuzco in untouched glory with its great Temple of the Sun literally covered with sheets of gold, and inspected the mummies of the dead Incas, each seated in state on a gold-encrusted chair. As Atahuallpa had warned them to do, they respected the sacred mummies, but they committed other outrages, such as raping some of the Chosen Women attached to the Temple of the Sun. In spite of this sacrilege no hand was raised against them. They returned to report that they had seen nothing but peace. Other missions brought the same report. If Atahuallpa was planning an uprising, he was doing it quietly.

The gold continued to stream into Cajamarca, and now the ransom room was nearly full. Some of the metal was in sheets stripped from temples, but there were also articles of marvelous workmanship, such as astonishingly lifelike golden llamas and ears of golden corn with silver leaves and tassels. Altogether, the gold heaped in the ransom room is now estimated to have been worth over eight million dollars. In the 16th Century this was a fantastic amount.

At last Pizarro declared the ransom paid and ordered that all the gold with the exception of a few objects of special artistic interest be melted into ingots. After one fifth had been allotted to the King of Spain (including the objects of art, nearly all of which were subsequently melted down) each of Pizarro's foot soldiers received gold worth $20,-000. Cavalry men got $50,000. Pizarro kept $425,-000 for himself. There is no record of the amount received by Pizarro's partner, Diego de Almagro, who arrived from Panama with reinforcements just in time to take part in the division of the spoils.

The division having been made, Atahuallpa demanded his freedom. To live up to their promise and give it to him would obviously be dangerous for the Spaniards; the Inca might very well rally the Empire. Nevertheless there seems to have been a genuine debate about this point of honor. De Soto declared flatly that the Inca must be freed. Other romantic cavaliers felt the same way, but they were in a minority. Most of the soldiers rated honor far below their personal safety; Pizarro himself was undecided, or pretended to be.

While the debate was going on, dark rumors of impending attacks began to circulate again through the Spanish camp. Some of the tales may have originated with Indians who had belonged to Huascar's faction, but their main source was Felipillo, an Indian interpreter who had been caught making advances to one of Atahuallpa's concubines. In Peru the usual penalty for this offense was death, so it was obviously in Felipillo's interest to make sure that the Inca did not regain his freedom.

Felipillo was ingenious, and his fluency in both Spanish and the Quechua spoken by the Peruvians gave him a good deal of power. He falsely reported that great concentrations of Indian troops had been seen gathering in the south. Terror swept the Spaniards; soldiers slept in armor; guards and patrols were increased. It did no good for Atahuallpa to protest that no attack was impending. He could not talk directly to Pizarro or any other Spaniard, and Felipillo misinterpreted everything he said.

At last, when the alarmed soldiers were close to mutiny, Pizarro yielded to their demands that Atahuallpa must die. He sent De Soto away on a scouting trip; then he arranged a trial of the captive Inca. Most of the charges dealt with idolatry, polygamy, incestuous marriage between brother and sister and other practices that were customary in the Inca Empire at the time. The only valid accusations were that Atahuallpa had usurped the throne and that he had ordered his half-brother Huascar to be killed. With the false Felipillo interviewing and misrepresenting Indian witnesses, the Inca was shortly pronounced guilty and condemned to be burned alive that same night, before De Soto could return and attempt to reverse the sentence.

A stake was set up in the great square. Atahuallpa was bound to it and the faggots piled around him. The Spanish soldiers gathered to watch by torchlight. Then Father Valverde approached the doomed ruler with his crucifix. Throughout his captivity the priest had tried to convert the Inca to the True Faith, but had failed. Now he told Atahuallpa that he would be strangled comparatively painlessly if he agreed to become a Christian. The Inca accepted and was baptized on the spot under the name of Juan de Atahuallpa. Then he was strangled by a cord passed around his neck.

So died the last of the ruling Incas, and the Inca Empire died with him. It shattered into helpless fragments, most of which passively accepted Spanish control. With no absolute monarch to issue commands, the elaborate machinery of the Peruvian state ceased to function. Its lesser officials, trained to carry out orders instead of issuing them, were incapable of taking over and banding together against the Spaniards, and there was no popular will to resist the invaders. To the Peruvian commoners the Spaniards seemed merely a new class of rulers, just as remote and probably no worse than the Inca and his nobility. Near Cuzco, the Inca heartland, stubborn resistance eventually developed, but it came far too late to prevent conquest.

The Peruvians were as wrong in their trusting passivity as the Mexicans had been wrong in actively aiding the invaders against the Aztec oppressors, but nothing that either people could have done would have delayed the outcome by more than a few years. The Spaniards brought more than conquest to the isolated civilizations of the ancient Americans; they also brought contact with the outside world, and this proved disastrous.

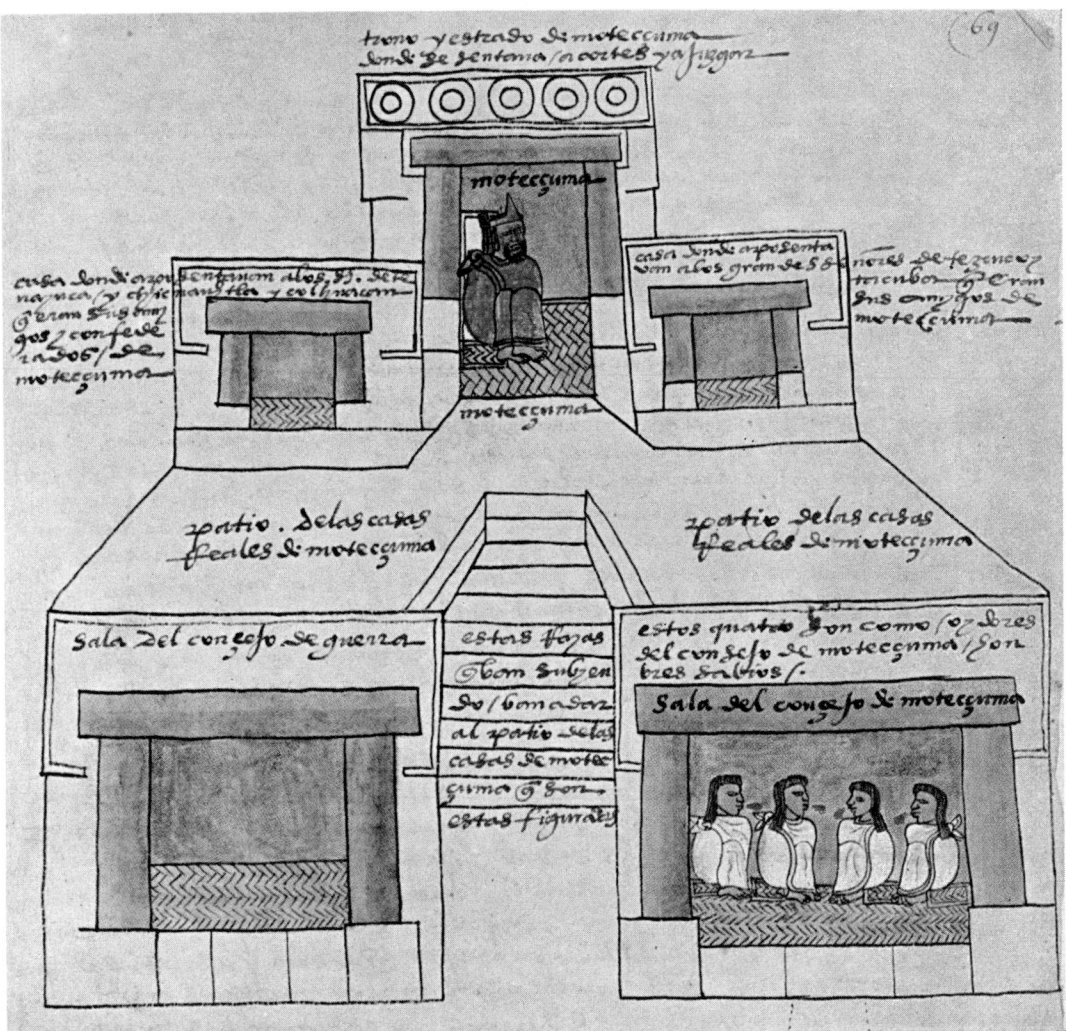

MOCTEZUMA'S PALACE *symbolized Aztec government: Emperor and chiefs sat above, war councils and courts below.*

# THE AZTECS' ORDERLY SOCIETY

The Spaniards landing in ancient Mexico were astonished by the high degree of social organization attained by the pagan Aztecs. "One may well marvel at the orderliness and good government which is everywhere maintained," the conqueror Hernán Cortés wrote Madrid. Under their Emperor, Moctezuma, the Aztecs had a well-regulated economy, a ruling class based on ability as well as birth, a system of low and high courts, and a strong moral code that held family and community above all. Fortunately, before destroying most of the old ways, the colonizers commissioned dozens of manuscripts to record Aztec society. One of the best is the Codex Mendoza, ordered in 1541 by the Viceroy Antonio de Mendoza to give Charles V a graphic account of His Majesty's new subjects. Drawn by an Aztec artist, with text by a Spanish priest, it vividly illuminates these people's lives.

Left to right:
Messenger
Father advising son
Musician and listener

Left to right:
Plow and basket
Farm laborer
Vagabond
Ball player

Overseer

Left to right:
Plow and basket
Farm laborer
Thief
Gambler

Left to right:
Woodcutter and son
Stoneworker and son

Far right: Gossip

Left to right:
Painter and son
Goldsmith and son

Left to right:
Featherworker and son
Couple drinking
Noose indicating
death penalty

154

THE MANY OCCUPATIONS *an Aztec boy could choose are shown in the figures above. At top center, a father tells his son about them*

# THE GUIDED STEPS OF CHILDHOOD

Home life for the ideal Aztec family was both well disciplined and warm. Parents had a close relationship with children and brought them up according to a strict regime. At the age of three a child was given lifelike toys such as a small loom or grinding stone and was assigned certain household tasks; at six he took on broader domestic responsibilities, and at 15 began regular schooling. In the pictures below, for example, a 13-year-old boy and girl receive instruction from their father and mother in bringing home rushes by canoe and grinding maize into meal, while 14-year-olds learn to net fish and work a loom.

As their children grew up, the parents were expected to counsel and guide them into honorable careers. At top left, a father is shown advising his son on desirable vocations such as that of messenger or musician, pictured on either side. He also warns of the pitfalls of becoming a gossip, a thief, a vagabond or a drunkard, depicted farther down.

DOMESTIC CHORES *are explained to children by their parents; dots signify the children's ages, ovals their prescribed ration of tortillas.*

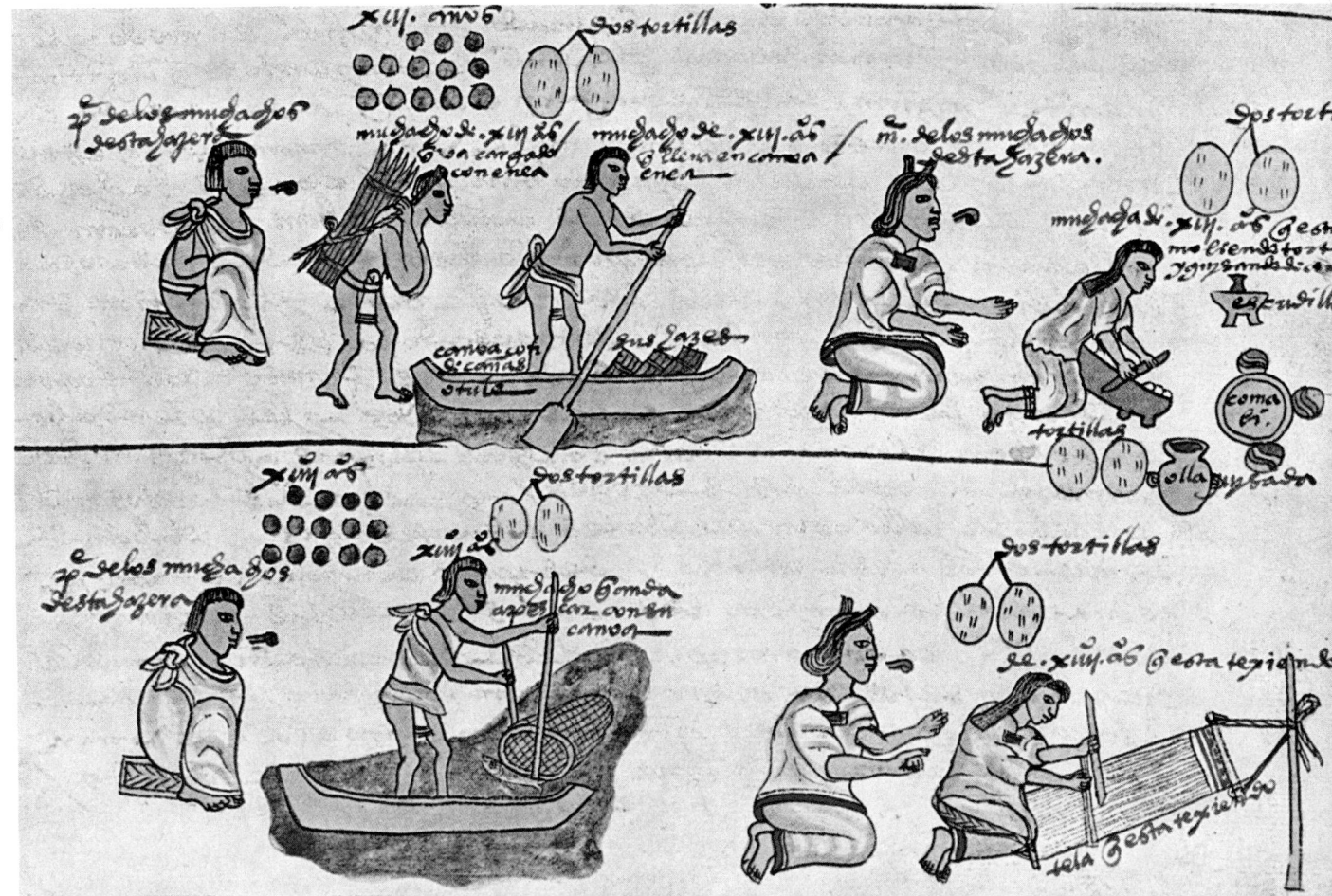

*Left to right:*
*Father teaching son*
*Son gathering rushes*
*Daughter grinding corn*

*Left to right:*
*Father teaching son*
*Son learning to fish*
*Daughter weaving*

155

# THE JOYS AND PENALTIES OF ADULT LIFE

The rigid order that governed an Aztec child's upbringing continued into his adult years. Marriage was expected when a young man reached 20 and a girl 16. Matches were arranged by the two families—presumably with some occasional *sub rosa* guidance from the young people. Once agreement was reached, the youth's relatives sent two old women to negotiate the marriage with the bride's parents.

On the evening designated for the ceremony the girl was

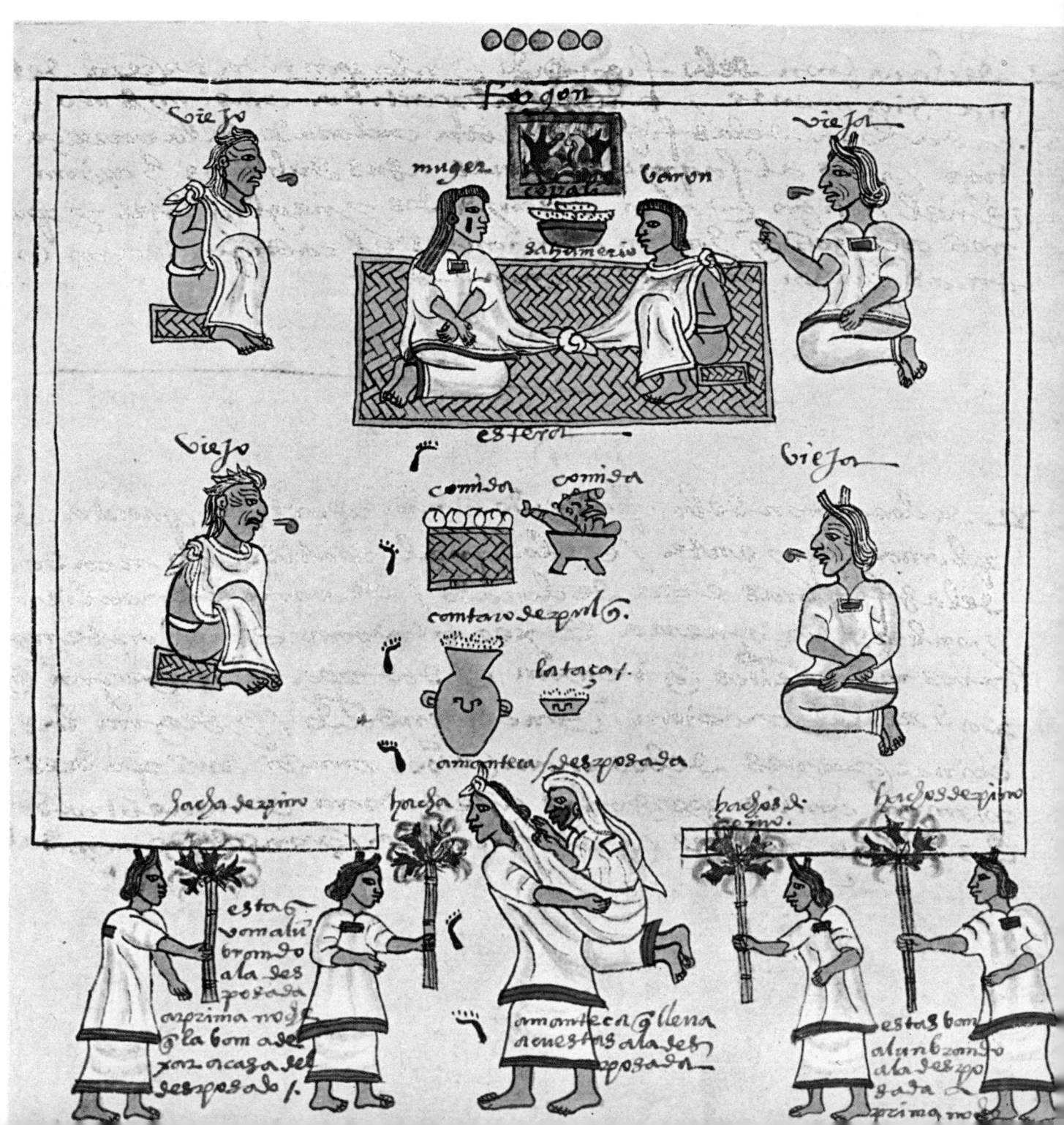

carried to the groom's home; daughters of the nobility were borne on litters, while poor girls rode on the back of an old woman, their path lighted by other women carrying burning pine branches. During a ceremony held before the hearth, the groom's tunic was knotted to the bride's blouse, officially uniting them. After a feast, accompanied by much beer for the older relatives, the couple retired to burn incense and pray to the gods for four days before consummating their marriage.

After marriage, the strict Aztec code continued to govern every aspect of family behavior. If their children stepped out of line, parents were entitled to give them the smoke treatment *(seen below)*, prick their flesh with thorns, or leave them outside all night to sleep in a mud puddle. When the adults themselves erred, the consequences were considerably more severe: thieves, drunkards and adulterous couples were put to death—commoners in public, aristocrats by private execution.

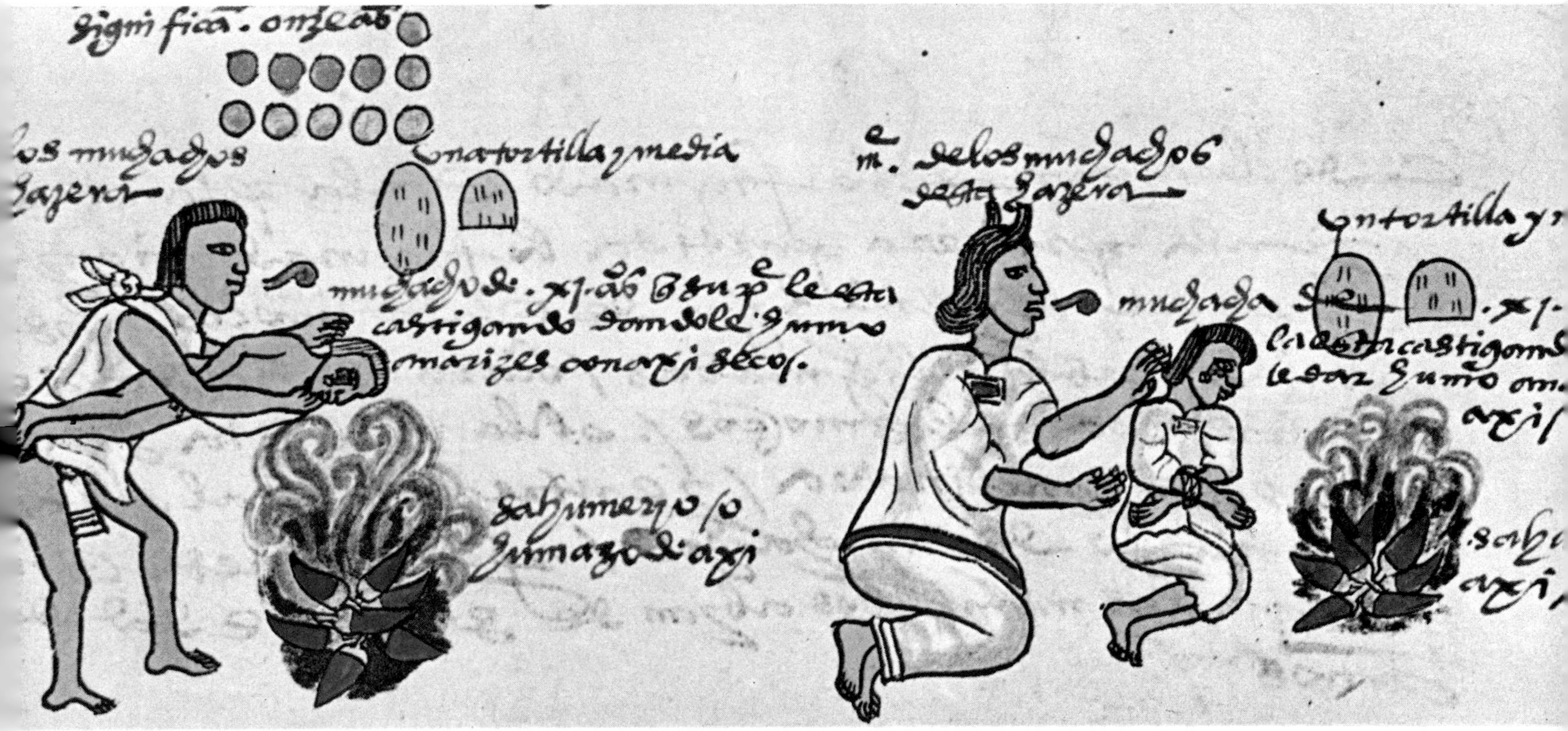

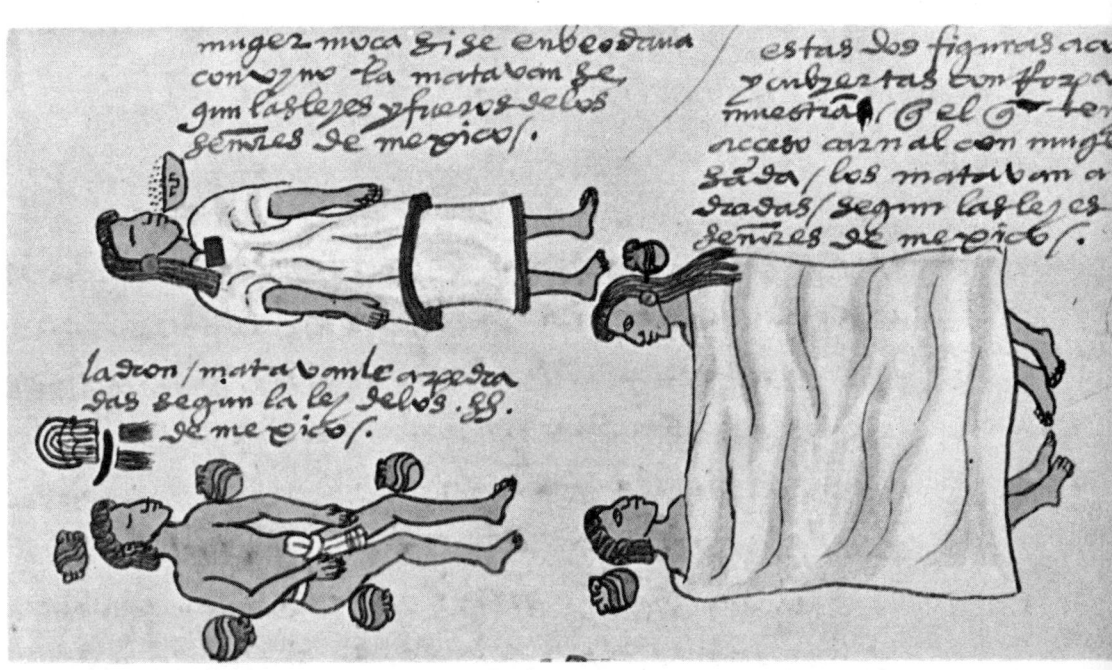

DISCIPLINING A CHILD, *a father holds his son over a fire of peppers to make his eyes smart. A mother, right, threatens her daughter with the same treatment.*

MARRIAGE RITUALS *(left) involved carrying the bride to the groom's house on an old woman's back, feasting on turkey and corn, and literally tying the knot (top).*

CAPITAL PUNISHMENT *for drunkards, adulterers and thieves usually meant death by stoning (right). Drunkenness was regarded as the root of most sinful acts.*

AN AZTEC STEAM BATH *was a stone hut with one wall of porous rock, against which an outside fire was built (left). Bathers inside splashed water on the h*

# PURIFYING RITUALS, SACRED GAMES

In the well-organized lives of the Aztecs even everyday activities such as taking baths and playing games were governed by ritual. Most respectable houses boasted a sauna-like building outside, but Aztecs usually did their daily washing in ponds and rivers, reserving steam baths for ceremonial occasions such as purifying newlyweds after marriage and mothers before and after giving birth.

Aztec games, while enjoyed for sheer sport, almost invariably had sacred connotations too. One widespread favorite, climbing the pole, was an important part of religious festivals. Another, *patolli*, a game not unlike Parcheesi, was played on a board of 52 squares, the number of years in the Aztec century; it was supposed to divine future events but was also an excuse for heavy betting.

ll, producing billows of steam.

CLIMBING THE POLE, men raced each other to reach the top with the aid of ropes. The winner, seen seated here at the summit, found prizes awaiting him and threw down pieces of sacred bread to the crowd.

PLAYING PATOLLI, competitors throw a form of dice in order to move beans around a cross-shaped board. Watching over the players at left is Macuilxochitl, the Aztec god of gambling, dance and music.

159

THE GOD OF THE DEAD *is honored by worshipers who approach the skull-faced deity, offering blood from self-inflicted wounds.*

# A POWERFUL RELIGION

Underlying and giving meaning to all of Aztec life was an elaborate set of deities and religious rites. At least half the month was taken up with sacred observances. A typical ceremony started at sunset with songs and dances. For hours warriors and women, holding hands, would weave among rows of torch holders, singing and chanting rhythmically until well into the night. After as many as 10 such nights, the rites were climaxed by sacrifices.

One deity frequently honored was Mictlantecuhtli, the God of the Dead, who ruled the Aztecs' afterlife from the ninth and lowest region of hell. Others were Huitzilopochtli, the God of the Sun, and Tlaloc, the God of Rain. To this day, in parts of backcountry Mexico, the old gods are worshiped along with the new, and sometimes when rain refuses to come, sacrifices of chickens and turkeys are made.

SACRIFICING TO THE SUN GOD, *a priest plung*

*fe into the chest of a warrior, whose soul is seen ascending skyward in a bloody trail. Another victim of the rite lies dead at the foot of the temple steps.*

# 8

# THE DEATHLESS HERITAGE

A REFLECTION OF THE PAST, *an ancient pottery figurine is seen in a mirror of obsidian, or volcanic glass, set in a carved frame some 700 years old. The figure itself, at least twice that old, depicts a dignified, straight-backed woman in the style peculiar to the sculpture of the west coast of Mexico.*

For most of the people of the Aztec and Inca Empires the Spanish conquest did not at first seem catastrophic. Warfare was a familiar part of their lives; cities had been destroyed before and ruling groups dislodged. What if it happened again? What if the strange men from the sea who displaced their native rulers looked a little different and had different customs? The rain would fall and the corn would grow and life would continue as usual.

But life did not continue as usual. The Spaniards who came with Cortés and Pizarro were only the forerunners of a many-sided invasion of men and ideas that would overwhelm both Indian Empires and basically change the lives of their peoples. The sheltered American civilizations, which had developed without contact with the rest of the world, would be forced to compete with vigorous Spain, at that time the most powerful and ambitious nation in Europe, and a nation whose technologies and institutions were superior in most respects to the Indians'.

Such cultural collisions have seldom been pleasant for the weaker participant. Before the Indian countries could become adjusted to membership in the world civilization, nearly all their inhabitants would be reduced to serfdom and great numbers of them would die before their time. Cities would dwindle to villages, and villages would disappear. Entire regions would be abandoned to death and emptiness. For centuries it would appear that the civilized Indians of ancient Mexico and Peru, along with their accomplishments and their rich traditions, would fade to a memory, and never again would people of Indian blood enjoy prestige.

The melancholy period of decline that followed the conquest has often been blamed on Spanish cruelty and oppression. This is only partially true. Some Spaniards were indeed spectacularly cruel, though probably no more so than any Europeans of the time would have been under similar circumstances. Others were greedy for wealth and power, and blind to the effects their acts were having on the Indians. But far more damaging than Spanish misdeeds were the invisible microorganisms that they unwittingly brought from Europe. Pestilence after pestilence took a shocking toll among the susceptible Indian population. Some of these devastating epidemics were smallpox, others probably measles and influenza.

The cumulative effect of the pestilences was horrible in the extreme. Accurate statistics do not exist, but many responsible observers reported the results of the plagues. Both the Gulf and Pacific Coasts of Mexico were swept almost clear of people. The Valley of Mexico lost about 80 per cent of its Indians by 1600. The same happened in Peru, where the dense populations of the coastal oases practically disappeared. The fertile Rimac Valley, where modern Lima stands, lost almost 95 per cent of its people in less than 50 years. There was no quick recovery. In 1685 the Spanish Marqués de Varinas, who had journeyed from Lima to Paita on the northern Peruvian coast, described what he saw: "One recognizes at very short intervals mounds of skulls and bones of these miserable beings, which horrify those traveling the road." He estimated that, of the two million Indians who once lived in the region through which he had passed, only 20,000 remained.

The plagues were not the fault of the Spaniards, but in other respects the Spaniards undoubtedly contributed to the decline of population. The delicately balanced economies of the Peruvian coastal valleys, for example, depended on keeping the irrigation systems in good working order, but because internecine strife raged for years among the Spaniards of colonial Peru, the strong, stable authority needed to maintain the canals was lacking. As the canals fell into disrepair, many areas where crops once flourished reverted to desert and the Indians starved. In both Mexico and Peru, hundreds of thousands of Indians were forced to work in Spanish mines, where they often died; other hundreds of thousands fled to remote mountains or jungles to avoid such killing labor.

It was on this insecure base of disease, despair and shrinking population that the Spaniards built their empire in the New World. However, their problems in Mexico and Peru were not the same, partly because of differences of climate and geography and partly because the Indian population of each region reacted in sharply different ways.

Cortés had won his victory in Mexico by taking advantage of the violent enmity between groups of subject Indians and their Aztec oppressors, and much of the fighting was done by his native allies. After the defeat of the Aztecs, which was hailed as glorious news by most of Mexico, Cortés and his successors extended the conquest by the same policy. Indian armies led by Spaniards and including the Tlaxcalans, who had helped win Tenochtitlán, sallied out of the Valley of Mexico just as the Aztecs had done before them and subjugated outlying regions. Especially stubborn resistance came from the Maya of Yucatán, who were decadent in culture but not in resolution. In 1535 they drove all Spanish invaders out of their country. During the next 10 or 12 years most of Yucatán was conquered bit by bit, but only after serious losses among the Spaniards; parts of the interior resisted conquest for more than a century.

The Maya were an exceptional case. Most of the civilized Indians of Mexico submitted to Spanish domination without prolonged resistance, and the Spaniards replaced the native ruling class with surprisingly little conflict. The common people were accustomed to obeying Indian overlords and they obeyed the Spaniards in the same way, passively paying tribute as they had done for native rulers. The great difference was that Indian overlords were often temporary and usually brought little change, whereas the Spaniards conquered permanently. They set up an elaborate administrative system centered in Mexico City, the capital that they established on the ruins of Tenochtitlán and founded towns that became strongholds of Spanish power. If a province revolted the Spaniards killed its leaders, enslaved most of its people and so made reasonably certain it would not revolt again.

Beyond the boundaries of Mexico's high Indian civilization the conquerors were less successful. Some parts of northern and western Mexico were fairly thickly inhabited, but the tribes were not accustomed to obedience and did not intend to obey the Spaniards. In the state of Jalisco on the Pacific Coast, for example, they revolted and defeated a Spanish army under Pedro de Alvarado, Cortés' captain. Some of the tribesmen retreated into the mountains where they held out for 200 years.

A factor that eased the conquest of many parts of Mexico was the Indian attitude toward religion. In the Indian view, gods were simply supernatural beings who conferred tangible benefits in return for rituals and sacrifices, and some were more generous and more powerful than others. Many a defeated Indian people had adopted the gods of its native conquerors. Why not? The very gods that caused the defeat might be persuaded to grant a future victory.

The victories of the Spaniards were proof in Indian eyes that they possessed an unusually effective set of gods which for some odd reason they were eager to share with others. After the fall of Tenochtitlán, the Spanish missionaries who set out to Christianize the Indians met little resistance. Converts pressed around them for baptism, which was often done in mass ceremonies. Some of Mexico's oldest churches have balconies from which the officiating priests baptized crowds of Indians packed into walled courtyards.

One Franciscan friar claimed to have baptized 400,000 Indians during his lifetime. Another baptized 14,000 in a single day. Few converts understood the subtleties of Christian theology, but there was no doubt about their devotion. They faithfully attended ceremonies and gave their labor to build elaborate churches. When they were convinced that a priest or friar was really devoted to their interests, as many were in the early years of Spanish rule, they defended him against all opponents.

The Spanish state and Church, working together, were quick to take advantage of Indian piety. They destroyed the blood-stained religious center of Tenochtitlán lest it become a rallying point for Indian backsliders. Its pyramids and wall decorated with snakes were leveled, and their stones and idols were dumped into the lake. There most of them remain today with Mexico City's cathedral holding them down.

Ancient Indian centers of worship that were no longer in use—such as the ruins of Monte Albán and the pyramids of Teotihuacán—the Spaniards ignored as harmless, but many active holy places they deftly transformed into centers of the new religion. Usually they dismantled the Indian shrine and built a church beside it or upon it, sometimes reusing the ancient stones. Even sacred trees were not neglected. A few miles from the city of Oaxaca stands an enormous and still-flourishing cypress that was a focus of worship in preconquest times, and beside it stands a beautiful old church that was built to benefit from the piety of the tree's congregation.

But in spite of determined efforts by the Christian clergy to erase the old religion, it did not entirely disappear. The Indians quickly, and probably gladly, abandoned human sacrifice and the bloodthirsty gods that demanded it, but they continued to worship their ancient nature gods of rain and corn, the harvest and springtime. Some of them still do, and many Indian traditions are incorporated into nominally Christian practices. The most popular shrine in modern Mexico is the basilica of the Virgin of Guadalupe in a suburb of Mexico City. Hundreds of thousands of Indian pilgrims come from all over the country to make small offerings to this celebrated Virgin who is depicted as a beautiful Indian woman, but their piety

is not exclusively Christian. The place was sacred in preconquest times as the shrine of Tonantzin, the mother of the gods, who was old before the Aztecs. It is doubtful that Mary of Nazareth is clearer in the pilgrims' minds than the ancient mother goddess whom their ancestors worshiped.

Providing a quasi-Christian religion for the Indians was easier than devising an efficient government for them. Cortés himself was a talented statesman, and he might eventually have accomplished this if the King of Spain had not curtailed his powers. Most of the Spaniards who came with Cortés were greedy, violent men interested solely in wealth and bitterly disappointed by the small amount of gold that was available in Mexico. To prevent their mutiny, Cortés awarded many of them *encomiendas*, or grants of Indians.

Theoretically, the Indians in an encomienda were not slaves. Urged by idealistic priests, the Spanish Crown had drawn up strict regulations to protect them. The owner of an encomienda was supposed to look out for the Indians' welfare, see that they became good Christians and require from them only a designated amount of tribute and labor. In some cases this system worked fairly well but more often the Indians were savagely exploited.

The Spanish Crown was well aware of these abuses, and some of its early viceroys made determined efforts to stop them. But communications with Spain were slow and uncertain, and later viceroys were often corrupt and weak. The officials whom they charged with protecting the Indians exploited them instead. The owners of great estates, haciendas, used legal subterfuges to take from Indian communities the land that supported them, and so forced the Indians to work for a bare subsistence. As the Spaniards acquired more land in this way, the richer parts of the country, where Indian centers of civilization had formerly flourished, came to be almost entirely oc-

cupied by their haciendas and towns, neither of which had any use for the higher aspects of Indian culture. So the Indian upper classes, the cultured chiefs and priests, were eliminated, leaving only peasants, laborers, artisans and small traders.

Though sharply reduced in numbers, the Indians of Mexico were still plentiful enough to make the land attractive to many Spanish colonists. These settlers came from a country that was still feudal-minded, where even men of lowly birth dreamed of becoming landed nobles who did no personal work but were supported by the labor of serfs. The civilized parts of Mexico suited them perfectly, and many a common soldier became an instant grandee with plenty of industrious Indians to feed, attend and amuse him. Few Spanish women came in the early years, but the conquerors had no race exclusiveness, and they found it easy to assemble collections of Indian girls. During later centuries more Spanish women were imported, but they were never sufficient to maintain a numerous population of purely Spanish blood.

Out of unions between Spaniards and Indians came a class of *mestizos* (mixed-bloods) which symbolically got its start when Cortés had a son by his beautiful adviser and mistress, Doña Marina. A few mestizos were accepted by the ruling

Spanish families, and their descendants became indistinguishable from aristocratic Spaniards. Others joined Indian communities, acquiring their outlook and customs. The majority adopted a mode of life part way between the Spanish and Indian.

This racial and cultural mingling would eventually make Mexico a unified nation, but it was slow to take effect. For nearly 400 years the country was dominated by a very few aristocrats of predominantly Spanish blood who treated the rest of the people badly. The Indians in particular were despised as lazy and hardly human. The occasional leader who rose from their submerged level—including Benito Juárez, a Zapotec Indian who in the 19th Century became Mexico's President—did not alter the belief of the landowners that Indians were not worth educating and that paying them higher wages would only permit them to spend more time in idleness.

With extraordinary tenacity in the face of contempt and mistreatment, the Indians preserved their special character, refusing to adopt the full range of Spanish culture and selecting only the parts that suited them. They continued some ancient handicrafts, notably pottery making, with only minor changes. They took over other crafts, such as glassmaking and leatherwork, from the Spaniards and imposed on them an unmistakably Indian look. Ancient dances and festivals persisted, often with Christian trimmings. Though most of its people spoke Spanish and had accepted some elements of Spanish culture, colonial Mexico remained predominantly Indian; only the very small ruling class looked and acted Spanish.

When it came to consolidating their conquest of Peru the Spaniards were helped by the fundamental character of the Inca Empire. Unlike Aztec Mexico, tense with explosive enmities and eager to revolt, Peru was too orderly for its own good.

After the capture of Atahuallpa, Pizarro found that he could act in the name of the Inca and have the obedient Empire at his beck and call. The execution of Atahuallpa, who might have agreed to become a puppet ruler, may have been a mistake as well as an act of barbarity, but for a while it did not seem to make much difference. The little army of Spaniards advanced to the Inca capital of Cuzco without great difficulty. They dispersed some remnants of Atahuallpa's forces and enlisted contingents of Indian soldiers on their side. There was no popular resistance. When the Spaniards pillaged Cuzco, raped its aristocratic women and combed other Inca centers for golden treasure, the Indians accepted the abuse with hardly a defensive gesture. They were trained to act only in response to commands from above, and the Spaniards now occupied the commanding position.

To ensure the continuance of his almost unbelievable power, Pizarro chose a puppet Inca, a young half-brother of Atahuallpa named Manco, and had him crowned with elaborate ceremony. For two years Manco accepted this humiliating role; then he fled from Cuzco to head a revolt. With an Inca to lead them again, the Indians of the Cuzco region awoke from their helpless trance. For a year they besieged Cuzco, which was garrisoned by only a few hundred Spaniards. Large armies of them surrounded the city and attacked repeatedly with reckless bravery. Most of Cuzco was destroyed, but the Spaniards managed to hold its center until reinforcements arrived to raise the siege. Manco retreated into the wilderness of the Urubamba Valley, where he and his successors held out for more than 30 years.

No other Indian revolt seriously challenged the conquerors, who soon split into factions and fell to fighting one another over the spoils of conquest. In 1541 Pizarro himself was murdered. Civil war among the conquerors continued, with dire consequences for the helpless Indians, until 1556 when a strong viceroy, the Marqués de Cañete, arrived from Spain and put a stop to it.

The subsequent development of Peru was largely dictated by its extraordinary and extreme geography. Even before the revolt of Manco, Pizarro had decided that Cuzco, separated from the sea by almost 300 miles over towering mountain ranges, was too high, cold, remote and susceptible to attack to make a good center of Spanish rule. Instead he founded his own capital, Lima, only eight miles from the coast. Lima was laid out in Spanish style with a rectangular grid of streets and a central plaza for the government headquarters and for the cathedral, where the body of Pizarro lies today, preserved in a glass coffin and recalling the Indian custom of displaying mummified Incas in Cuzco.

With this fresh beginning and no Indian antecedents, Lima became a Spanish city in spirit as well as in appearance. Many of the officials who arrived from Spain in colonial times brought their wives and daughters with them. Since Lima was new and small, these women were numerous enough to breed not only a ruling class but an appreciable part of the capital's population. The bulk of its citizens were Indians or mestizos, but they spoke Spanish and followed Spanish customs that were only slightly modified to fit the country.

From Lima the Spaniards spread along the coast, setting up haciendas in the fertile valleys, many of which had been almost emptied of their Indians. Most of the coastal valleys were gradually repopulated by highland Indians recruited to work on the haciendas. The migrants learned Spanish and retained few Indian attributes. Except for its racial background, the coast of Peru was effectively hispanicized.

The Andean highlands were not. Remote from the sea, the source of Spanish strength, they remained predominantly Indian, although the Indians were by no means in control. Much of their best land was taken over by Spanish-owned haciendas and was sometimes cleared of people so cattle could graze more freely. Whole provinces in the mountains were nearly depopulated by the forced recruiting of men to work in Spanish mines. The Peruvian Indians diminished in number, and, like the Mexican Indians, lost most of the higher aspects of their ancient civilization, but they were neither exterminated nor hispanicized. With stubborn persistence they clung to their old customs, preserving even more of them than the Mexicans did. Early in the 19th Century the declining highland population reached a turning point. The Indians began to increase. Today the highlands of Peru (and of adjacent Ecuador and Bolivia) are almost solidly Indian, and are probably more thickly populated than they were in Atahuallpa's time.

Though colonial Mexico and Peru differed widely in detail, they shared one factor of overriding significance: the persistence of their indigenous culture. Only where the Indians had achieved their highest civilizations, in Middle America and the Central Andes, did they retain important features of their ancient ways.

Even the most casual glance at modern Mexico and Peru shows that both countries have preserved a great deal from their Indian past and that their long-submerged Indian population is fast rising to the surface. To achieve this, Mexico had to pass through a violent revolution that gave its society a fairly modern structure. Peru had no such revolution.

The Mexican dictator Porfirio Díaz was overthrown by a series of popular revolts which began in 1910, some of them led by Indians, others by mestizos. Years of anarchy followed; the landed aristocrats were despoiled and many of them killed or exiled. But when the country finally quieted down, it had a new social order, the first that accorded property, hope and dignity to its largely Indian and near-Indian population. The effect of the reforms was immediate and extraordinary. Within a few years the people of Indian blood had become more responsible, orderly and industrious than they had been since the Spanish conquest of 1521.

Modern Mexico is prosperous and progressive, with a stable and generally efficient government. Mexico City has over three million people and is growing rapidly. The country is full of new houses, schools, hospitals, roads, factories, dams, airports and universities.

In this scene of feverish, optimistic activity, where are the Indians? The answer is that since the revolution of 1910 most of them have become Mexicans. In some parts of the country isolated villages can still be found where the people speak an Indian language, shun the outside world and cling to customs that have changed hardly at all since preconquest times, but such picturesque anachronisms are becoming fewer. Many Indians now live in industrial cities or on their outskirts, or in modernized villages. These retain their charming old churches, their cactus fences, their cheerful weekly market days and their small, carefully tended fields of corn. But they also have electricity, a school, perhaps a government clinic. On weekdays the girls may wear the local Indian costume, a long skirt and shapeless blouse, but on Sundays they blossom out in short modern dresses.

Traditionalists deplore such changes, but welcome others. The Indian past of Mexico, no longer despised or ignored, has become fashionable. On holidays the people of Mexico City stream out by thousands to Teotihuacán to admire the pyramids built by their ancient ancestors. Indian festivals are revived and Indian dances performed in brand-new city squares. Indian art forms are popular, even among Mexicans who have little or no Indian blood. Students are taught preconquest history; some of them study Náhuatl, the Aztec language.

The Mexican government encourages Indianism as a source of national unity and supplies funds to explore and reconstruct the ruins that are so plentiful throughout the country. Tlaltelolco, Tenochtitlán's twin city in Lake Texcoco, is a good example of such government-sponsored reconstruction. Out of the lake-bottom silt, a complex of Aztec religious buildings is emerging, with many of its strange stone carvings looking as fresh as when they were made. At Tlaltelolco the Spanish conquerors had partially destroyed a tall pyramid, using its stones to build beside it an enormous, fortresslike church. For centuries both pyramid and church were neglected, but a program of restoration was recently started. A new stone pavement covers an area at the base of the pyramid and is used for festivals and dances of Indian, colonial or modern origin. Skyscraper apartment houses stand roundabout, finished in gay pastel colors. This place is called the Plaza of the Three Cultures: the Indian past, colonial Spain and today's urban industrialism. Modern Mexico has succeeded in happily blending them all.

Peru's modern development diverges sharply from that of Mexico, mostly because of its geography. Lima is more Spanish than Mexico City, but the highlands that formed the core of the Inca Empire are about as Indian as ever. The provincial cities tucked away in formerly remote mountain valleys once had a Spanish upper class, but many of its members have departed for Lima, leaving the mountains almost entirely to Indians and mestizos.

There are no reliable statistics to tell how numerous the highland Indians actually are, but the Peruvian government estimates that about half of the country's 12 million inhabitants speak Quechua, the ancient Inca language, and a third of the total population speak nothing else. Only a scattering of the population, mostly around Lima on the coast, is fully Spanish; the rest is Indian or of mixed blood.

Some highland Indians wear European clothes, speak Spanish and work at modern white-collar or industrial jobs. Others own a few acres of fertile land and are prosperous in an archaic way; they wear gay, homewoven clothes and appear well fed, healthy and cheerful. But most are not so lucky. Landless Indians who work on highland haciendas are usually ill paid and pitifully poor. Many live far up twisting valleys where only tiny patches of land can be cultivated or in villages that perch on sterile slopes steeper than the roofs of their houses. They scratch a precarious living from the soil and go hungry when crops fail. Despite their generally harsh life, the mountain Indians are increasing rapidly. Driven by population pressure, large numbers of them are flooding down to the coast, where they live in squatter towns outside the cities.

Poor though most of the Indians are, they have one possession that gives them enormous comfort: their close community life. Nearly every individual belongs not only to a widely ramified family but to a larger group whose members intermarry, organize humble festivals, work together, help one another and try as best they can to face together the hostile outside world. These communities are ingrowing and intensely conservative, but they are descendants of the ancient *ayllus*, the social unit on which the Inca built their Empire. They survive today as little oases of warmth and friendship and make life endurable for the Indians.

Other cultural assets besides the communities have survived from Inca times. Indian handicrafts, especially textiles, are still made in large quantities for Indian use, not merely to sell to tourists. Indian music, which has its own strange scale and sounds like no other music, is still played on native Pan-pipes, drums and trumpets, and also by modern orchestras and, loudly, by brass bands. In Cuzco, where Indianism is pursued by intellectuals, Inca religious ceremonies have been revived. One of them celebrates the winter solstice in June when the sun, the dominant god of the Inca, begins to return from the north.

After centuries of oppression and poverty, a brighter future now seems to be in the making for Peru's Indians. The country is exceedingly prosperous; its cities and industries are growing so fast that jobs are available for almost anyone who wants to work. The government is sincerely trying to give the Indians a better economic life, a feeling that they are appreciated and a sense of identification with the nation's future.

The results of this effort have been encouraging. The upper class is broadening, the middle class is growing rapidly, and Peruvians of Indian ancestry are proving that they can handle with ease all the skilled jobs offered by modern industry. Peru appears to be well on its way toward revising its social structure without ever having had to pass through an Indian-mestizo revolution like the one that shaped modern Mexico.

The strange civilizations of the ancient Americans will never rise again. Developed in isolation, they were imperfect and could not compete with the dynamic world culture that crossed the Atlantic with the Spaniards. Mexicans will never revert to human sacrifice; Peruvians will never again keep their accounts with knotted strings. But in both Mexico and Peru—and in Guatemala, Ecuador and Bolivia—Indian traditions are still very much alive and are even extending their influence. For the foreseeable future the Indian countries of Middle America and the Andes will be islands of distinctiveness in an increasingly uniform world.

A FLUORESCENT SUN, *lighting the museum's entrance hall, is a modern version of an old Aztec symbol.*

# A PEOPLE'S PRIDE

Modern Mexico rings with echoes of its Indian past. Families proudly cite their Aztec ancestry, students flock to courses in Maya art, and contemporary architects find inspiration in the monumental stonework of Toltec cities. Nowhere are the echoes so strong as in Mexico City's National Museum of Anthropology, which houses the world's largest collection of Pre-Columbian art treasures. The building itself is less a museum than a stage setting for a pageant of stone sculpture arranged to dramatize the whole legacy of native Mexican culture. Ancient and modern quotations inscribed on the museum's walls reflect the pride of its builders in their great heritage. One near the entrance sums up their intent: "People of Mexico, look at yourselves in the mirror of that greatness."

In the main courtyard of the museum, where an inscription evokes the grandeur of the Aztec capital, the works of modern and ancient Mexico are seen in striking juxtaposition. A stone statue of the Aztec God of Night stands before a low modern sculpture resembling a conch shell, an ancient water symbol. In the background a huge, umbrellalike canopy supported by a single column shelters the courtyard.

Tenochtitlán will never perish''

AZTEC MEMORIAL

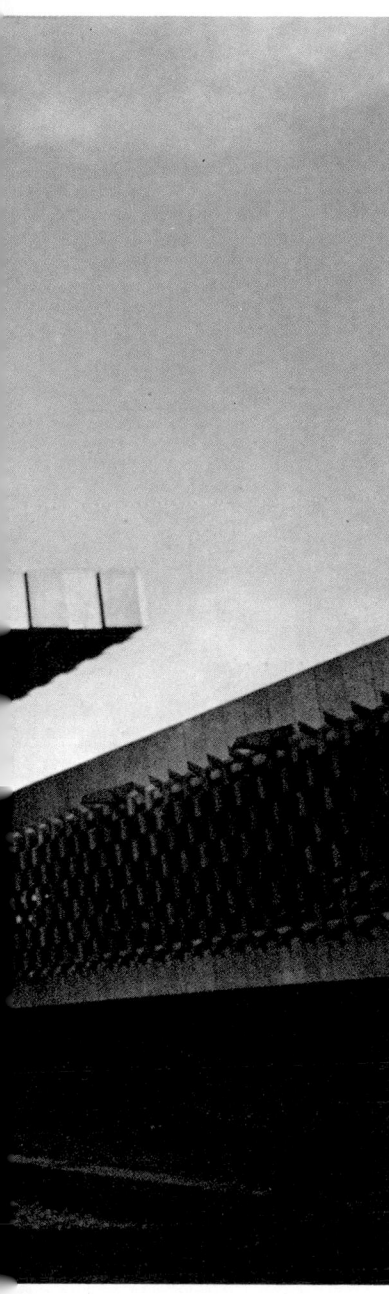

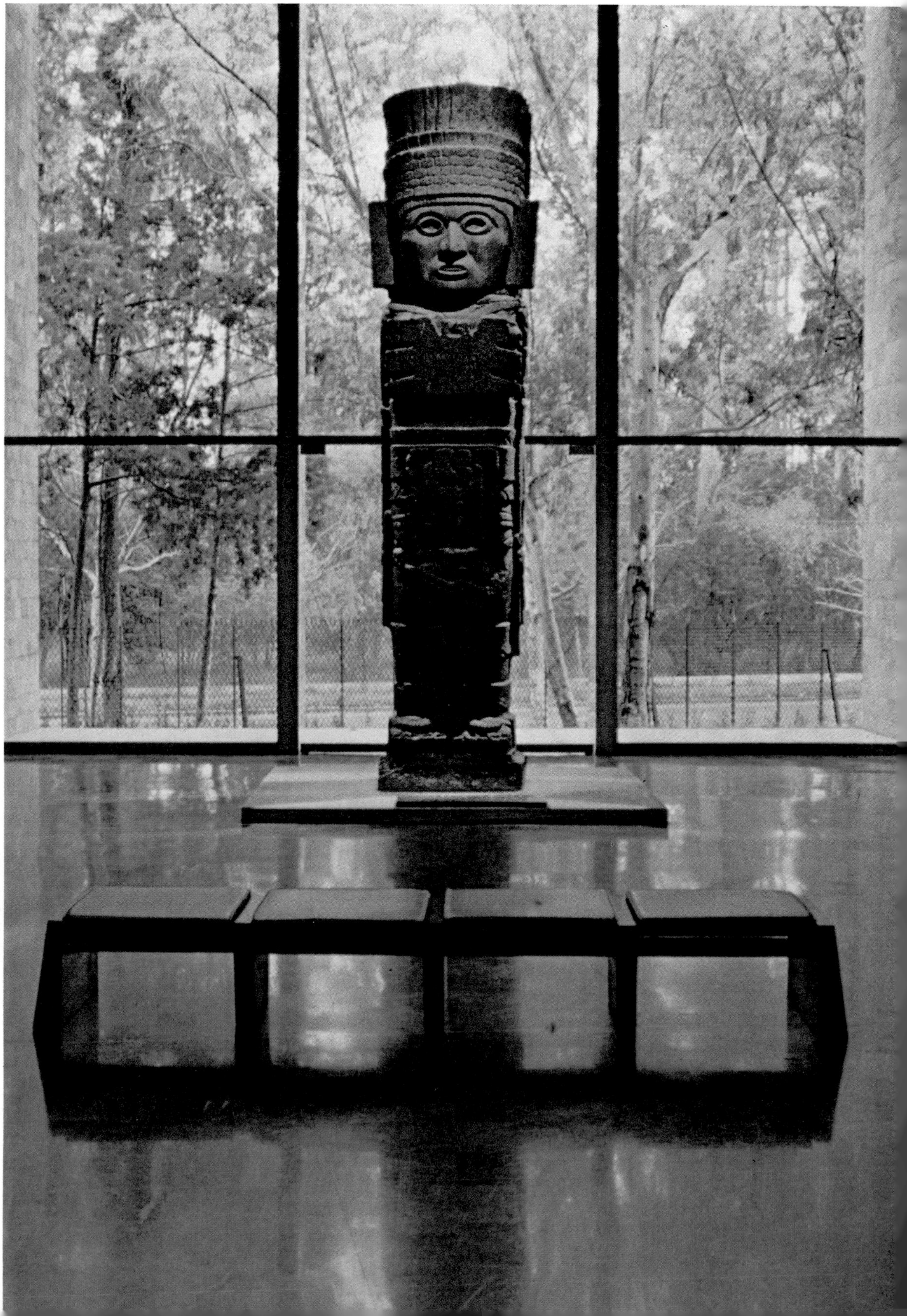

Atlas-like figure of an 800-year- Toltec warrior is framed by a plate- s window in the museum's Toltec ery. The 15-foot-high stone piece e served as a column to help sup- the roof of a temple at Tula, the ecs' capital. The stark, powerful n, hewn from four blocks of stone ed one on top of another, is deco- d by a traditional butterfly breast- e and a stylized feather headdress.

"Even though it was still night . . . the gods gathered together, there in Teotihuacán"

—AZTEC CHRONICLE

To dramatize one of Mexico's early cultures, the museum has duplicated part of the Temple of the Feathered Serpent at Teotihuacán, a city the Aztecs thought was so old it had been built by gods. Flanked by stone statues and architectural ornaments brought from the city, the temple's painted façade is brilliantly reflected in the museum's black marble floor.

"Civilizations pass away, but the glory

of the men who toiled to build them remains forever"

—MODERN INSCRIPTION

The greatest Aztec ruin, the imperial capital of Tenochtitlán, lies buried under the streets of Mexico City, some of whose major public buildings stand on the rubble of the older city's monuments. Modern builders, scooping out foundations for new structures, often resurrect impressive carved stones, like those shown spotlighted above in the museum's Aztec gallery.

Deep inside a pyramid at Palenque in the Mexican jungle, archeologists found the tomb of a high priest in 1952. The tomb is regarded as one of the most important relics of Maya culture. This replica in the museum's Maya gallery, including copies of the jade death mask and jewelry that adorned the body, preserves the original tomb's aura of deep mystery.

"There will be neither glory nor greatness on earth until the creation of man"

—MAYA LEGEND

Some of the earliest known sculptures in the Americas are depictions of men, ranging from small clay figurines to huge monolithic heads carved by the Olmecs almost three thousand years ago. The head seen here, originally found at an Olmec settlement in Veracruz, was fashioned from a single 16-ton piece of rock. The same feeling for monumental stonework is echoed at right in the façade of the museum itself, which is built of marble blocks rough-hewn by Indian craftsmen.

"Men find, in the greatness of their past, courage and confidence for the future"
—MODERN INSCRIPTION

At the museum's core, a remarkable tour de force of contemporary architecture celebrates Mexico's marriage of present and past, as well as her hopes for the future. It is a vast canopy of gleaming ribbed aluminum, supported with the help of cables from a single bronze-clad mast. Through central openings in the canopy, which extends 250 feet over the museum's courtyard, a fountain cascades to a pavement of volcanic stone.

Though the canopy on its single column is a bold statement of modern engineering, it also suggests aspirations rooted in a unity with Mexico's past. Like the stone pillars that held up the roofs of ancient temples, the column is covered with bas-relief sculpture. Symbolic figures suggest the fusion of Indian and Spanish cultures and Mexico's emergence into the modern world, which is represented by a stylized atom. At the top, the figure of a man, flanked by olive branches and crowned with a dove, emphasizes the nation's continuing quest for prosperity and peace.

# GREAT AGES
# OF WORLD CIVILIZATION

The chart at right shows the approximate duration of the major ancient American civilizations in relation to the important cultural periods of the Western world, the central, Near Eastern and African regions, and the East. It is excerpted from a more comprehensive world chronology which appears in the introductory booklet to the Great Ages of Man series.

On the following two pages there appears a chronological table of some of the more important events that took place throughout the Americas during the era covered by this book. The table is divided geographically into the three major regions where high civilizations developed in the New World: Central Mexico, the Maya Region and Peru. Significant cultures within these regions are indicated by capital letters.

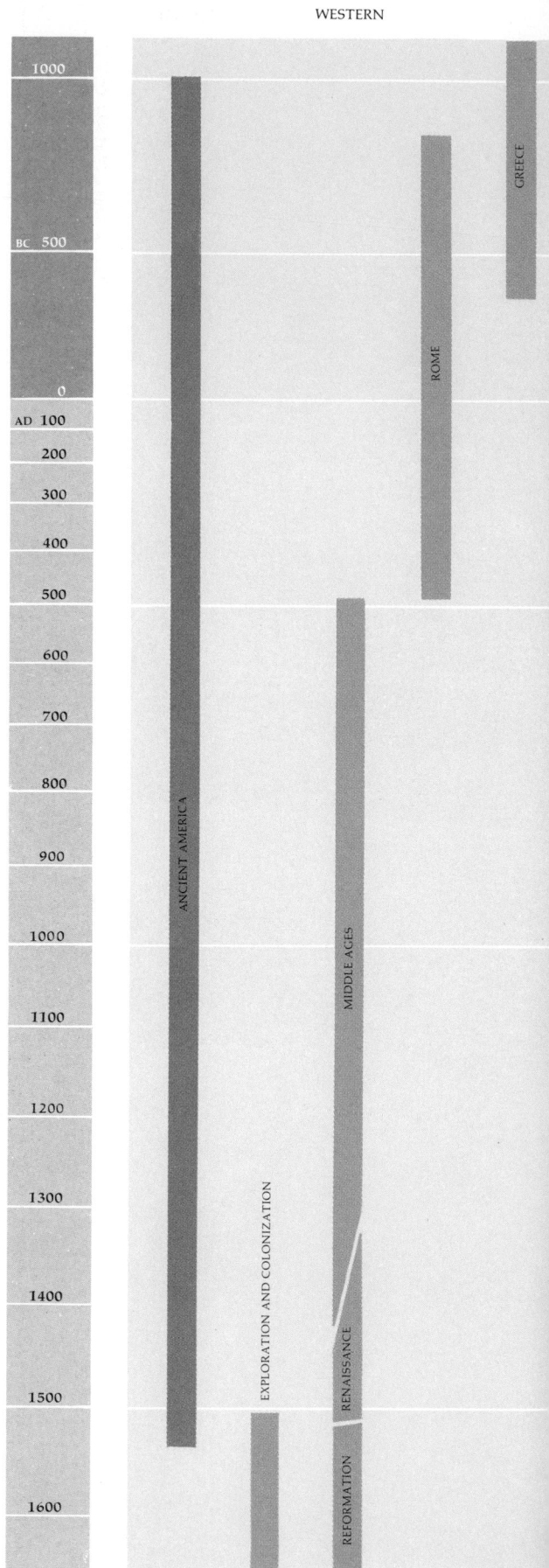

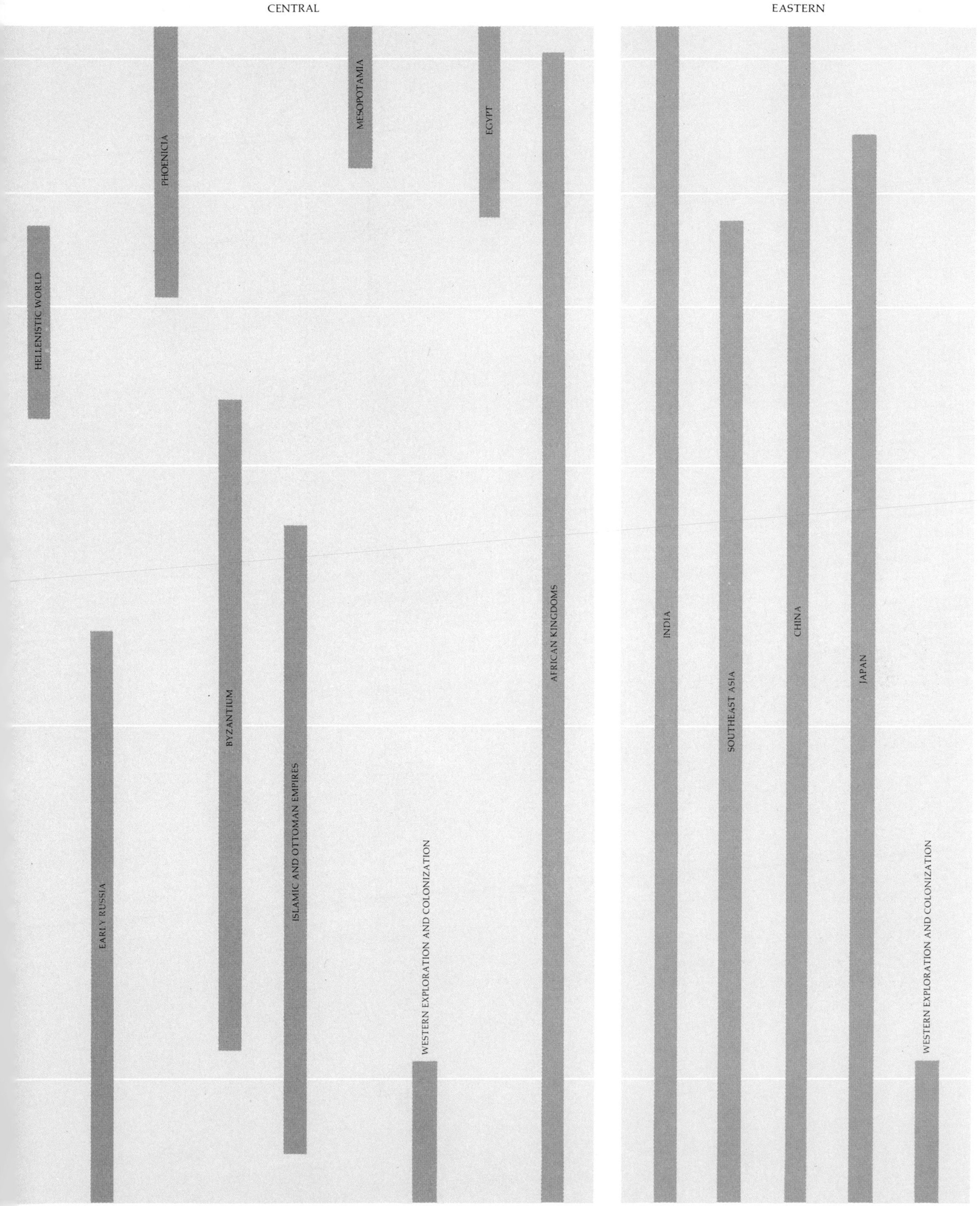
CENTRAL
EASTERN
HELLENISTIC WORLD
PHOENICIA
MESOPOTAMIA
EGYPT
AFRICAN KINGDOMS
EARLY RUSSIA
BYZANTIUM
ISLAMIC AND OTTOMAN EMPIRES
WESTERN EXPLORATION AND COLONIZATION
INDIA
SOUTHEAST ASIA
CHINA
JAPAN
WESTERN EXPLORATION AND COLONIZATION

CHRONOLOGY: A summary of significant developments in ancient America

|  | Mexico | | | Maya Region | Peru | | |
|---|---|---|---|---|---|---|---|
|  | OAXACA | GULF COAST | VALLEY OF MEXICO |  | NORTH COAST | HIGHLANDS | SOUTH COAST |
| 1000 |  | OLMEC civilization, Mexico's first, originates the man-jaguar cult. Olmec culture spreads widely, produces jade and basalt sculptures and hieroglyphic writing, and large ceremonial centers like La Venta |  |  |  | CHAVIN culture, based on worship of man-jaguar gods, flourishes in northern Peru. Chavin peoples build imposing stone ceremonial centers and spread their religious influence and art style throughout Peru |  |
| 900 |  |  | Figurines at Tlatilco display features typical of Olmec art | Villages based on a slash-and-burn agriculture take first steps toward civilization under Olmec influence | Gold ornaments, earliest known metalwork in ancient America, are buried in graves at Chongoyape |  |  |
| 800 |  |  |  |  |  |  |  |
| 700 |  |  |  |  |  |  |  |
| 600 | MONTE ALBAN, a major ceremonial center, is begun, probably by Zapotecs; its bas-reliefs show Olmec influence |  |  |  |  |  |  |
| 500 |  |  |  |  | *Unity of Chavin culture gives way to rise of local cultures* |  |  |
| 400 |  | Invaders destroy La Venta |  |  |  |  |  |
| 300 |  |  | Cuicuilco pyramid becomes a focus of Olmec-style religion |  |  |  |  |
| 200 |  |  |  |  |  |  |  |
| 100 BC |  | Tres Zapotes flourishes as an important religious center |  | Temples and pyramids at Uaxactún and Tikal show primitive Maya features |  |  | PARACAS culture produces brilliant textiles and elaborate funeral offerings |
| AD 100 |  |  | Ostcyahualco begins as a sacred center with a large settled population |  |  |  |  |
| 200 |  |  | CLASSICAL TEOTIHUACAN, built near Ostoyahualco, evolves into a true city, with huge pyramid complexes and an urban population supported by improved agricultural techniques | MAYA civilization, ruled by a priestly elite, develops in loosely federated city-centers throughout southern Mexico, Guatemala and Honduras | MOCHICA peoples of Peru's northern coast federate several adjoining valleys, build huge pyramids and produce highly realistic sculptural portraits |  | NAZCA peoples continue Paracas textile traditions, crisscross desert with mysterious designs and make multicolored pottery |
| 300 | Classical Monte Alban develops as major temples are built |  |  |  |  |  |  |
| 400 |  |  | Typical Teotihuacán orange pottery spreads, probably through trade, over most of Mexico and as far south as Guatemala | Teotihuacán influence extends into the Maya region, and Mexican-style pyramids are built at Kaminaljuyú. Maya custom of erecting hieroglyphic-dated monuments spreads from Guatemala to Yucatán |  |  |  |

| Year | Peru / Andes | Maya | Central Mexico |
|---|---|---|---|
| 600 | ...ceremonial center near Lake Titicaca, achieves religious domination of Peru. Huari, a satellite center, helps to disseminate Tiahuanaco religion | Maya culture revives and enters a period of new vigor | |
| 700 | | Major temples are built at Tikal. Astronomers convene at Copán | CHICHIMEC nomads from northern Mexico invade and overthrow Teotihuacán, inaugurating a long era of warfare and cultural decline |
| 800 | | Bonampak frescoes are painted | |
| 900 | | Classical Maya civilization suffers a widespread decline, halting abruptly in parts of Mexico and Guatemala but continuing to flourish in Yucatán | TOLTECS, a Chichimec people, subjugate the Valley of Mexico and make Tula their capital. Monte Albán is abandoned as a ceremonial center |
| 1000 | Tiahuanaco empire disintegrates, but the tradition of political and cultural unity that it established continues in Peru | Toltec armies from Mexico reach Guatemala and invade Yucatán, bringing warlike gods and large-scale human sacrifice; Chichén Itzá becomes a Toltec city | Marauding Toltec armies overpower many small independent states and extend their domination over most of Mexico. MIXTEC peoples expand under Chief Eight-Deer Ocelot Claw |
| 1100 | CHIMU peoples create a coastal empire 600 miles long | | Tula is ravaged by northern tribes |
| 1200 | Inca tribesmen led by Manco Capac settle in Cuzco valley. Inca bridge Apurímac River, allowing westward expansion | Toltecs abandon Chichén Itzá and their influence ceases. Invaders from the south found Mayapán, which becomes the capital of Yucatán; art declines, but ceremonial centers evolve into true cities | Monte Albán is used for royal burials by the Mixtecs. City-states compete for power throughout Mexico. AZTECS enter the valley of Mexico and settle on islands in Lake Texcoco |
| 1300 | Inca fight inconclusive wars with neighboring tribes | | Tenochtitlán, the Aztec capital, is built |
| 1400 | Chancas attack Cuzco, but are defeated by the Inca Pachacuti. Pachacuti rebuilds Cuzco and begins the fortress of Sacsahuamán. INCA EMPIRE begins to expand as its armies conquer Central Highland tribes. Topa Inca builds roads and sends armies to Chile. Topa Inca conquers Kingdom of Quito and Chimu Kingdom. Inca Empire reaches its maximum extension, stretching from southern Colombia to the Maule River in central Chile | Mayapán is destroyed and its rule gives way to independent states | Aztecs under Itzcóatl begin wars on nearby tribes. Territories in southern Mexico are conquered by Aztec armies. Ahuitzotl sacrifices 20,000 victims at dedication of a temple to Huitzilopochtli in Tenochtitlán |
| 1500 | Huayna Capac consolidates the Empire, but succumbs to a mysterious plague possibly introduced by early Spanish explorers. Civil war breaks out between Atahuallpa and Huascar, Huayna Capac's sons and heirs, and disrupts the Empire. SPANISH CONQUEST of Peru by Pizarro begins (1532), Atahuallpa is executed and replaced by a puppet ruler, Manco II, who revolts and leads Indian troops against Spaniards. VICEROYALTY OF PERU is established in 1542 by Spain's Charles V | Hernández de Córdoba arrives on the coast of Yucatán. SPANISH CONQUEST of Guatemala (1525) and of Yucatán (1541) destroys the waning Maya civilization | Moctezuma II ascends Aztec throne. Aztec attempts to subjugate Mixtecs and Zapotecs are unsuccessful. SPANISH CONQUEST begins as Cortés lands in Mexico (1519) and conquers Tenochtitlán (1521) with the aid of Indian allies. VICEROYALTY OF NEW SPAIN is established in 1535 by Charles V |

# BIBLIOGRAPHY

*These books were selected during the preparation of this volume for their interest and authority, and for their usefulness to readers seeking additional information on specific points.*

*An asterisk (\*) marks works available in both hard-cover and paperback editions; a dagger (†) indicates availability only in paperback.*

## GENERAL HISTORY

†Augur, Helen, *Zapotec*. Dolphin, Doubleday, 1954.
Bennett, Wendell C. and Junius Bird, *Andean Culture History*. Natural History Press, 1964.
Bushnell, G.H.S., *Peru*. Frederick A. Praeger, 1957.
Coe, Michael D., *Mexico*. Frederick A. Praeger, 1962.
Herring, Hubert, *A History of Latin America*. 2nd edition, Alfred A. Knopf, 1962.
Jennings, J. D. and Edward Norbeck, eds., *Prehistoric Man in the New World*. University of Chicago Press, 1964.
Kosok, Paul, *Life, Land and Water in Ancient Peru*. Long Island University Press, 1965.
Macgowan, Kenneth and J. A. Hester, Jr., *Early Man in the New World*. Anchor, Doubleday, 1962.
Mason, John Alden, *The Ancient Civilizations of Peru* (rev. ed.). Penguin, 1964.
Means, Philip A., *Ancient Civilizations of the Andes*. Gordian, 1964.
Parkes, Henry Bamford, *A History of Mexico*. 3rd edition. Houghton Mifflin, 1960.
\*Peterson, Frederick A., *Ancient Mexico*. Capricorn, 1962.
Reichel-Dolmatoff, G., *Colombia*. Frederick A. Praeger, 1965.
Tax, Sol, ed., *The Civilizations of Ancient America*. University of Chicago Press, 1951.
†Wolf, Eric, *Sons of the Shaking Earth*. University of Chicago Press, 1959.

## MAYA, AZTEC, INCA

Baudin, Louis, *A Socialist Empire: The Incas of Peru*. Van Nostrand, 1961.
Bingham, Hiram, *Lost City of the Incas*. Duell, Sloan & Pearce, 1948.
Caso, Alfonso, *The Aztecs: People of the Sun*. University of Oklahoma Press, 1959.
Goetz, Delia and S. G. Morley, *Popol Vuh*. University of Oklahoma Press, 1950.
Leon-Portilla, Miguel, *Aztec Thought and Culture*. University of Oklahoma Press, 1963.
Morley, S. G., *The Ancient Maya*. Stanford University Press, 1958.
Soustelle, Jacques, *Daily Life of the Aztecs*. Macmillan, 1962.
Spinden, H. J., *Maya Art and Civilization*. Falcon's Wing Press, 1957.
Thompson, J. Eric, *The Rise and Fall of Maya Civilization*. University of Oklahoma Press, 1954.
Vaillant, George C. (rev. by Suzannah B. Vaillant), *Aztecs of Mexico*. Doubleday, 1962.

## ART, ARCHITECTURE AND ARCHEOLOGY

Arroyo de Anda, Luis and Gordon F. Ekholm, "Clay Sculpture from Jaina." *Natural History*, April 1966.
Bennett, Wendell C., *Ancient Arts of the Andes*. The Museum of Modern Art, 1954.
Bushnell, G.H.S., *Ancient Arts of the Americas*. Frederick A. Praeger, 1965.
Coe, Michael D., *The Jaguar's Children: Pre-Classic Central Mexico*. The Museum of Primitive Art, 1965.
Coe, William R., "Tikal." *Expedition*, Fall 1965.
Covarrubias, Miguel, *Indian Art of Mexico and Central America*. Alfred A. Knopf, 1957.
Disselhoff, H.-D. and Sigvald Linné, *The Art of Ancient America*. Crown, 1960.
Drucker, Philip, "Gifts for the Jaguar God." *National Geographic*, September 1958.
Ekholm, Gordon F., "Is American Indian Culture Asiatic?" *Natural History*, October 1950.
Emmerich, André, *Art Before Columbus*. Simon & Schuster, 1963.
Emmerich, André, *Sweat of the Sun and Tears of the Moon*. University of Washington Press, 1965.
Kubler, George, *Art and Architecture of Ancient America*. Penguin, 1962.
Lothrop, Samuel K., *Essays in Pre-Columbian Art and Archaeology*. Harvard University Press, 1961.
Lothrop, Samuel K., *Treasures of Ancient America*. Skira, 1964.
Meggers, Betty J. and Clifford Evans, "A Transpacific Contact in 3000 B.C." *Scientific American*, January 1966.
Paddock, J., *Ancient Oaxaca*. Stanford University Press, 1966.
Proskouriakoff, Tatiana, *Classic Maya Sculpture*. Carnegie Institution, 1950.
Proskouriakoff, Tatiana, *An Album of Maya Architecture*. University of Oklahoma Press, 1963.

Robertson, Donald, *Mexican Manuscript Painting of the Early Colonial Period*. Yale University Press, 1959.
Robertson, Donald, *Pre-Columbian Architecture*. Braziller, 1963.
Rowe, John Howland, *Chavin Art, An Inquiry Into Its Form and Meaning*. Museum of Primitive Art, 1962.
Sawyer, Alan R., *Ancient Peruvian Ceramics*. The Metropolitan Museum of Art, 1966.
Steward, J. H., ed., *Handbook of South American Indians*, Vol. II. Smithsonian Institution, 1946.
Stirling, Matthew W., "Expedition Unearths Buried Masterpieces of Carved Jade." *National Geographic*, September 1941.
Stirling, Matthew W., "La Venta's Green Stone Tigers." *National Geographic*, September 1943.
Ubbelohde-Doering, Heinrich, *The Art of Ancient Peru*. Frederick A. Praeger, 1952.
Wauchope, Robert, ed., *Handbook of Middle American Indians*, Vols. I, II and III. University of Texas Press, 1964.
Wauchope, Robert, *Lost Tribes and Sunken Continents*. University of Chicago Press, 1962.
Willey, Gordon, *An Introduction to American Archaeology*, Vol. I. Prentice-Hall, 1966.

## TECHNOLOGY AND CRAFTS

Coe, Michael D., "The Chinampas of Mexico." *Scientific American*, July 1964.
Easby, Dudley T., Jr., "Early Metallurgy in the New World." *Scientific American*, April 1966.
Johnson, Lieut. George R., *Peru from the Air*. American Geographical Society, 1930.
Kosok, Paul, "The Mysterious Markings of Nazca." *Natural History*, May 1947.
MacNeish, Richard, "Ancient Mesoamerican Civilization." *Science*, February 1964.
Reiche, Maria, *Mystery on the Desert*. Lima, 1949.
Ruppert, K., J. Eric Thompson and Tatiana Proskouriakoff, *Bonampak, Chiapas, Mexico*. Carnegie Institution, 1955.
Vaillant, George C., *Artists and Craftsmen in Ancient Central America*. American Museum of Natural History, 1935.
Von Hagen, Victor, *Highway of the Sun*. Duell, Sloan & Pearce, 1955.

## CONQUEST AND COLONIALISM

Bernal, Ignacio, *Mexico before Cortez: Art, History and Legend*. Dolphin, 1963.
Blacker, I., *Cortés and the Aztec Conquest*. Harper & Row, 1965.
Cieza de León, Pedro de, *The Travels of Pedro de Cieza de León, 1532-1550*. Hakluyt Society, 1864.
Cieza de León, Pedro de, *The Second Part of the Chronicle of Peru*. Hakluyt Society, 1883.
Díaz del Castillo, Bernal, *The Discovery and Conquest of Mexico, 1517-1521*. Farrar, Straus and Cudahy, 1956.
Garcilaso de la Vega, *The First Part of the Royal Commentaries of the Yncas*. 2 vols. Hakluyt Society, 1869-1871.
Gibson, Charles, *The Aztecs Under Spanish Rule*. Stanford University Press, 1964.
Haring, Clarence Henry, *The Spanish Empire in America*. Oxford University Press, 1947.
Lopez de Gómara, Francisco, *Cortés*. Transl., ed. by Lesley Byrd Simpson. University of California Press, 1964.
Means, Philip A., *Fall of the Inca Empire and the Spanish Rule in Peru: 1530-1780*. Gordian, 1964.
Morison, Samuel Eliot, *Admiral of the Ocean Sea*. Little, Brown, 1942.
Prescott, William H., *History of the Conquest of Mexico and History of the Conquest of Peru*. Modern Library.
Sahagún, Fray Bernardino de, *General History of the Things of New Spain*. (Florentine Codex). Transl., ed. by Arthur J. O. Anderson and Charles E. Dibble. School of American Research and the University of Utah, 1955.
Squier, George E., *Peru: Incidents of Travel and Exploration in the Land of the Incas*. Harper and Brothers, 1877.
Stephens, John Lloyd, *Incidents of Travel in Yucatán*. University of Oklahoma Press, 1962.

# ART INFORMATION AND PICTURE CREDITS

*The sources for the illustrations in this book are set forth below. Descriptive notes on the works of art are included. Credits for pictures positioned from left to right are separated by semicolons, from top to bottom by dashes. Photographers' names which follow a descriptive note appear in parentheses. Abbreviations include "c." for century and "ca." for circa.*

Cover—Xipe Totec, Mixtec cast gold pendant from Coixtlahuaca, Oaxaca, 13th-15th c. A.D., National Museum of Anthropology, Mexico City (Lee Boltin courtesy Editions d'Art Albert Skira, Geneva).

CHAPTER 1: 8—Maya jade mosaic death mask from the Funerary Crypt, Temple of the Inscriptions, Palenque, Chiapas, Mexico, ca. 7th-8th c. A.D., National Museum of Anthropology, Mexico City (Lee Boltin courtesy Editions d'Art Albert Skira, Geneva). 10-11—Messengers, painted decoration from a Mochica vessel, 3rd-6th c. A.D., reproduced from Rafael

Larco Hoyle, Los Mochicas, Lima, Peru, 1939. 13—Clovis point, drawing by Leslie Martin after original found at Lehner Site, Arizona, now at the Arizona State Museum, Tucson. 19—Olmec jade figure from southern Mexico, 9th-4th c. B.C., The Brooklyn Museum, Guennol Collection. 20-21—Olmec ritual cache from La Venta, Tabasco, 9th-4th c. B.C., National Museum of Anthropology, Mexico City (Lee Boltin courtesy Editions d'Art Albert Skira, Geneva); Olmec jadeite head, fragment of a statue, from Tenango del Valle, Mexico, 6th-1st c. B.C., National Museum of Anthropology, Mexico City (Lee Boltin courtesy Editions d'Art Albert Skira, Geneva). 22—Drummer, Colima style clay sculpture from western Mexico, 3rd-

9th c. A.D. formerly on loan to National Museum of Anthropology, Mexico City (Lee Boltin); Reflective man, Colima style clay sculpture from western Mexico, 3rd-9th c. A.D., American Museum of Natural History (Lee Boltin)—Woman with metate, Colima style clay sculpture from western Mexico, 3rd-9th c. A.D., formerly André Emmerich Gallery, New York (Andreas Feininger). 23—Musicians, Nayarit style painted clay sculptures from western Mexico, 3rd-9th c. A.D., Diego Rivera Museum, Mexico City (Lee Boltin courtesy Editions d'Art Albert Skira, Geneva); Kneeling girl, Nayarit style clay sculpture from western Mexico, 3rd-9th c. A.D., National Museum of Anthropology, Mexico City (Lee Boltin)—Seated woman, Nayarit style clay sculpture from western Mexico, 3rd-9th c. A.D., Collection of Dr. Kurt Stavenhagen, Mexico City (Lee Boltin courtesy Editions d'Art Albert Skira, Geneva); Warrior or ballplayer, Nayarit style clay sculpture from western Mexico, 3rd-9th c. A.D. Private Collection, Switzerland (Irmgard Groth Kimball). 24-25—Maya clay figurine with doughnut shaped earrings from Jaina, Campeche, 7th-10th c. A.D., National Museum of Anthropology, Mexico City (Lee Boltin); Maya painted clay figurine with large hat from Jaina, Campeche, 7th-10th c. A.D., National Museum of Anthropology, Mexico City (Irmgard Groth Kimball). 26-27—Teotihuacán painted clay mask, originally part of an incense burner, 3rd-7th c. A.D., National Museum of Anthropology, Mexico City (Lee Boltin courtesy Editions d'Art Albert Skira, Geneva); Zapotec clay sculpture from Tomb 113, Monte Albán, Oaxaca, 3rd c. B.C.-3rd c. A.D., National Museum of Anthropology, Mexico City (Irmgard Groth Kimball); Las Remojadas style clay sculpture of Xipe Totec, 11th-13th c. A.D., Collection of Jay C. Leff, Uniontown, Pa. (Lee Boltin); Aztec mask of green diorite found at Castillo de Teayo, Veracruz, 13th-15th c. A.D., American Museum of Natural History (Lee Boltin). 28—Nazca clay effigy vessel, ca. 6th c. A.D., formerly on loan to American Museum of Natural History (Lee Boltin)—Seated cripple, Mochica clay effigy vessel, 3rd-5th c. A.D., Collection of Rafael Larco Hoyle, Lima, Peru (Lee Boltin courtesy Editions d'Art Albert Skira, Geneva). 29—Portrait head, "The Ruler," Mochica clay vessel with stirrup spout, 3rd-5th c. A.D., Art Institute of Chicago (Lee Boltin courtesy Editions d'Art Albert Skira, Geneva).

CHAPTER 2: 30—Zapotec painted clay sculpture of a jaguar from Monte Albán, Oaxaca, 3rd c. B.C. to 3rd c. A.D., National Museum of Anthropology, Mexico City (Lee Boltin courtesy Editions d'Art Albert Skira, Geneva). 32—Olmec jade ceremonial ax, 9th-4th c. B.C., Courtesy Trustees of The British Museum, London (Derek Bayes). 36-37—Tlalocán, the rain god's paradise, fresco from the painted palace at Tepantitla, Teotihuacán, 4th-6th c. A.D., painted copy courtesy the Peabody Museum, Harvard University (Lee Boltin). 38-39—Teotihuacán, site plan by Jim Alexander, drawings of pyramids by Otto van Eersel. 43—Dick Davis. 44-45—Editions Arthaud, Paris; Roger-Viollet. 46-47—Fritz Goro; Roloff Beny. 48-49—Dmitri Kessel. 50-51—Dick Davis. 52-53—Dick Davis; Roger-Viollet—Martin Weaver from Camera Press-Pix, London. 54-55—Roloff Beny.

CHAPTER 3: 56—Giselle Freund. 64—Courtesy the Mexican Consulate of New York. 67—Drawing of *chinampas* by Leslie Martin. 69-77—Illustrations from *Codex Nuttall, Facsimile of an Ancient Mexican Codex belonging to Lord Zouche of Harynworth, England, with an Introduction by Zelia Nuttall,* Peabody Museum of American Archaeology and Ethnology, Harvard University, Cambridge, Mass., 1902, courtesy The Museum of Primitive Art, New York, except 70-71, photograph by Donald Miller and 72-73 top and bottom right courtesy Trustees of the British Museum, London (John R. Freeman).

CHAPTER 4: 78—Mythological demon carrying a trophy head, Paracas Necropolis embroidery, 1st c. B.C.-1st c. A.D., National Museum of Anthropology and Archaeology, Lima, Peru (Lee Boltin courtesy Editions d'Art Albert Skira, Geneva). 83—Shang marble tiger found at Anyang, China, 18th-12th c. B.C., Academia Sinica, Taiwan (James Burke); Chavín stone mortar in the form of a jaguar, 10th-5th c. B.C., University Museum of the University of Pennsylvania (Robert Crandall)—Stone sculpture from Mahoba, India, 8th-9th c. A.D., reproduced from Benoytosh Bhattacharyya, *Indian Buddhist Iconography,* London, Oxford University Press, 1924, courtesy Dr. Gordon Ekholm; Sculptured stone slab on the wall in the western corridor of House E in the Palace at Palenque, Chiapas, Mexico, 7th-8th c. A.D., reproduced from Alfred P. Maudslay, *Biologia Centrali-Americana,* London, R. H. Porter, 1896-1899, courtesy Dr. Gordon Ekholm—Lotus rhizome with flowers and leaves drawn from the jaws of a *makara* by a dwarf *Yaksa,* from a 2nd c. A.D. sculptured frieze at Amaravati, southern India, reproduced from Ananda K. Coomaraswamy, Yaksas, Washington, Smithsonian Institution, Freer Gallery, 1931, courtesy American Museum of Natural History; Lotus panel animated by human figure, from sculptured chamber reproduced from wall of the Great Ball Court, Chichén Itzá, Yucatán, 10th-11th c. A.D., Alfred P. Maudslay, *Biologia Centrali-Americana,* London, R. H. Porter, 1896-1899, courtesy American Museum of Natural History—Bronze 19th c. wheeled representation of the God Indra riding an elephant from India, courtesy American Museum of Natural History; wheeled clay dog from Tres Zapotes, Veracruz, 8th-9th c. A.D., National Museum of Anthropology, Mexico City (Antonio Halik). 87—Chief in house receiving captives borne in litters, painted decoration from a Mochica vessel, 3rd-5th c. A.D., courtesy American Museum of Natural History. 91—Early Nazca hammered sheet-gold ornament, 1st-3rd c. A.D., The Museum of Primitive Art, New York (Lee Boltin). 92-93—Chavín repoussé sheet gold ornament of a feline, 9th-5th c. B.C., The Textile Museum, Washington, D.C. (Lee Boltin); Inca (possibly Chimú) beaker in the form of a head, 13th-15th c. A.D., The Art Institute of Chicago (Lee Boltin)—Mochica repoussé gold head ornament with the face of a feline deity, 2nd-7th c. A.D., Museo Rafael Larco Herrera, Lima, Peru (Lee Boltin courtesy Editions d'Art Albert Skira, Geneva). 94—Mochica gold puma effigy, 4th-8th c. A.D., Miguel Mujica Gallo Collection, Lima, Peru (Lee Boltin); Pair of gold Ica beakers, 14th-16th c. A.D., Art Institute of Chicago (Lee Boltin)—Chimú gold ceremonial hand (one of a pair), 12th-13th c. A.D., Miguel Mujica Gallo Collection, Lima, Peru (Lee Boltin); Mochica gold female effigy, 4th-8th c. A.D., Brüning Museum, Lambayeque (Cornell Capa from Magnum). 95—Chimú gold ceremonial knife with turquoise and shell inlay,12th-13th c. A.D., National Museum of Archaeology and Anthropology, Lima, Peru (Lee Boltin); Inca gold figurine of a woman, 14th-16th c. A.D., Collection of Mrs. Bertram Smith, New York (Lee Boltin)—Chimú gold ceremonial vessel in the form of a bird, 12th-13th c. A.D., formerly John Wise Collection, New York (Nelson Morris for TIME). 96—Tolima cast gold and copper alloy pectoral found at el Dragón, Quindio, Colombia, 1st-9th c. A.D., Museo de Oro, Banca de la República, Bogotá, Colombia (Lee Boltin courtesy Editions d'Art Albert Skira, Geneva). 97—Quimbaya cast gold human effigy figure found at Finlandia, Colombia, 5th-8th c. A.D., Museo de América, Madrid (Michel Des Jardins, courtesy *Réalités*); Muisca cast-gold votive figurine, ca. 14th-15th c. A.D., Cleveland Museum of Art, in Memory of Mr. and Mrs. Henry Humphreys, gift of their daughter Helen (R. S. Crandall for TIME)—Coclé breastplate with repoussé design of anthropomorphic alligator god from Sitio Conte, Coclé province, Panama, 3rd-10th c. A.D., University Museum of the University of Pennsylvania (Lee Boltin courtesy Editions d'Art Albert Skira, Geneva). 98—Mixtec cast gold pendant in the form of a ceremonial shield *(chimalli)* with turquoise mosaic inlay, 14th-16th c. A.D., National Museum of Anthropology, Mexico City (Irmgard Groth Kimball)—Mixtec necklace of pearls, turquoises, coral, red spondylus shell, and gold, found in Tomb 7 at Monte Albán, Oaxaca, 15th-16th c. A.D., Regional Museum of Oaxaca, Mexico (Frank Scherschel). 99—Mixtec gold deity pendant with calendrical notations in cast filigree, found in Tomb 7, Monte Albán, Oaxaca, 15th-16th c. A.D., Regional Museum of Oaxaca, Mexico (Frank Scherschel).

CHAPTER 5: 100—Zapotec clay urn representing a Maize God, from Monte Albán, Oaxaca, Mexico, 5th-8th c. A.D., Collection of Lola Olmeda de Olvera, Mexico City (Lee Boltin courtesy Editions d'Art Albert Skira, Geneva). 105—Inca cast silver figure holding corn, 14th-16th c. A.D., Collection of Mr. Nasli Heeramaneck, New York (Lee Boltin). 109-117—Maya murals from Bonampak, Chiapas, 9th c. A.D., paintings copied by Antonio Tejeda for the Carnegie Institution of Washington, D.C. (Robert Kafka), except 110, bottom, diagram by Otto van Eersel.

CHAPTER 6: 118—Glyphs from decoration around the entrance to Temple XVIII at Palenque, Chiapas, Mexico (Lee Boltin). 120—Inca silver alpaca and llama with gold appliqué, 14th-16th c. A.D., American Museum of Natural History (Andreas Feininger). 125—Weavers, design from the interior of a Mochica vase in the British Museum, 3rd-6th c. A.D., courtesy American Museum of Natural History. 127—Sergio Larrain from Magnum. 128-129—Servicio Aerofotografico Nacional, Peru; Cornell Capa from Magnum—Cornell Capa from Magnum. 130-131—Inca road map by Leslie Martin after *Highway of the Sun,* ©, 1955 by Victor von Hagen; Victor von Hagen; drawing of suspension bridge by Leslie Martin—Servicio Aerofotografico Nacional, Peru, courtesy *Life, Land and Water in Ancient Peru* by Paul Kosok, Long Island University Press, 1965. 132-133, Servicio Aerofotografico Nacional, Peru; Servicio Aerofotografico Nacional, Peru—Victor von Hagen. 134-135—Drawing by Leslie Martin adapted from photograph by Marc and Evelyne Bernheim from Rapho Guillumette; Cornell Capa from Magnum—Cornell Capa from Magnum. 136-137—Martin Chambi, Lima, Peru.

CHAPTER 7: 138—Gilded silver bowl, Spanish, 16th c., Kunsthistorisches Museum, Vienna (Erich Lessing from Magnum). 143—Cortés, 19th c. lithograph after 17th c. anonymous portrait in the Hospital de Jesús Nazareno, Mexico City (Culver Pictures). 149—Pizarro, 19th c. oil on canvas painting, from a series of portraits of the Incas of Peru, courtesy The Old Print Shop, New York. 153-157—Illustrations from Codex Mendoza, 16th c. early colonial manuscript, Bodleian Library, Oxford. 158-161—Illustrations from Codex Magliabechiano, 16th c. early colonial manuscript, Biblioteca Nazionale, Florence.

CHAPTER 8: 162—Jalisco style clay figure of a woman, 3rd-9th c. A.D., and Aztec obsidian mirror in early colonial gilded wood frame, American Museum of Natural History (Andreas Feininger). 166-167—Photograph by Lee Boltin. 171-181—Photographs by Peter Turner courtesy National Museum of Anthropology, Mexico City.

# ACKNOWLEDGMENTS

The editors of this book are particularly indebted to Gordon R. Willey, Bowditch Professor of Mexican and Central American Archeology, Peabody Museum, Harvard University; Gordon F. Ekholm, Curator of Mexican Archeology, and Junius Bird, Curator of South American Archeology, American Museum of Natural History, New York; Harry Bernstein, Professor of History, Brooklyn College, City University of New York; Thomas C. Patterson, Professor of Anthropology, Harvard University; John O. Outwater, Professor of Mechanical Engineering, University of Vermont; John B. Glass; Pedro Ramírez Vázquez, Designer, Ignacio Bernal, Director, Jose Chávez Morado, Designer of Umbrella Column and Margarita Laris, Director of Public Relations, National Museum of Anthropology, Mexico City; Lorenzo Fuentes Ogario, Director, Hospital de Jesús, Mexico City; Lola Olmedo de Olvera, Director, and Carlos Pellicer, Diego Rivera Museum, Mexico City; Alberto Ruz Lhuillier, Justino Fernández, Salvador Novo, Josué Saenz, and Kurt Stavenhagen, Mexico City; Luis Rodríguez López, University of Trujillo; Luis Barreda Murillo, University of Cuzco; Frederic Engel, Lima; Miguel Mujica Gallo, Lima; Vatican Library, Rome; Victor von Hagen, Rome; Irma Merolle-Tondi, Director, Biblioteca Laurenziana, Florence; Emanuele Casamassima, Director and Eugenia Levy, Biblioteca Nazionale, Florence; Victor Velen, Florence; Kurt Krieger, Museum für Völkerkunde, Berlin; Violetta Becker-Donner, Museum für Völkerkunde, Vienna; Erwin M. Auer, Kunsthistorisches Museum, Vienna; Cottie Burland; The Department of Ethnography at the British Museum, London; The Bodleian Library, Oxford; Madeleine David, Conservateur Adjoint, Musée Cernuschi, Paris.

# INDEX

*This symbol in front of a page number indicates an illustration of the subject mentioned.*

✗

PRODUCTION STAFF FOR TIME INCORPORATED

*John L. Hallenbeck (Vice President and Director of Production),*
*Robert E. Foy, Caroline Ferri and Robert E. Fraser*
*Text photocomposed under the direction of Albert J. Dunn and Arthur J. Dunn*